INFLATABLE BOATS

INFLATABLE BOATS

Selection, Care, Repair, and Seamanship

Jim Trefethen

Illustrated by Clint Trefethen

International Marine
Camden, Maine

International Marine/
Ragged Mountain Press
A Division of The McGraw-Hill Companies

4 6 8 10 9 7 5 3

Library of Congress Cataloging-in-Publication Data

Trefethen, Jim, 1942-
Inflatable boats : selection, care, repair, and seamanship /
Jim Trefethen ; illustrated by Clint Trefethen.
p. cm.
Includes index.
ISBN 0-07-065252-X
1. Inflatable boats. I. Title.
VM360.T74 1996
623.8'202—dc20 95-52697
CIP

Questions regarding the content of this book should be addressed to:

International Marine
P.O. Box 220
Camden, ME 04843
207-236-4837

Questions regarding the ordering of this book should be addressed to:

The McGraw-Hill Companies
Customer Service Department
P.O. Box 547
Blacklick, OH 43004
Retail customers: 1-800-262-4729
Bookstores: 1-800-722-4726

Inflatable Boats is printed on 60-pound Renew Opaque Vellum, an acid-free paper that contains 50 percent recycled waste paper (preconsumer) and 10 percent postconsumer waste paper. ♻

Printed by R.R. Donnelley

Design by Chris McLarty

Production and page layout by Janet Robbins

Edited by James R. Babb, John J. Kettlewell, and Don Casey

To my son, Jay

Contents

Acknowledgments

This book was hard to write. The recent recession hit the inflatable-boat industry particularly hard, and several major inflatable-boat distributors went out of business or switched to more profitable products while I was working on the manuscript. But the inflatable-boat industry is always in turmoil. A highly competitive business, it is controlled at the top by a few large companies that manufacture the materials and fabricate the boats under a variety of brand names. The boats themselves are distributed and retailed by small companies, many with only a few employees. The market is tiny compared with that for products like skis, tennis rackets, or walking shoes. And recently the entire industry was turned on its ear by the out-of-court settlement for an undisclosed sum of a class-action lawsuit claiming one of the world's largest manufacturers of inflatables deliberately misrepresented the quality of its boats.

Competition in the rubber-boat business is stiff, profits are low, suspicions are high, animosity flares, and paranoia reigns supreme. An outsider asking for information to be compiled into a book is likely to be viewed as an industrial spy and is about as welcome as a Greek knocking on the gates of Troy asking to take Helen for a walk on the beach. The several industry insiders who responded to my letters or accepted my phone calls and answered my questions with candor and honesty have indicated that it might be best not to mention their names in this acknowledgment. They know who they are, however, and my heartfelt thanks to all of them.

There are others I can name, without whose assistance I could never have written this book. My editors, Jim Babb, John Kettlewell, and Don Casey, whose collective patience was tested to the limit when deadlines came and passed into history without an acceptable manuscript; my mentor, Captain Dick Bunker, who provided moral support, editorial commentary, and the air-conditioned luxury of his yacht, *Sans Souci*, as a place to plug in my Macintosh; and my friend Mary, who provided proofreading, editorial commentary, and a fellow writer's perspective on a potentially dry and dull subject—all share equally in the success of this venture.

Introduction

If it happened today as it happened nearly 20 years ago, our very first trip in our very first sailboat would surely have been our last. But we were in love and under the spell of that peculiar condition that allows young people to turn the most miserable circumstances into joyous memories. "Well honey, here we are," I happily announced to Susan, my bride-to-be, as we dropped the anchor just outside the surf line, a few hundred yards off the white, sandy expanse of Crane's Beach in Ipswich, Massachusetts. We had just made our first open-water passage in our brand-new 21-foot sailboat, and we were flush with the heady success of having completed a tortuous and adventuresome journey fraught with dangers and excitement. We had survived the fearsome tidal rips of Bass Rock and avoided foundering on the foul shores of Castle Hill. We had crossed the bar at the mouth of the Ipswich River under full sail without being pounded to pieces in the surf, escaping the fate of many brave souls who had preceded us. Indeed, having read *Chapman's* from cover to cover several times, I was pleased that we had managed our first trip like the true salts we aspired to be. Our journey of about 10 miles (nautical miles, of course) had taken us from the Ipswich Yacht Club on Plum Island Sound to a long-planned picnic at the western end of the Crane's Beach Reservation, a remote spit of unspoiled dunes accessible only to those fortunate enough to own a new sailboat, except for a few unhappy landlubbers with a penchant for long beach hikes.

"Oh darling, isn't this just the most beautiful spot on earth?" Susan bubbled, with a delightful enthusiasm that intoned that I, as self-appointed captain of our little expedition, was somehow responsible for the whole splendid panorama.

"It sure is," I answered from the starboard shrouds, shading my eyes against the glare of the sun the way I imagined Leif Eriksson must have done after successfully navigating the North Atlantic and bringing craft and crew safely to anchor off the rocky coast of Vinland.

"And now my darling," Susan said, without the slightest hint that she suspected I didn't have a ready answer for the obvious question, "how are we going to get the picnic basket and the blanket to the beach?"

"Quite easily, my dear, . . . quite . . . easily," I answered calmly, scanning the boats anchored nearby for a hint of how others were handling this particular problem. The answer was not encouraging as I noticed that each and every party on the beach had a dinghy pulled high above the waterline. "We'll just . . . well we'll . . . what we'll do is. . . . " We had considered buying a dinghy, but even the smallest one on the market would be hard to manage with a 21-foot sailboat. My mind raced through the options: swimming through the surf would soak the blanket and ruin our lunch; beaching the boat in the surf would ruin the boat; and paddling ashore on the cockpit cushions would deal an ignominious death blow to my rapidly deflating self-image. What would Leif have done?

"Well, we better haul anchor and move on," I announced with an authoritative scan of the sandy bottom. "This holding ground doesn't look too good to me, and we're wide open if a blow should blow up," I went on, happy to have found a use for some of the new words I recently learned from reading Richard Henderson's *Sea Sense*.

"But darling, the other boats aren't having any trouble holding the ground."

"The poor fools probably don't know any better. We'll go around to the other side where it's more protected."

So we hauled anchor, which was a chore because the ground was holding it quite well, started our little outboard, and motored around to the other side of the peninsula where the bottom turns from clean sand to a muddy flat covered with acres of mussels, and the Essex River broadens into a wide marsh. Though the scenery was not as idyllic, it was a beautiful and lonely spot, and since there was no surf, we were able to bring our little boat close enough to the high-water mark to enable us to wade ashore with lunch, blanket, and skipper's ego unscathed.

"But sweetheart, won't the tide go out and leave the boat stranded on the beach?"

"Of course not my dearest. We'll just shove her out to deeper water every 15 minutes or so—just enough to keep her afloat."

And that's what we did—at least for the first half hour. Then we became involved with those various activities young people indulge in when they are terribly fond of each other and they find themselves alone in a secluded spot on a beautiful day in the middle of the summer.

"Shouldn't you go check on the boat?" a whisper whispered in my ear through a somnolent haze.

"Naw, the boat is fine," I whispered back before drifting off into the oblivion of a noontime nap on the hot, sunny beach.

When we awoke, the sun was still hot but not nearly as high in the sky, and needless to say, our boat was higher and very much drier than it was before. "We'll kedge her off," I said, remembering a passage from Eric Hiscock's *Around the World in Wanderer III,* but even a lubber could see that there was nothing to kedge her off to: the river was as dry as a teetotaler's convention in the Sahara Desert.

"How long before the tide comes back in?" Susan asked, her confidence in my grasp of things nautical only slightly diminished.

"Oh, only an hour or so . . . I think."

That was at 3 P.M. At 3:30 the first advance scouts of that most vicious of nature's creatures, the green-head fly, arrived, followed by waves of mosquitoes. After the breeze died, clouds of hungry midges joined the feast. We built a fire from driftwood and sat swatting at small unseen vampires as we watched the sun set across a vast expanse of mud flat and mussel shells.

"You're right," Susan said softly, without a trace of sarcasm. "The ground is holding much better on this side."

At 7 o'clock a cold drizzle started to fall; at 8 our supply of driftwood gave out; at 9 the beam of our only flashlight flickered and died. Finally, at 10 P.M., the mast of our sturdy craft began a slow, nearly imperceptible return to vertical, and at 11:30 we floated free.

I will spare you the details of our midnight trip across the bay in the rain and fog. Suffice it to say that when, through some freak accident or the kindness of the Supreme Navigator, we finally managed to locate our mooring at the yacht club, the launch operator had long since retired to the cozy comfort of his bed, and we were left shivering in the wet darkness with no way to get to the landing. We pulled our new boat up to the fuel dock, and while I struggled with a damp pencil and wet paper to write a note to the dockboy to please put her on her mooring, Susan tied the bow line to a cleat on the floats.

"Shall I secure the stern, Captain?" The emphasis was on "Captain," and I thought it had a bit of an edge to it.

"Hell no. Just tie the damned thing to the dock and let's get out of here."

We finally made it home at dawn, just in time to trade our sopping boat clothes for business suits and go to work.

The amazing conclusion of this long-winded anecdote is that Susan married me anyway, but not before I made four important purchases: a large bottle of Cutter's insect repellent, a powerful flashlight with lots of extra batteries, a current copy of the *Eldridge's Tide and Pilot,* and an inflatable dinghy. We have been sailing together ever since, near and far, through fair seas and foul, but we would rather leave the mains'l home than ever go anywhere without these four items.

If the reader will forgive my lapse into romantic nostalgia, it was not without purpose, pointing out the impact inflatable boats have had on the lifestyle of the cruising sailor. Our first inflatable was an 8-foot Avon Redstart that, when deflated, just barely fit into the lazarette of the 21-footer. It was just right for the two of us then, but since that memorable first trip, our crew list has grown to four with the addition of Sarah (now age 14) and Phillip (age 11). Our current boat, *Sultana,* is a 40-foot cruising ketch, and our current inflatable is a 12-foot Achilles with a 25-horsepower Mariner outboard.

Between that first inflatable and the one we now own, we have owned several other boats, enjoyed many experiences (some good, some bad, and some really bad), and learned a lot. Though the title of *old salt* eludes us yet, we're still working on it. This book is about some of what we have learned and a little about how we learned it. It is my hope that sharing it with you reinforces the point made many times by many others that where you go isn't nearly as important as how you get there.

A bit of talcum
Is always walcum.

—Ogden Nash

CHAPTER 1

Inflating History

One of the favorite pastimes of academic speculators with fancy-sounding letters following their names is the theorization of "firsts." Historians, anthropologists, paleontologists, paleoanthropologists, and a slew of others who like to pretend an insight into the early adventures of our species are endlessly theorizing on who first did what, and how. In the marine field, a speculative consensus on the origins of the first boat was reached early on: early man learned to propel himself across a lake or stream by straddling a floating log. This consensus was shaken a bit by Thor Heyerdahl's hypothesis that the first boats were constructed from bundles of papyrus reeds. I have my own theory on the nature of the first boat, and in sharing it with you, I hope to settle the argument once and for all.

The Dead Pig Theory

The seed that would sprout and grow into the flower of this theory was planted during a solitary fishing trip on the turbid waters of the Potomac River above Great Falls, an area of small islands and raging rapids interspersed with isolated sloughs and quiet backwaters. It was the mid-1950s, and this area, now swallowed and mostly digested by the rapacious Washington suburbs, was then as wild and remote as when the settlers landed at Jamestown; white-tailed deer browsed on the grassy shore, red fox stalked cottontails in the thickets, snapping turtles waddled along the muddy banks, and giant sycamores dotted the river's edge, dipping their branches into the water as if trying to escape the humid summer heat.

Accompanied by a small beagle named Rambler and a large tobacco tin filled with night crawlers, I paddled my little canoe between the islands and into the shade of the backwaters. When we found a likely spot, I tied the bow line to a drooping branch, Rambler clambered onto the bow seat where he could sleep without missing anything, and I lounged in the stern, trailing one of the worms in the current. As I lay honing my skills of inactivity to a razor's edge, I noticed a large cylindrical object caught in the current in midstream. The unidentified floating object was about a half mile away, bobbing along in the rushing water. I could see four protrusions pointing skyward, much like the legs of a table turned upside down. Four large black crows rode atop the UFO while a dozen others followed milling and cawing above. Was this mysterious object some sort of tank broken loose from a farm wagon? Gradually curiosity overcame lassitude, so with Rambler barking encouragement, I cast off the bow line and dug

The origin of watercraft.

my paddle deep into the roily water. With the hapless worm skipping along behind, we took up the chase.

A short period of energetic paddling halved the distance to the UFO, which was drawing dangerously close to the rapids above Great Falls—where only a fool would follow. We redoubled our efforts, me paddling furiously, Rambler barking frantically, and the worm following resignedly. As we pulled abreast of the object, we could see that it wasn't a tank at all but the bloated carcass of a large hog. Above the waterline, the skin was stretched tight by the expanding gases of corrupting flesh and had been dried hard by the relentless summer sun. Below the waterline . . . well, it's just as well that part was out of sight. A tentative poke with my paddle sent the corpse bobbing in the current like a cork.

A solid whack brought forth a resonant hollow sound, like a poorly tuned kettledrum crossed with an empty oil tank. When the carcass reached the first line of rapids, I had to backpaddle to avoid joining it on its journey through the falls. As I watched its progress through the rapids, bobbing violently and bouncing off boulders and snags, I admired the dead hog's remarkable stability. Had we been caught in the rapids, we would have been better off aboard the hog than aboard my flimsy canoe. Rambler agreed as always; the worm declined comment.

You can see that as an improvised watercraft, the corpse of a hog is far superior to a fallen tree with its snaggle of roots on one end and a bundle of unruly branches at the other. As for bundled reeds, that requires sufficient advancement to join together related material in a cohesive manner—a problem we are still struggling with. However, a dead pig (or a wart hog, or even a deceased hippo for large groups), readily available to our ancestors, would have made a fine and stable boat after a few days in the sun, offering the advantages of a large bony head for ballast and upright legs for handy stanchions. This theory not only explains the origin of the first boat, but perhaps the origin of the term *stinkpot* as well.

Thus we have the Trefethen Theory of the Origin of Watercraft: the first boat was obviously an inflatable—self-inflating, in fact. Because this book just happens to be about inflatable boats, adherents to the now discredited Floating-Tree Theorem may argue that this theory is self-serving, but the historical significance of the inflatable boat is merely a fortuitous coincidence. So as historians rush to correct their texts, we can continue to examine the history of inflatable boats.

The Inflatable Boat in Ancient History

While a dead pig made a fine boat by Lower Paleolithic standards, it did have several drawbacks. A bothersome odor may have been one, although it is unlikely that early man smelled much better. In the days before agriculture and take-out food, early humans may well have chosen to eat the pig before it became bloated. And the most serious drawback must have been that a dead pig had a short life span as a seaworthy craft.

The answer to all these problems, which doubtless occurred to our ancestors in time, was to separate the pig from its skin, eat the pig, then fill just the skin with air. Here we have our first man-made inflatable boat. Herodotus describes the soldiers of Cyrus the Great using inflated bullock hides in an amphibious assault on the forces of King Croesus of Lydia about 550 years B.C. On his way to attack Rome in 218 B.C., Hannibal transported his elephants across the Rhône River on vast wooden platforms supported by inflated ox hides. Even today in the remote backwaters of the Third World, one may encounter inflated animal skins, proofed with tallow, pitch, or tar, being used as crude boats.

The Modern Inflatable

Question: What does a dirigible have in common with a raincoat? Too easy? Well, what do they both have in common with an automobile tire? The answer is that the development of the modern inflatable boat borrowed from the technology of all three.

The very first rubber boat—two tubular bladders of rubber-impregnated cotton cloth protected by a canvas cover—was made in 1847 by Charles Macintosh, inventor of the macintosh raincoat. The technology developed by Macintosh for his famous raincoats, allied with Charles Goodyear's vulcanization process combining raw latex rubber with sulfur, also made possible the development of the giant airships called *dirigibles*. Invented in 1852, dirigibles didn't become practical until Ferdinand von Zeppelin flew his first rigid airship in 1900.

As an early producer of dirigibles, a French company named the Société Zodiac prospered during the early part of the century, but when the 1937 *Hindenburg* crash ended the era of the giant airships, the company found itself without a market. Fortunately, the difference between a dirigible and an inflatable boat is essentially a matter of scale, and the Société Zodiac switched to making small inflatable rubber boats—just in time to capitalize on the growth market in life rafts created by World War II.

Zodiac had introduced an inflatable kayak as early as 1934, and the private-market success of this two-person craft encouraged the company to begin production of a 12-foot inflatable catamaran. This more substantial craft caught the eye of the French Navy, and the fortunes of the Société Zodiac and the entire inflatable-boat industry took off on a wave of government contracts that continues today.

These early boats employed the same vulcanized-rubber-over-canvas-duck technology that Charlie Macintosh had developed for his raincoats back before the War Between the States. But when Japanese hegemony began gobbling up the world's rubber-producing countries, the rubber-boat industry found itself with a huge market and no raw materials—a situation guaranteed to bring tears to the eyes of any self-respecting capitalist.

A Brief Chemistry Lesson

As a direct result of the collapse in raw-rubber supplies, the US government, military, and rubber-dependent industries initiated a crash program to develop synthetic rubber based on the 1860 discovery of British chemist Charles Williams that natural rubber was a polymer of the monomer isoprene, which can be extracted from turpentine.

After a year and a half of research and $700 million of government money, scientists at DuPont came up with the first successful artificial rubbers—neoprene and Hypalon. Both are still used today in the manufacture of inflatable boats. To make neoprene, scientists polymerized ethylene (a clear hydrocarbon gas grocery stores spray on your oranges to make them orangier) into polyethylene, which was then reacted with sulfur dioxide (another colorless gas used by your grocer to make you think your vegetables are fresh). Chemically, a Hypalon molecule is a neoprene molecule with three chlorine atoms added, but this seemingly slight difference is misleading because neoprene and Hypalon have a number of differing charac-

After the war. . . .

teristics, all of which are important to inflatable boats, as we will discover in a later chapter.

Other developments of WWII were the expanded use of nylon (a synthetic thermoplastic resin developed by DuPont in 1935) and polyester fibers. Both are used in inflatable-boat construction under various trade names. Less important for our purposes but still significant was the development of fiberglass—filaments of melted glass spun into yarn and woven into a cloth, which, embedded in polyester resin, is used in inflatable boats for transoms, floorboards, and (increasingly) hulls. Besides providing the impetus for the development of these synthetic materials, WWII also served as the testing ground for inflatable life rafts, which saved the lives of thousands of combatants on both sides of the argument.

After the war, military life rafts were sold to the public as surplus. Their universal availability at low prices stifled further development of inflatable boats for private use until the supply was finally depleted sometime in the mid-1950s. My own first boat was a bright yellow two-man life raft I bought from a friend for a dollar (serious money for a 10-year-old in 1952). With it the friend and I explored, in one day, the entire length of the rain-swollen Paint Branch River. The news of this intrepid journey, which to us outstripped John Wesley Powell's conquest of the Colorado, came as quite a shock to our parents when they were advised by the Prince George's County Police Department that if they wanted us, they had to come get us.

Nineteen fifty-two was significant for another notable voyage by inflatable boat: Dr. Alain Lewis Bombard, a flamboyant and vociferous champion of inflatable boats as survival craft, set out from the Canary Islands to row and sail an inflatable dinghy across the Atlantic to prove that a shipwrecked mariner could survive for months on plankton and fish. He used a standard Zodiac 15-footer built from 18-inch tubes and outfitted with a lugsail, lee boards, and a steering oar. He departed without food or water on board. After 65 days at sea, Dr. Bombard made landfall on Barbados on Christmas Eve. That he was nearly dead when he arrived has not detracted from his achievement one bit.

When the supply of war-surplus inflatable life rafts was finally exhausted about 1955, Zodiac reentered the pleasure-boat market with a commercial version of the boat that Dr. Bombard had sailed across the Atlantic. Called the Mark III, it was 15 feet 6 inches long, 6 feet wide, and had a plywood floor. In 1959 a British tire company named Avon Rubber Products attempted to diversify its product line by introducing an 8-foot fabric-bottomed dinghy designed for rowing. Later that same year, Avon added a 12-foot version of the same boat. Other tire companies, such as Pirelli and Goodyear, also began to manufacture inflatable boats. Since the 1960s, dozens of other companies have entered the market with a bewildering assortment of types and models.

Today inflatable boats have evolved from the general to the specific. We now have inflatable boats designed to match the requirements of a wide variety of activities and varying in size from one-person dinghies to huge industrial barges. But with the exception of inflatable life rafts, there is no such thing as a single-use inflatable boat; all types can be used for a variety of activities. For example, besides serving as a dinghy to our sailboat, my 8-foot Avon was also used successfully as a whitewater river raft and as a freshwater fishing boat. In the next chapter we will first discuss the general categories of blow-ups available, then explore the activities appropriate for each.

CHAPTER 2

How Inflatable Boats Are Made

We have already mentioned that the original inflatable boats (excluding the putrid pig), such as the one made by old Charlie Macintosh from raincoat material, were built from fabric made airtight—"proofed" in the vernacular of the rubber-boat trade—by the application of thin layers of vulcanized rubber. The fabric was usually cotton, but silk, used a lot in airships, was also used for boats when light weight was critical. Many early life rafts, particularly those made by Goodyear and other tire companies, enclosed a rubber bladder—resembling a truck-tire inner tube—inside a protective shell of heavy canvas.

Natural rubber and cotton fabric combine to make a serviceable inflatable boat, but they have serious drawbacks. Natural rubber is quite soft, but when vulcanized with sulfur it becomes stronger and tougher while retaining its elasticity. Unfortunately, the more rubber is vulcanized, the more flexibility it loses. In a rubber boat, where flexibility and toughness are both important, a compromise has to be reached; a boat made from rubber-impregnated cotton is neither as tough nor as flexible as might be desired.

With repeated use, a boat made from vulcanized rubber delaminates where the fabric is folded. If it is put away without a proper drying, the rubber surfaces fuse where they touch, leading to further delamination when the boat is unfolded. The little WWII veteran my friend and I used in our adventure on the Paint Branch showed large areas where the yellow rubber had peeled away from the fabric. This necessitated frequent stops for emergency reinflation. Natural rubber is also photodegradable—subject to attack by ultraviolet radiation—and it is oxidized by ozone, so any boat exposed to the elements for longer than a few hours would be damaged.

Today no boats are made from natural rubber. The materials of choice are neoprene, Hypalon, and a corrupted form of polyvinyl chloride (PVC). Neoprene and Hypalon are closely related forms of artificial rubber that are often used together. PVC is a plastic. The differences between artificial rubber and plastic may seem academic, but they are significant for inflatable-boat manufacture and need to be examined in detail.

Neoprene and Hypalon

As we learned in Chapter 1, neoprene was developed during WWII as a practical replacement for natural rubber. It is truly a miraculous product, displaying most of the desirable properties of natural rubber and correcting a few of the negative ones. Neoprene is as elastic as rubber, much tougher, not as photodegradable, and it resists heat, hydrocarbon fuels, and many chemicals that turn natural rubber into a sticky goo.

When three chlorine atoms are added to the neoprene molecule, we get Hypalon, which retains most of the desirable qualities of neoprene with a dramatic increase in toughness and resistance to abrasion. It is even less vulnerable than neoprene to photodegradation, and it is less thermoelastic—meaning it won't soften when you leave your boat out in the hot sun. On the down side, Hypalon doesn't hold air quite as well as neoprene, and it's harder to glue.

The original inflatable dinghies introduced in this country by Avon and Zodiac were made from fabrics impregnated with neoprene and Hypalon. The Avons used Hypalon on both sides of the fabric. Zodiac used Hypalon on the outside, where abrasion resistance was most important, and neoprene on the inside, where airtight qualities were paramount. Today Avon maintains the same construction techniques as in the original boats while Zodiac has switched to the new kid on the block, polyvinyl chloride.

Polyvinyl Chloride

Polyvinyl chloride—or just plain PVC as it's called by legions of happy plumbers who no longer must wrestle with heavy copper, steel, or cast-iron pipes—is one of the most important of modern plastics. It is the material used to make phonograph records (remember them?), the tough, durable insulation around household electrical wire, and the shiny covering on your kitchen floor. We members of a technologically advanced society can't get by a single day without dozens of encounters with PVC, and it's safe to say our society wouldn't be the same without it. But hold on there. This is a book about inflatable boats, not about the socioeconomic implications of the polymerized synthesis of acetylene and hydrochloric acid, so let's get back to the subject at hand and talk about PVC as it applies to inflatable boats. Here we start to have a few problems.

The PVC used to make inflatable boats is essentially the same stuff used to make plastic drain pipes. The primary difference is that the material used to make boat fabrics airtight has various plasticizers added to make it more flexible and softer than the average sewer pipe. Dyes are also added to give the material the desired colors.

PVC-covered fabric is cheaper than Hypalon fabric, but the big advantage of PVC over Hypalon, in fact the only significant advantage, is that seams can be thermoelectrically welded quickly and efficiently by machines operated by semiskilled workers. Seams on a Hypalon or Hypalon and neoprene boat, on the other hand, must be painstakingly hand-glued by highly skilled workers using a glue pot and brush. The wisdom of sending one more segment of the world's skilled-labor force to the unemployment office is another societal question we can't address here, but we can't deny the savings to the manufacturer and ultimately to the consumer from the greatly reduced cost of the labor required to assemble PVC boats.

Unfortunately PVC has several problems as a boat material. For one thing, it is highly photodegradable—that is to say, in direct sunlight PVC quickly breaks down. If you leave a PVC boat out in the sun, it will begin to lose its flexibility, cracks will appear, and the boat will eventually leak air right through the fabric. Most manufacturers of PVC boats protect their products with ultraviolet protective coatings similar to the UVAs (ultraviolet absorbers) in marine varnishes and paints, but the long-term effectiveness of these coatings is subject to considerable debate.

Another problem with PVC is that the plasticizers used to make the normally rigid plastic appropriately soft and flexible also destabilizes it. Nearly all makes of PVC inflatables have had problems with quality consistency, with some boats being noticeably more durable than others made by the same manufacturer from a different batch of material.

Welded seams on PVC boats are indeed strong, but the seams where the fabric is attached to a wooden transom or a rigid bottom are not nearly as strong as those on Hypalon boats because while PVC welds very well, it doesn't glue well at all. This reluctance to accept conventional cold glues also makes repairing punctures and small tears more difficult.

Another potential problem with PVC is its susceptibility to damage from hydrocarbon fuels and other chemicals. The damage isn't cataclysmic in that gasoline won't eat your boat away, but it will stain and can shorten the life of the fabric. Hypalon is impervious to hydrocarbons and many other chemicals, as witnessed by the industrial use of the stuff as flexible liners for chemical and fuel tanks.

While neoprene and Hypalon display many important improvements over natural rubber, PVC enjoys only one significant advantage over neoprene and Hypalon: it's cheaper. Okay, it's a lot cheaper, and at least part of that cost advantage is passed on to you when you buy your boat, but there is a price to pay for this reduced cost.

I interviewed about a dozen full-time liveaboard cruising sailors and their families in the Caribbean regarding their choice of a dinghy. The responses to my questions about PVC boats were both startling and unanimous: a lip curled into a sneer and a string of adjectives unprintable in family-oriented literature. I heard several emotional accounts of PVC boats self-destructing in less than two seasons, and no one I spoke to who had purchased a PVC boat had any intention of ever buying another. The only bright spot in this admittedly unscientific survey was the willingness of several manufacturers to quickly replace damaged boats without question.

The opinions of the Caribbean cruising sailors I talked with are borne out by three recent surveys on inflatable boats—one taken by Jimmy Cornell in his *World Cruising Survey*, a second by *Practical Sailor* magazine, and a third by the Seven Seas Cruising Association (SSCA). None of these surveys were influenced by the substantial power of the advertising dollar, which neutralizes just about anything you might read on the subject in popular boating magazines. The results were unanimous, with well over 90 percent of the all the respondents favoring Hypalon over PVC, even at higher prices. The two top manufacturers in all three surveys were Avon and Achilles. Avon took the top prize with an incredible three-to-one advantage over Achilles.

Does this mean you shouldn't consider a PVC boat for your new inflatable? No, it doesn't, and here's why. My Caribbean survey, the SSCA survey, and the Jimmy Cornell survey all were conducted among full-time cruisers who had done most of their sailing and spent most of their time in the tropics—a virtual torture chamber for everything nautical. The constant assault on boats and equipment from blazing sun, persistent trade winds alternating with rainy-season gales and squalls, sopping humidity, and corrosive salinity is worse in the tropics than anywhere else on earth. And aside from the harsh environment, these full-time cruisers use their inflatables every day of the year. Cruisers in the tropics favor Hypalon boats because they last much longer under adverse tropical conditions. These surveys clearly suggest that if you're headed south of Bimini, you should avoid PVC boats unless you're willing and able to keep your boat covered most of the time. However, it is unfair to judge the suitability of a PVC boat for more temperate regions based on tropical experience.

The *Practical Sailor* survey was not centered in the tropics and contained a representative sample from a variety of geographical areas. Neither was it centered around full-time cruisers, representing instead a cross section of the boating public, less than 10 percent of which use their boats more than 10 percent of the time. The results still favored Hypalon boats, but the margins weren't as great, the distinctions weren't as clear, and the reactions to the problems with PVC were not as dramatic. Casual users also placed greater importance on the potential savings in initial purchase price.

First of all, photodegradation of PVC boats doesn't seem to be the problem in temperate areas—north of about 23°N (or south of 23°S)—that it is closer to the equator. The *Practical Sailor* survey included calls to several repair shops not associated with dealers and failed to detect a bias for either material. Nor was the frequency of repair greater for boats made of one material over the other. My own calls to New England dealers and repair shops met with similar responses. Avon and Boat/U.S. dealers, who sell Hypalon boats, claimed that every PVC boat that came through the doors was practically beyond repair because of ultraviolet degradation. Zodiac and West Marine dealers, who sell PVC boats, were equally adamant that their welded seams were a tremendous advantage over the hand-glued seams of Hypalon boats. But those who repaired both and didn't sell either couldn't report any difference one way or the other.

In the frigid Northeast where we sail *Sultana* during those few brief months of summer when the sun actually shines, the reason ultraviolet radiation is less of a problem is distressingly obvious: there is a lot less of it. Our sailing season is short by any reasonable standard, and inflatable boats used in the Northeast don't spend as much time exposed to the elements as those farther south. Boats in New England spend six to eight months in storage waiting for the snow to melt, and it's a pretty good bet we don't get as much sunlight in our entire summer season as a tropical island gets in a good week in the winter. The inference is that if you take reasonable care to avoid leaving your boat in direct sunlight for extended periods and you wipe up gasoline spills promptly, the lower price of PVC boats can make them an excellent buy.

The truth is that how long your new inflatable boat lasts is likely to depend more on how you use it and the care you give it than the material from which it's made. The most expensive boat on the market will quickly become a piece of junk if it's abused and neglected, while an inexpensive boat conscientiously maintained and carefully used will give the happy owner years and years of trouble-free service. A Hypalon boat—or a PVC boat, provided it is conscientiously protected from the sun—in constant daily use as a dinghy to a full-time cruising boat should last about five years before it needs replacing. The same boat used occasionally for fishing or family boating may be in good shape after 20 years or more. We don't really know how long the new generation of inflatable boats will last because they haven't been around that long.

The warranty can be a clue to the comparable life expectancies of different boats. Hypalon boats from Avon currently come with a no-hassle 10-year warranty on the fabric (five years on seams) that is even transferable from owner to owner. PVC boats from West Marine have a comprehensive five-year warranty. Both have excellent reputations for prompt and efficient warranty service. But a good warranty doesn't necessarily assure a good boat. Some inflatable manufacturers, including one of the largest producers of PVC boats in the world, have good warranties on paper, but they have acquired reputations of being insensitive, even disdainful, to warranty claims—to the extent of generating lawsuits.

Fabrics

While the coatings discussed above are critical to the ability of an inflatable boat to hold air in and water out, they don't do much to add strength to the boat. That is the function of the fabric to which the PVC, Hypalon, or neoprene is bonded. Cotton and silk have been supplanted by cloth woven from polyester or nylon yarns. There are distinct differences between these two synthetics, but they aren't as dramatic or important as the differences between Hypalon and PVC.

Most yachtsmen are familiar with the characteristics of both polyester (usually Dacron, a trademark of DuPont) and nylon because both are used as cordage, each fulfilling specific purposes according to its special properties. Polyester is the material of choice for running rigging, where its minimal stretch and its ability to survive extended periods in the sun are substantial assets. Nylon rope is used as anchor rode, the dinghy painter, and for docklines because of its great strength and its incredible ability to absorb energy by stretching.

The strength and stretch of nylon rope became apparent to me several years ago on a fishing trip to northern New Hampshire. I was driving my Jeep with my inflated Avon on the roof along a remote dirt road north of Errol when I came upon a couple who had driven their very small Volkswagen into a very large ditch. The only thing I had that resembled a tow rope was the ⅜-inch nylon painter from the dinghy, and figuring it was better to try something than to do nothing, I gave it a go. To everyone's amazement, that little piece of nylon stretched to about twice its normal length, and the Volkswagen skipped out of that ditch quicker than spit out of a hot skillet.

Most boaters also know that nylon is photodegradable. A new soft and flexible dinghy painter becomes stiff and unmanageable after a few weeks of exposure to the elements. This susceptibility to ultraviolet radiation, along with nylon's propensity to stretch, make it nearly useless as a material for sails (spinnakers excepted). Polyester cloth, on the other hand, makes wonderful sails because it doesn't stretch and it resists ultraviolet attack.

The majority of inflatable boats on the market today are built with polyester fabric, usually Dacron. Most of the others use nylon. While an argument can be made that polyester's lack of stretch is important to obtaining the stiffness that makes an inflatable boat manageable, my own opinion is that, except for riverboats that may benefit from the stretch of nylon, it doesn't matter what kind of fabric is used.

What does matter is the weight of the fabric, but this is hardly ever printed in the sales brochures, nor is it always available from the salesperson trying to sell you a boat. It's not that it's a secret or anything like that; it's just that the average salesperson often isn't informed of such things. If you are able to determine the weight of the fabric, it will be a figure expressed in either denier (pronounced *den-yea*) or decitex—the weight in grams of a 9,000-meter-long or a 10,000-meter-long piece of yarn, respectively, from which the fabric is woven. Denier is the industry standard by which all fabrics are measured. Expect a denier of 800 to 1,200 or a decitex of 900 to 1,300 on better-built boats, less on less-expensive boats. Nearly all life rafts are constructed of 400- to 600-denier fabric (nylon or polyester) because heavier fabric would make the raft cumbersome and hard to launch and because life rafts are designed for very infrequent use.

Heavy fabric makes for a tough and durable boat, but of course, the heavier the fabric, the heavier the boat. Everything is a trade-off. Another minor problem with heavy fabric is the tendency for air to leak from inflation chambers by following a strand of yarn from one end where it terminates inside a chamber to the other end where it terminates outside the chamber. This phenomenon, called *wicking*, results in a very slow pressure loss that is usually no more than a minor annoyance, but it is the primary reason your boat may need to be topped off every so often when it is left inflated for a long period of time. Heavier fabrics are more prone to wicking than the lighter ones because they use thicker yarns, and Hypalon boats are more prone to wicking than PVC boats because thermowelding tends to seal the ends of the yarns better than cold gluing.

Many less expensive inflatables and all play boats are made from PVC or PVA (polyvinyl acetate) without any reinforcing fabric. These plastic materials often have an embossed texture and are dyed to make them look like a reinforced fabric. Most are constructed from sheet stock with heat-welded seams of varying quality. Some, like the Sevylor kayaks, are made from material heavy enough to stand up to fairly rough treatment and can represent a good value for those of us without a lot of money to spend on a boat. Others are so poorly made as to be useless outside the shallow end of a swimming pool.

Color

The first mass-produced life rafts used by flyers in World War II were yellow because yellow was thought to be the easiest color for rescuers to spot. (We have since determined that orange is even easier to spot, and that's now the color of most life-raft canopies.) For years any serious inflatable, life raft or no, had to be yellow. The first commercial neoprene/Hypalon boats were black, the natural color of those materials, but black makes for a solemn-looking boat that reaches amazingly high temperatures when left in the sun. In a matter of minutes, a black boat left in direct sunlight will be too hot to touch. So the industry fiddled around and came up with a way of adding a white coloring agent that turned Hypalon and neoprene a dark gray. This was a significant improvement, and for many years most inflatable boats were gray.

When PVC boats were first introduced in the late '70s and early '80s, they mimicked the gray of Hypalon boats. But it is easy to add dyes to PVC, so it wasn't long before lighter shades of gray, then white (the natural color of PVC), then two-tone boats began to appear. Achilles and a few other manufacturers make red boats. West Marine and HBI both use a distinctive blue fabric that appears to be stable and resistant to fading.

What color is best for you? Well, dark colors are hotter. White is cool but soils easily, and if you plan to use your dinghy as a life raft, white is hard to see in an ocean of whitecaps. Red is more visible, and probably easier to find if the dinghy breaks loose from the mother ship. Duck hunters will want a color that is easy to camouflage. But without a compelling reason for a particular color, it comes down to personal preference. Just pay your money and make your choice.

By the way, if you're buying an inflatable to use as a dinghy for your yacht, don't worry about the black rubrails and oarlocks making marks on your hull. This was an annoying problem with older boats, but the neoprene used for these parts on modern boats is very stable, and I haven't recently seen a problem with it transferring color to other materials. However, some strong solvents and silicone treatments can degrade the surface of the rubber to the point that it will leave marks on everything it touches.

The Future Is Yet to Come

I have come to hold a strong mistrust for technology. It seems that every time I buy anything complicated or electronic or trendy, the relevant industry introduces a new model, and the one I bought becomes old-fashioned and obsolete. This happens every time I buy a computer, and I stopped trying to keep up with the changes in camera gear years ago. You can bet that as you're reading these words, major companies are working overtime to develop or adapt new technology that will define the next generation of inflatable boats. Inflatable boats have proven themselves superior in a great many ways to traditional rigid boats, and the market for them continues to grow. But the best boats still carry price tags far greater on average than do equivalent hard boats, and cheap inflatables deteriorate so quickly that they aren't really a consideration for the serious buyer. The industry is busy searching for a material as tough and durable as Hypalon and neoprene and as easy and inexpensive to manufacture as unreinforced PVC. Should you wait for this miracle fabric before you buy a new boat? No, because search as they might, they may never find it.

Construction Details

How a boat is put together is nearly as important as the fabric in determining how long it will last and how much you'll have to pay for it. All inflatables made today use similar construction techniques, but there are enough differences to warrant our going over them one-by-one.

Multiple Chambers

All boats are constructed from airtight tubes arranged around some type of floor system, and all but the cheapest play boats have the tubes arranged to form more than one flotation chamber. Multiple chambers provide a measure of safety that allows inflatables to be used with confidence in circumstances where trusting a boat with a single chamber would be foolish.

On many quality boats, chambers are separated by conical baffles that can extend from one chamber into the other to equalize pressure. For example, if there is a slow leak in one tube, the differential pressure will force the cone-shaped baffle from the intact tube into the leaking tube, maintaining equal air pressure in both. The conical baffle also provides additional flotation in a boat with a deflated chamber by increasing the volume of air in the intact chambers, at a slight reduction in total air pressure.

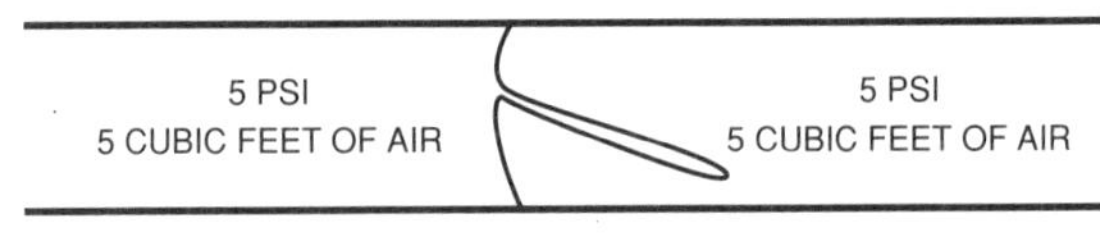

BOTH CHAMBERS INFLATED TO PROPER AIR PRESSURE
BAFFLE DEFLATED

SMALL LEAK IN ONE CHAMBER
PRESSURE IS REDUCED IN BOTH CHAMBERS
VOLUME REMAINS THE SAME
BAFFLE IS PARTLY INFLATED

LARGE LEAK IN ONE CHAMBER
ONE CHAMBER DEFLATED BUT THE OTHER CHAMBER HAS 8 CUBIC FEET OF AIR BECAUSE THE PRESSURE HAS BEEN REDUCED TO 3 PSI.
BAFFLE COMPLETELY INFLATED

Cone-shaped baffles.

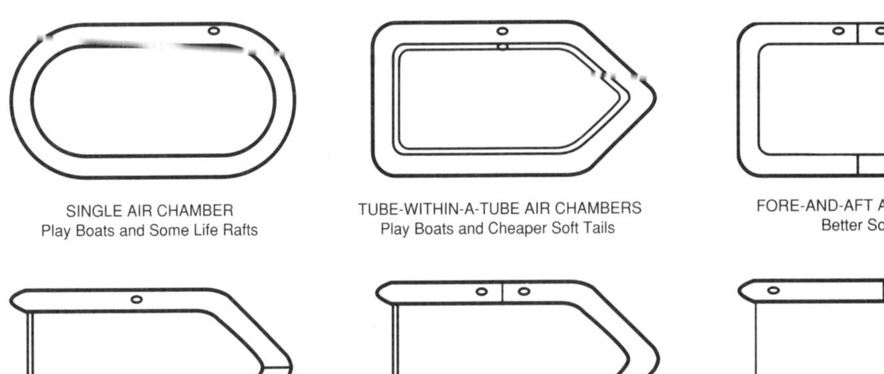

Air chamber configurations.

Seam Construction

There are probably as many different inflatable-boat designs as there are manufacturers, but all are made from sheets of rubberized fabric formed into tubes. The tubes are divided with baffles into chambers, formed into a boat shape, and attached to some type of floor. All manner of things—dodgers, handles, lifelines, valves, transoms, towing rings, pockets, sockets, and beer-can holders, to name a few—are attached to this basic hull. Forming the tubes and attaching the other parts requires various types of seams, and since pictures are worth a lot of words, here's what some of them look like:

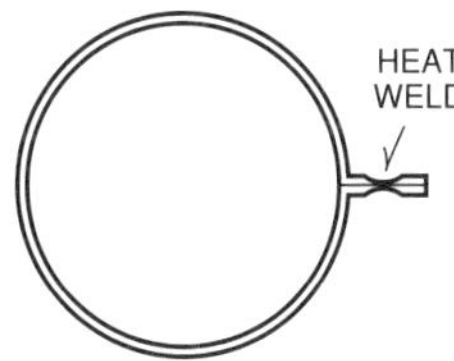

HEAT-WELDED FLANGE
PLAY BOATS ONLY
• **ADVANTAGES:** CHEAP TO BUILD
• **DISADVANTAGES:** CHEAP, CHEAP, CHEAP, AND UGLY!

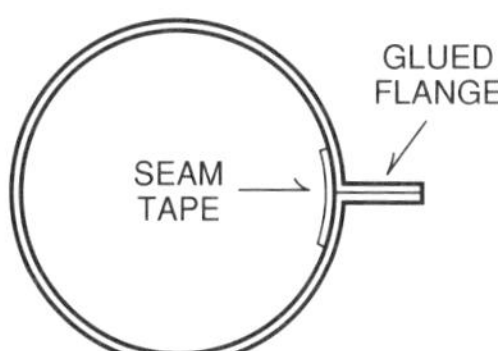

REINFORCED LAP SEAM
• OLD-FASHIONED LIFE RAFTS
• **ADVANTAGES:** STRONG AND EASY TO BUILD BY HAND
• **DISADVANTAGES:** UGLY, VULNERABLE TO ABRASION

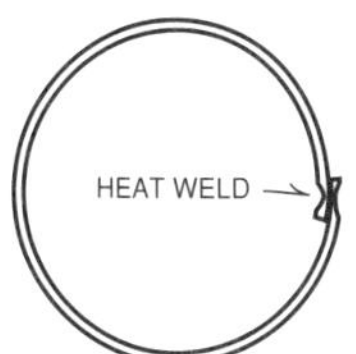

HEAT-WELDED SIMPLE LAP
PLAY BOATS AND REINFORCED PVC SOFT TAILS AND KAYAKS
• **ADVANTAGES:** EASY TO BUILD WITH MACHINERY AND QUITE STRONG
• **DISADVANTAGES:** WICKING CAN BE A PROBLEM WITH RUBBERIZED FABRICS

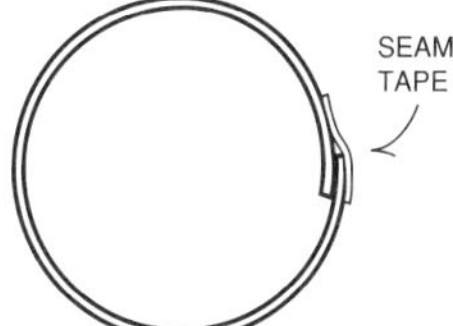

REINFORCED LAP SEAM
MANY LESS EXPENSIVE BOATS IN CURRENT PRODUCTION AND A FEW TOP-OF-THE-LINE BOATS
• **ADVANTAGES:** STRONG. CAN BE HAND GLUED OR WELDED
• **DISADVANTAGES:** PRONE TO WICKING AND QUALITY CONTROL PROBLEMS WITH WELDED PVC BOATS

DOUBLE REINFORCED LAP SEAM
TOP-OF-THE-LINE BOATS
• **ADVANTAGES:** STRONGEST SEAM FOR HYPALON, PRACTICALLY ELIMINATES WICKING
• **DISADVANTAGES:** EXPENSIVE TO BUILD

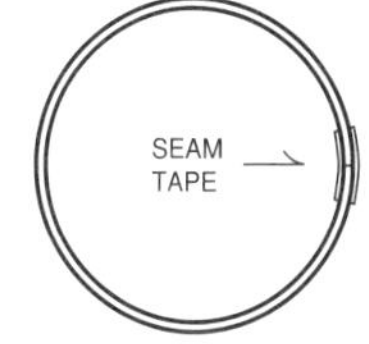

DOUBLE REINFORCED BUTT SEAM
MANY GOOD HYPALON BOATS AND A FEW TOP-OF-THE-LINE BOATS
• **ADVANTAGES:** STRONG, MOST ATTRACTIVE AND SMOOTHEST SURFACE
• **DISADVANTAGES:** EXPENSIVE AND NOT QUITE AS STRONG AS DOUBLE REINFORCED LAP SEAM

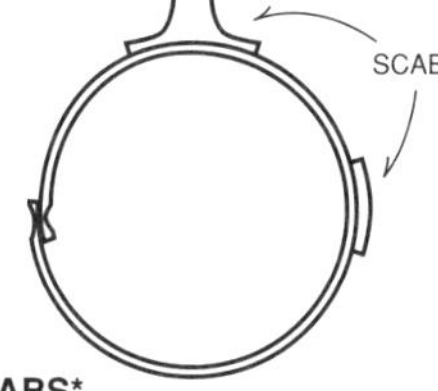

SCABS*
• USED TO ATTACH OARLOCKS, TOW RINGS, AND THAT SORT OF THING
• CAN'T BE WELDED AND MUST BE COLD GLUED SO THEY MAY TEND TO FALL OFF PVC BOATS
* "SCABS" IS A TERM USED IN THE SHOP NOT LIKELY TO MAKE IT INTO THE SALES BROCHURES!

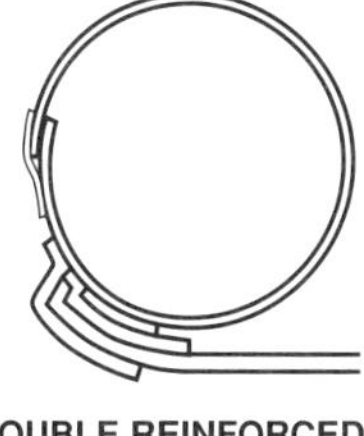

DOUBLE REINFORCED BOTTOM SEAM

Seams.

Calendering

The unreinforced PVC material used to make inexpensive boats is rolled into sheets of the desired thickness, but reinforced fabrics have the rubberizing material bonded to the woven cloth. A knifing technique was used in the past, similar to the process a plasterer uses to skim-coat a wall with finishing mix. Natural or synthetic rubber was heated and thinned with solvents until it was liquid enough to be spread with a long, thin knife blade, sometimes in one coat and sometimes in as many as 10. Knife-coating was the only way natural rubber could be applied to fabrics and it worked fairly well with vinyl. However, even the best knife-coated fabrics are subject to delamination, so today better boats are all built from calendered fabric.

Calendering involves running the fabric through a set of rollers under intense pressure and heat while introducing a pelletized rubberizing material such as PVC, Hypalon, or neoprene. The resulting fabric is one piece and very stable. Calendering can accommodate layers of different materials, such as Hypalon on the outside and neoprene on the inside, and it allows for layers of alternating colors. Delamination of calendered fabrics is rare.

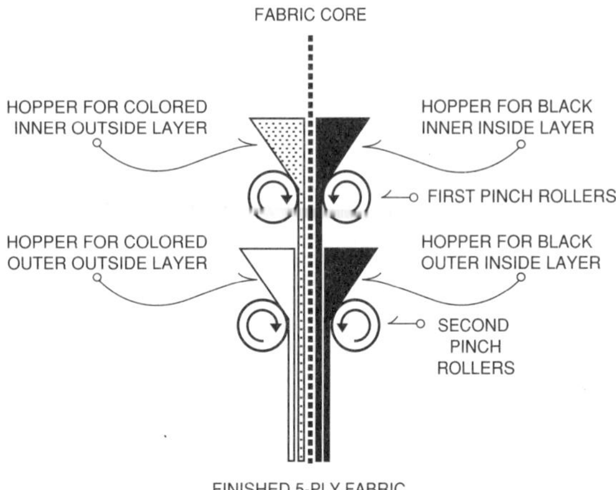

Calendering a five-ply material.

Valves

My old Zodiac had the most complicated inflation valve I've ever seen. It was beautifully machined from stainless steel and phenolic plastic, and it provided for inflating all three major inflation chambers from a single valve. Turning the valve to the inflate position magically connected all the chambers to the inlet at the same time. Turning it to the navigate position just as magically isolated the chambers. The valve also had a pressure relief that bled off excess air if the boat was overinflated, and you could equalize the pressure among all chambers by turning the closed valves to the *inflate* position. To deflate the boat, you pulled on the pressure relief valve, which let the air out in a rush, or you removed the cap. The most amazing thing about this complicated valve was that in 10 years it never once failed. When it got a little sticky, a shot of WD-40 was all that was required, and that's the only maintenance it ever got.

The inflation valves on my old Avon Redstart were a study in contrast—a lot like comparing French *haute cuisine* with English roast beef and boiled cabbage. The Avon valve was simply a reinforced hole with a flapper valve and two screw caps. To inflate the boat you removed the outer cap, inserted the hose, and pumped away. Each chamber had to be pumped separately, and there was nary a sign of a relief valve. To deflate the boat you removed both caps, which removed the flapper valve and allowed the escaping air unrestricted flow.

Today most boat manufacturers use some variation of the Avon design. I expect they are a lot cheaper to build than the old French valves, and they are certainly a lot easier to use. The absence of a relief valve isn't really a problem since quality boats today are built to withstand limited overinflation.

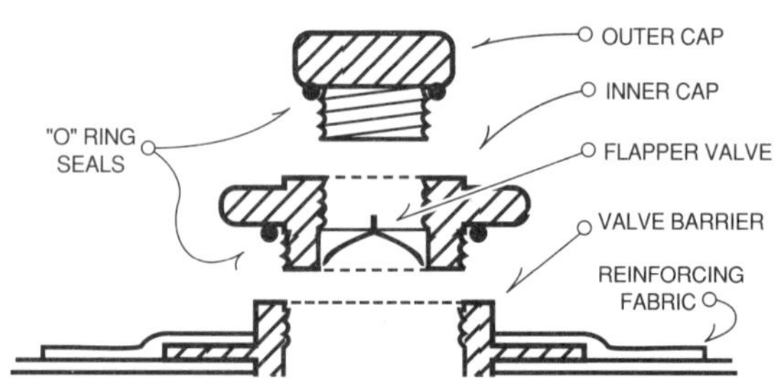

A typical inflation valve.

CHAPTER 3

Why an Inflatable?

If you are considering the purchase of a small motorboat for activities such as waterskiing, scuba diving, or just motoring around the harbor, there are a great many reasons why you should consider an inflatable. If you're a yachtsman considering the purchase of a new tender, you should evaluate the relative merits of hard dinghies versus inflatables. If you are a whitewater enthusiast, your choices range from one-person rafts to inflatable riverboats that carry a dozen paddlers. If you are a bluewater cruiser or an offshore racer, you would be foolish not to consider an inflatable life raft; indeed, you will be forbidden by the rules from participating in almost all organized offshore activities without one. And if you're an apartment-dwelling city slicker who just happens to enjoy backpacking into the deep woods to paddle among beaver ponds, a small inflatable kayak is worthy of your consideration.

Types of Inflatable Boats

My personal experience over the years has included all these activities except waterskiing, so I feel with all appropriate humility that I can speak with some authority on each. But before we proceed with a closer examination of activities appropriate to inflatables, let's take a moment to look at the types of boats available. It will be helpful to divide the throng of inflatable boats into a handful of categories, but the lines between these categories aren't clearly drawn, and there is considerable overlap.

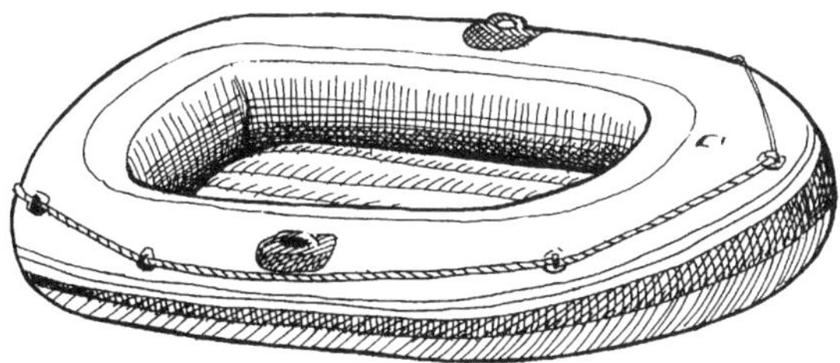

Play boat.

Play Boats

There are a lot of small inflatable boats on the market made from soft, unreinforced PVC or other vinyl plastic and available from Kmart or even a full-service grocery store for between $25 and $100. Notable for their bright colors, these boats often feature lively pictures of mermaids, sea horses, or even Mickey, Donald, and (my personal favorite) Goofy. Since this is a serious book about serious boats, my first impulse was to treat these inexpensive boats as toys and ignore them, but that is also to ignore the fact that thousands of people get a great deal of on-the-water enjoyment from these boats. Omitting them is also unfair to their manufacturers, who are trying to deliver good value at affordable prices.

The important thing about play boats isn't so much what they will do as what they won't do. They don't make good dinghies (although thousands are used in this way) because they are simply too flimsy. Only a fool would depend on one of these boats as a life raft. They lack the rigidity required to motor well with even the smallest outboard—though larger play boats come with outboard brackets. And rowing or paddling one even a short distance is a study in frustration.

What these boats do very well is to provide a tremendous amount of fun for unrestrained children of all ages (including your frolicsome author) who enjoy splashing around in the protected waters of a public beach, a pond or small lake, or a swimming pool. This is the use for which these boats are designed. If you expect anything more from them, you are bound to be disappointed, and you may even place yourself at unreasonable risk.

Soft Tails (Dinghies)

Some intrepid wordsmith recently coined the term *soft tail* to refer to the smallest of the serious inflatable boats—previously called *dinghies*. Since these boats have many uses other than as dinghies, and since I can't improve on "soft tail," let's adopt it.

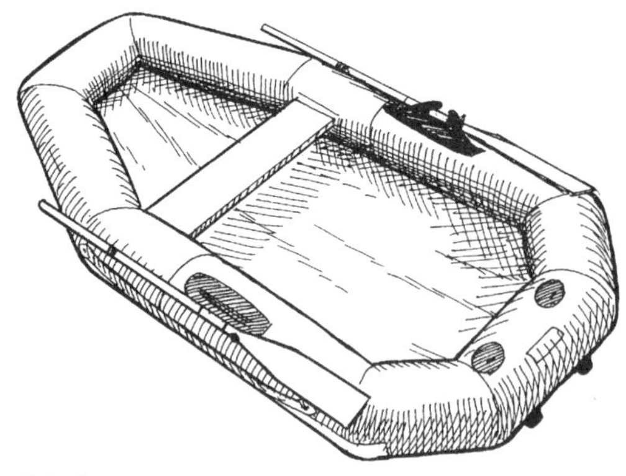

Soft tail.

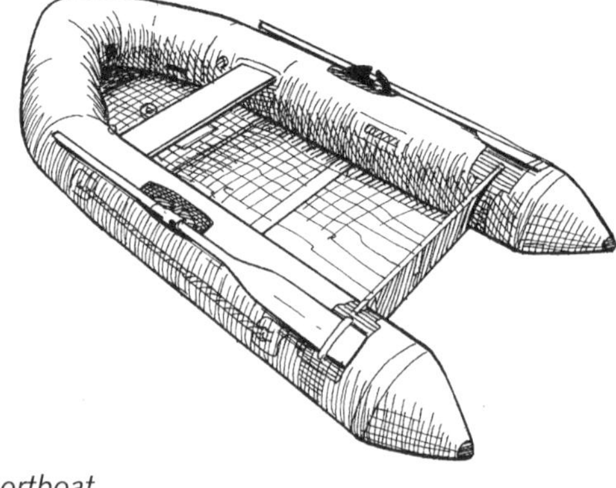

Sportboat.

Soft tails are usually constructed from two tubes or chambers, perhaps with an inflatable seat as a third. They don't have transoms and are designed for rowing or paddling, although most will accept, with varying degrees of success, a small outboard on a bracket. For the cruising boat that needs a small tender but lacks the space to stow a conventional dinghy on deck, a soft tail can provide an ideal alternative to towing a dinghy astern. They are also excellent for apartment and condo dwellers, or anyone else who wants to own a boat but doesn't have room for a conventional craft. These small inflatables can be used successfully for fishing, scuba diving, exploring, camping, swimming, or that most enjoyable of all outdoor activities, just messing about in a boat.

Soft tails are available in a wide variety of materials and at varying costs. The simplest and least expensive are made from heavy-duty unreinforced PVC and would be considered play boats but for their larger size, more rugged construction, and greater utility. The Sevylor Caravelle is one of the most popular of this type. The next step up takes you into reinforced fabrics coated with PVC or Hypalon—bigger and heavier boats that are naturally more expensive but also offer a wider variety of use options. You can expect to pay about $150 for a good-quality Sevylor to about $1,200 for a top-of-the-line Achilles or Avon.

Sportboats

Sportboats are a step up from the soft tails, and their added utility makes them popular as dinghies as well as general-use runabouts, fishing boats, and dive boats. They are distinguished by rigid, integral transoms, rigid floors, and (usually) some sort of keel to improve handling under power. Unlike soft tails, these boats are designed for use with outboard motors and are available in sizes and configurations that can safely handle motors from 1 horsepower (hp) up to about 50 hp. All sportboats are made from fabrics rubberized with either PVC or Hypalon, all have multiple air chambers, and most have floorboards that lock in place over fabric bottoms. The transoms and floors have traditionally been high-grade plywood, but plastic, aluminum, and fiberglass have become more evident in newer models.

Sportboats, especially larger ones, can be fitted with accessory windshields, wheel steering, dodgers, and running lights, and may lend themselves to transportation on a trailer. Self-defeating, you say? Not necessarily, and we'll talk more about storing and transporting inflatables in Chapter 7.

Sportboats are distributed under a great many trade names and in a wide range of quality and price. A bit of study will be required before you purchase one. The smallest sportboat retails for about $800; the largest will set you back over three grand.

ROLL-UP SPORTBOATS. The biggest problem with sportboats, especially the small ones used as dinghies, is the floorboards. Soft tails used as dinghies are often purchased without floorboards because there isn't space to stow them on the mother ship. A soft tail without floorboards is marginally useful; it can still be rowed, after a fashion. A sportboat without floorboards is useless, so floorboards aren't an option but come with the boat.

Floorboards are fine when the boat is in use, but problems arise when the thing is deflated. The bag holding just the floorboards is likely to be almost as big and heavy as the one holding the boat. Furthermore, the average yacht doesn't have the large flat surface needed for proper installation of floorboards. Installing them in even the smallest sportboat on the deck of a yacht can be a frustrating experience, resulting in flaring tempers and, too often, damage to the inflatable.

What to do? Well, for many years Henshaw Inflatables Limited of Somerset, England, has been marketing both the doughty little Tinker Tramp and the larger (and doubtless doughtier) Tinker Traveller with integral floorboards. It isn't necessary to install the floorboards in a Tinker because they aren't removed. You deflate the boat, roll it up, and stuff the whole thing into its bag. And it inflates as easily as a soft tail; just pump it up and off you go.

The rest of the industry is finally following Henshaw's lead, and most major brands of small sportboats now offer one or more versions of their products with integral floorboards. Collectively, roll-ups make up one of the hottest-selling segments of the inflatable-boat market.

Roll-ups do have a few drawbacks, and loath as I am to interject the dark specter of negativity into what has heretofore been a paragon of plaudits, I would be remiss were I to allow them to pass without a whisper of warning. Roll-ups cost about 20 percent more, on average, than an equivalent boat with removable floorboards. Low-end roll-ups, those with widely spaced slats sewn into the floor fabric, produce additional drag. (I'm not saying you shouldn't buy one—many offer quite good value—but just be aware that they require a little more energy to row or motor.) And the fabric floors of many roll-ups are easier to damage than conventional floors, with the damage more difficult and costly to repair.

Even with these drawbacks, roll-ups have to be the best thing to happen to inflatable dinghies since compressed air, and you can bet that the next time *Sultana* needs a new dinghy, roll-ups will get first consideration. If I were buying one today, I'd pick the Avon 3.15 because of its rugged construction, large tubes (16¼ inches), and ingenious floor design, but don't let me choose for you. Look at them all and decide for yourself. You may find one you like better, and you'll surely find several that cost a lot less.

INFLATABLE FLOORS. Another type of roll-up has an inflatable floor. Some less expensive soft tails (such as the Sevylor Voyager—about $200), smaller sportboats (Bombard AX Plus—about $1,500), and most of the kayaks, riverboats, and offshore life rafts have inflatable floors. Besides being quick and easy to deflate and stow, these have several important advantages over slat-type roll-ups:

- Because the floor is an independent air chamber, these boats provide additional flotation and safety.
- The best can be inflated very hard to give superior stiffness and therefore better performance than some slat-bottom roll-ups.
- The air layer in the floor provides welcome insulation for cold-water use.
- The inflated floor floats high, greatly improving the boats self-bailing ability (provided the boat has scuppers).
- The longitudinal orientation of the floor tubes increases lateral resistance, which improves motoring and rowing characteristics.

Rigid Inflatable Boats (RIBs)

A big problem with sportboats has been their fabric floors. It is difficult to fashion an effective keel out of fabric. If the bottom fabric is not absolutely taut, the drag of the loose fabric inhibits "stepping up" to planing speed. The bottom has greater exposure to abrasion and damage than the rest of the boat. Since the bottom on all but a few models isn't pressurized, it is difficult to find leaks when they occur. And the more efficient and durable sportboat bottoms are designed to be, the more difficult the boats become to assemble and inflate.

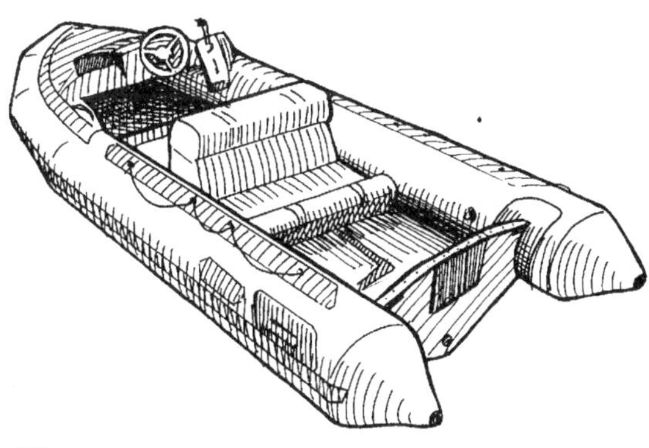

RIB.

To correct these faults, designers have combined the desirable inflatable-boat qualities of light weight, high-volume buoyancy, and stable tubular construction with the equally commendable rigid-boat qualities of durability and efficient keel design. To this new type of boat, they have attached the somewhat oxymoronic title of *rigid inflatable boat*—RIB for short.

RIBs are constructed much like sportboats, but in place of fabric-covered plywood or aluminum floorboards, they have a molded fiberglass or formed aluminum hard bottom resembling the bottom of a traditional boat with a "deep-V" hull. This hard bottom greatly extends the RIB's durability, utility, and performance under power. There are now RIBs designed for sport use that will accept outboard motors up to about 100 hp—enough to satisfy the most outrageous speed freak. HBI Hard Bottom Inflatables company of Sherborn, Massachusetts, produces a 40-foot monster that carries advertised loads of 800 hp and 40 passengers.

The HBI RIBs carry the hard-bottom concept one step farther: instead of gluing a hard bottom into an inflatable boat, they have attached inflatable tubes to a fiberglass boat. The tubes attach to the hull with a boltrope-and-groove system that makes them removable for maintenance, repair, or replacement.

We can't ignore the one major drawback to RIBs—the loss of the ability to deflate and stow the boat in a small space. Deflating the tubes when you put a RIB away for the season won't save that much space because of the hard bottom, and most manufacturers recommend storing the boats with the tubes inflated. Furthermore, because the tubes are an integral part of the boat, RIBs retain the requirement of all inflatable boats for special care and delicate handling in storage; you can't just flip one onto a set of sawhorses in back of the garage and expect it to survive more than a year or two.

Expect to pay more for a RIB than you would for a soft tail or a sportboat. As this is written, one of the least expensive is the 8-foot Caribe (a sweetheart) at about $2,000, and from there the prices go right through the roof. You can have one of those 40-foot HBIs for only $99,500. A foot pump is included. Engines, of course, are extra.

RIB JET BOATS. One recent development in RIBs is inboard power. Most such boats are a marriage of an inflatable and a Jet Ski, combining the stability of a hard-bottom inflatable with the seat, handle-bar steering, and propulsion of a jet ski. Typically these hybrid craft are a cooperative effort between a personal watercraft (PWC) manufacturer (such as Kawasaki) and an inflatable boat manufacturer (such as Avon). The idea seems like a good one, combining the fun and performance of a PWC with the safety and carrying capacity of an inflatable.

Some inflatable manufacturers have accomplished much the same thing in their RIBs by replacing the outboard with an inboard-mounted jet-drive engine. Such boats come in a range of sizes and powers, and they typically have side-by-side seating and wheel steering. Novurania (and probably others by print time) offers a RIB with twin jet drives. RIB jets like these resemble jet riverboats more than PWCs, and they can operate safely (and fast) in shallow water. These boats aren't cheap, but they may not be that much more expensive than a RIB and a comparably rated outboard.

Despite being reviled by a sizable segment of the boating public, including yours truly, personal watercraft have become the most popular boats in America—a point not lost on inflatable-boat manufacturers. Those that don't already have a RIB jet on the market undoubtedly have one in the pipeline. The inboard inflatable is a relatively new and still-emerging product in America, but it may merit your consideration.

Riverboats

Riverboats are a specialized version of inflatables designed for use in the rapids and whitewater of the world's wild rivers. They resemble large, poorly inflated soft-tail dinghies, but they have many unique features not immediately obvious.

Riverboats are usually designed to be inflated to lower pressures than other inflatable boats, and most are made from nylon fabric, which stretches more than polyester. Both features give added flexibility and resilience. High ends give riverboats a pronounced rocker that keeps the nose from digging into haystacks and rooster tails (river talk for big waves). Large scuppers drain the huge quantities of water that slosh aboard during a trip down the rapids. Inflatable floors increase buoyancy, facilitate draining, and protect the passengers from impacts with rocks, logs, and casualties thrown from the boat ahead.

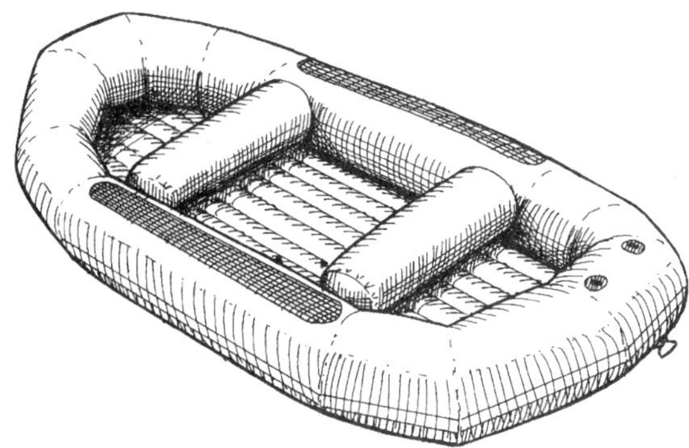

Riverboat.

Most riverboats are designed to meet the needs of professional outfitters and guides running whitewater river trips for large groups of adventurers. Several manufacturers, however, make smaller versions suitable for individuals or for small groups with a collective passion for the sport. Northwest River Supplies makes a one-person raft. Achilles make one for four. Avon's smallest riverboat is for seven. If you buy one of these little beauties, there's no reason you can't use it for more than bouncing down the Snake River. Because of the inflatable floor, a riverboat will row or paddle better than a soft tail, it makes a stable fishing platform, and the high ends make it more seaworthy in all waters. Many can be fitted with an outboard bracket and can be expected to motor better than a regular soft tail—again because of the inflatable floor. The high ends mean most riverboats require a long-shaft outboard.

If they're such great boats, why aren't more used for water sports other than whitewater rafting? Because they're expensive. The four-person Achilles, at just under $2,000, costs about twice as much as their four-person soft tail. The top-of-the line Avon—big enough for the whole neighborhood—sells for about $6,500.

Kayaks and Canoes

I was attending a kayak race in New Hampshire when I ran into Larry, a leftover hippie from the Sixties everybody knew by his old yellow Jeep with six battered kayaks on top. Larry never went near the water, just drove the Jeep for one of the clubs that never missed a New England meet. But lack of in-the-boat experience didn't stop Larry from being an expert on whitewater. With this book in mind, I asked him what he thought of the inflatable kayaks becoming more and more popular with recreational paddlers (never with racers). Larry thought for a moment, spat about a quart of tobacco juice into the river, then proceeded to set me straight.

"Them ain't kayaks. Them's canoes."

"The manufacturers call them kayaks," I said.

"Well, them manufacture dudes is full of pig feathers [he didn't say feathers, but this is a family book]. A canoe's somethin' ya rides in—like a washtub or a rowboat—but a kayak, that's different. Ya wears a kayak just like ya wears a pair of Levi's, and whereas ya jest climbs in a canoe an' paddles off, ya needs to put on a kayak." Here Larry went through the motions of pulling on an imaginary pair of pants, then spat another wad at a rock near my feet.

"An' that ain't all," he continued. "Whaddaya think would happen if ya put one of them rubber duckies in there?" He gestured toward the stream raging with the melted snows of early spring—Class IV and V all the way, expert only and no place for a rubber boat.

"Well . . . I don't know. . . . "

"Shore ya do. You'd drown quicker'n a rabbit in a pump house an' tha worl'd be a lot better off fer bein' done with such a fool." He was getting up another wad and looking about for a target. I stepped back a bit.

"An' whaddaya think would happen if ya tried to roll one of them things? What then?" He was referring to an Eskimo roll, an expert kayak maneuver where the paddler intentionally capsizes to one side, rolls 360 degrees underwater, and pops up on the other side. He glared at me waiting for an answer. Juice was starting to dribble down his chin.

"Well . . . ," I began.

"Well, hell. You'd drown all over again, that's what you'd do." He let loose a monstrous stream of

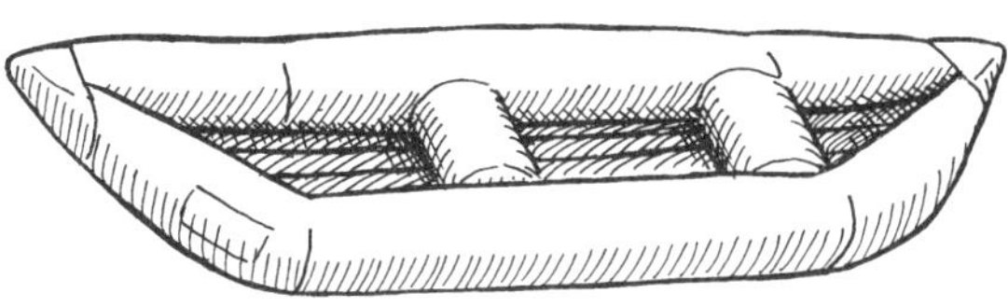

Kayak.

juice into the river. "Damn, now look what ya made me do. I done lost my chaw."

If you're a loner by nature, or if you prefer your whitewater adventure shared with one kindred spirit rather than a boat-full of howling strangers, you might consider one of the delightful little inflatable boats "manufacture dudes" call *kayaks*. Kayaks or canoes, these boats accommodate one or two paddlers in style and comfort. Granted, if you're a hard-core whitewater buff like Larry, or if your idea of recreation is a quiet paddle up a meandering stream in an antique Old Town canoe, you may not be entirely happy with a blow-up model. While they paddle better than a soft tail or sportboat and are more stable than a conventional canoe or kayak, they won't win any races against a hard-shell boat. But if you're faced with space and storage problems, an inflatable kayak might be the boat for you.

The light weight and compact package of the smallest inflatable kayaks make them ideal for backpackers. Sevylor makes a slick two-place kayak that fits onto a standard pack frame and still leaves plenty of room for sandwiches and fishing tackle. It weighs about 35 pounds with pump and paddles, and costs under $150 from discount houses. Other models are larger, heavier, more durable, and a lot more expensive—up to about $2,000. For more information about these boats, read *The Complete Inflatable Kayaker* by Jeff Bennett (International Marine, 1995).

Life Rafts

We have already discussed how inflatable life rafts were developed as survival craft for airplane crews during WWII. Today the progeny of those early survival craft, refined and improved, are available for those of us who venture offshore in aircraft and boats. Inflatable life rafts have become standard equipment on many small planes venturing over water. Nearly all bluewater cruising boats and offshore fishing boats carry life rafts. Approved life rafts are mandatory for participation in virtually any organized offshore sailboat race. And boats carrying passengers for hire often carry inflatable life rafts to satisfy stringent Coast Guard regulations for survival craft on commercial vessels.

Generally, life rafts for private use are available in three sizes: one-person rafts for small-plane pilots, four-person rafts for offshore boats with small crews, and six- or eight-person rafts for boats with larger crews. Confusing the issue somewhat, many manufacturers offer life rafts in both inshore or offshore models. Inshore rafts are generally constructed of lighter fabric with a single inflation chamber or tube and a single-layer fabric floor. Offshore models are heavier, have two or more tubes or inflation chambers, and most have a double-layer floor that is inflated for insulation from cold water. Inshore models are designed for coastal waters where there is a high likelihood of being found within a few hours. Offshore models, as the name implies, are more appropriate for use in extended voyaging where you might expect to drift for days, weeks, or even months before being picked up.

Life raft.

One-person rafts are of primary interest to small-plane pilots. Even the lightest four-person model is much too heavy to be practical in an aircraft, and deploying one through the door of a floating Beechcraft or Cessna would be practically impossible. Small-plane pilots who feel the need for a life raft will need a separate one for everyone aboard.

Similarly, boats that require room for more than eight people in a life raft may be better off with two smaller rafts rather than one of the big commercial jobs. Rafts larger than the standard eight-person size are heavy, difficult to store and deploy, and they cost more than those designed for recreational use. Smaller rafts are every bit as effective as the larger ones.

Because life rafts are designed as single-use craft, they don't require the rugged construction of a soft tail or a sportboat, and sensitivity to ultraviolet degradation and abrasion are not as significant. They must also be convenient to store yet accessible at an instant's notice; a small package and light weight are crucial. Life rafts are typically constructed of light polyester fabric coated with PVC, vinyl, or urethane, or of light nylon fabric coated with neoprene. The choice of materials is mostly a matter of manufacturing expediency. Since they all seem to work fine, you can concentrate instead on features and price.

All life rafts come with a compressed gas (usually CO_2) inflation system activated manually by a tug on a lanyard or automatically by hydrostatic pressure. They all have a canopy that either deploys when the boat is inflated or is erected after the fact. All have some sort of drogue or sea-anchor system that limits the raft's movement from the site of deployment. Most also have a water-ballast system that makes them less likely to flip over in big waves and strong winds.

One-person life rafts are stored for use in a small package shaped like a cushion on which the pilot of a plane can sit. Four-, six-, and eight-person rafts come packaged in your choice of a canvas bag called a *valise,* or in a fiberglass or plastic canister. The valise is designed to be stored below and must be brought on deck prior to deployment. The canister is designed to be mounted on deck and can be set up for automatic deployment with a hydrostatic release. The valise costs slightly less than the canister, but the danger is that most things stowed below eventually get shoved to the bottom of a locker and covered with other stuff, making them anything but handy in an emergency. *Sultana* is equipped with a four-person offshore Avon packed in a valise, but if I had it to do over, I'd get the canister.

Periodically—as often as once a year but no less than once every three years—life rafts must be delivered to a licensed facility for a test inflation, inspection, repairs, and replacement of dated materials such as flares and rations. Sometimes the inspection facility will allow the owner of the raft to be present when the raft is "popped." This is an excellent idea if you can arrange it because it's just about the only way you'll get to see your raft before you need it. Inspections aren't cheap. Depending on the size and type of your raft, figure on paying up to \$175 for an annual checkup, \$400 or more for a three-year inspection. The cost of an inspection can be significantly affected by the cost of replacement supplies packed with the raft.

Workboats

The light weight, tremendous buoyancy, seaworthiness, stability, and high speed of inflatable boats are being used to advantage by nearly all segments of the commercial waterfront. Barge and towboat companies are using them for tenders. Commercial fishermen are using them as yawl boats and net tenders. The construction industry is using them for temporary pontoon bridges and to transport supplies, materials, and personnel. The Defense Department uses them for surreptitious raids on despotic potentates (are there any other kind?). And municipalities with large harbors are using them as pilot boats and for law enforcement.

Workboat.

The manufacture, design, and use of inflatable workboats of all types is growing rapidly. That being said, we will drop the subject entirely. Inflatable workboats as a topic is just too vast to be covered here, and it is unlikely they were your interest when you bought this book. But the next time you see a Coast Guard vessel, it will likely be one of their big, bright-orange Avon RIBs that they use for everything from chasing down nefarious perpetrators of felonious misdeeds to fetching pizza for the dog watch.

Coast Guard RIB.

The Uses of Inflatable Boats

Now that we know the types of boats available, let's take a closer look at what we can do with them. We'll examine each activity in its turn and explore the reasons you should or shouldn't consider an inflatable for each.

As a Tender

Almost since their inception, inflatables have proven superior as the small boat used to tend to the needs of a large boat. The first American-market offerings from Avon and Zodiac were specifically designed as dinghies and tenders, and the majority of inflatable boats sold today are still used for these purposes. In the past few years, however, there has been a substantial shift in what we expect from a dinghy.

Early inflatable dinghies were usually purchased for their capacity to be deflated and stowed out of sight, intended only for occasional use in getting ashore when a more convenient means wasn't available. Following our ill-fated maiden cruise (detailed in the Introduction), it was just this line of reasoning that led us to the purchase of our first Avon Redstart. But times have changed and so have inflatable boats.

When we bought that first Avon, we were junior members of the Ipswich Bay Yacht Club and had the farthest mooring from the dock, but it was still an easy row to our 21-footer, even in a hard-to-row inflatable. That particular club, like most others, has expanded dramatically. Today the farthest boat appears to be more than a half mile away from the club floats—a piece of cake in a good pulling boat, but another matter in a soft tail, especially when the current isn't going your way.

In those days, when we went cruising to popular harbors like Edgartown, Hyannis, or Woods Hole, we cranked up the centerboard and, with 2 feet of draft, snuggled into the most restrictive anchorage. Today our boat is 52 feet from the tip of the bowsprit to the end of the mizzen boom, and while she draws only 5 feet and is surprisingly maneuverable, she isn't too good at snuggling into tight spaces. Since we have an aversion to renting moorings (this after diving on several and seeing first hand what you get for your 30 bucks), we often find ourselves anchored out of sight of the closest landing. The best anchorages are often miles away from the places we want to visit.

The old soft tail works fine for a row of 100 yards or so, and equipping it with a 2-hp motor provides the additional range to make most runs within an average harbor. But more and more cruising sailors are discovering that the advantages of a small sportboat over a soft tail far outweigh the added cost and more difficult stowage. With a 10-hp outboard, a lightly loaded sportboat easily reaches planing speed and laughs at a run of several miles.

Our Achilles is really too big to be called a dinghy (that function is served quite well by a 10-foot Dyer with a sailing rig and a 2-hp Johnson). *Tender* is a more appropriate term, but whatever it's called, it allows us the flexibility of anchoring away from the crowds. We have ready access to the shops, stores, and marinas in the most popular harbors without being subjected to the crowds, noise, and pollution of the adjacent anchorages. When we visit Southwest Harbor, Maine, for example, we anchor in Valley Cove at the entrance to Somes Sound. The Zodiac gets us to the town landing in a little over 10 minutes, where a short walk takes us to the fresh lamb chops at Sawyer's Market—by themselves worth the trip.

When we are cruising in far-off places like Canada or Central America, the high-speed sportboat becomes the family car, extending our horizons and expanding our ability to explore new territory.

An inflatable tender.

HARD VERSUS SOFT DINGHIES. In his latest *World Cruising Survey* (International Marine, 1989), Jimmy Cornell found that 80 percent of the cruisers surveyed had inflatable dinghies. This was up from 56 percent in his 1986 survey, indicating a significant trend away from hard dinghies toward their softer cousins.

One reason for this trend is the phenomenal load-carrying capacity of inflatables; it is virtually impossible to sink one by overloading it. Perhaps if you filled it with chain or lead ingots you could sink it, but loaded with cases of beer, coils of rope, canned food, the ship's dog, and two or three crewmembers—the normal boat stuff—the average inflatable will retain adequate reserve flotation even if swamped. Compare this with the typical 10-foot hard dinghy—easily overloaded with two people and a six-pack.

Another advantage of inflatables is their remarkable stability. Most of us learned early on to step into the center of a dinghy. If I heard it once, I heard it a thousand times: "Don't step on the gunwales." Well, you can step on the gunwales of inflatables all you want—jump up and down on them if you want to.

Their stability makes inflatables remarkably seaworthy in bad weather. I've negotiated some fearsome seas in my old Zodiac, seas that would be unthinkable in an ordinary dinghy. Swamp a hard dinghy and you're in trouble. (Don't panic, though; just tighten your life jacket, stay with the boat, and hope rescue arrives before Jaws does.) Swamping an inflatable boat is no big deal; you can keep rowing or, if you're so inclined, stop and bail the water out.

Inflatables can be deflated, and most can be bundled and stowed—either on deck or in a locker. In the off season they can be stored in a corner of the garage or up in the attic. The larger and more complex they become, however, the harder they are to deflate and stow. Deflating and folding a soft-tail dinghy is quick and easy, but add a set of floorboards to make rowing easier or allow the use of a small outboard, and assembly becomes difficult, stowage a nuisance. We long ago resigned ourselves to towing the cumbersome Achilles about 90 percent of the time, hauling it inflated onto the top of the deckhouse when the weather turns nasty or we are faced with a long passage. Newer roll-up inflatables, equipped with slatted or inflatable floors, solve many of the assembly and stowage problems that come with solid floorboards.

In spite of the substantial advantages a modern inflatable enjoys over the old-fashioned hard dinghy, there are stubborn traditionalists (cantankerous old codgers stuck in the past) who insist on hanging on to the old ones—and I'm one of them. Now hold on! Before you start calling me a hypocrite and go marching back to the bookstore for a refund, let me explain.

The dinghy we use on *Sultana* is an old Dyer equipped with a sailing rig. We have this boat instead of a small inflatable for two reasons: I like to row, and Phillip and Sarah like to sail. Inflatables don't row worth a damn, and while they will sail, they're not that good at it.

A well-designed hard dinghy will glide forward about three boat lengths for each skilled stroke of the oars. A good pulling boat will shoot forward six or seven boat lengths. A racing shell or scull will glide as far as 10 or more lengths for each stroke. With an inflatable, however, each stroke of the oars moves you forward only slightly more than the length of the stroke, and between strokes the damn thing practically stops. You don't really row an inflatable, you sort of lever it through the water using the oars as pry bars—like trying to row a scow with a net full of mackerel through oatmeal.

Sailing an inflatable isn't quite as hopeless. Dr. Bombard sailed his 15-footer across the Atlantic, and for a number of years Avon offered a sailing option for its Redcrest dinghy. I've never seen an inflatable that Sarah couldn't sail rings around with her Dyer, but they can be rigged to sail well enough to have some fun. The Avon sailing rig worked quite well, especially off the wind. Since it's no longer commercially available, I've included plans in Chapter 6 for a modified, easy-to-build version that is adaptable to just about any inflatable.

These days the only inflatable I know of available from the manufacturer with a sailing rig is the Tinker (see illustration on page 22). With its Marconi rig and overlapping jib, it is quite sophisticated and reportedly sails well. Still, if anyone with a sailing Tinker wants to challenge Sarah and Phillip around a standard triangular course, you're on. I'll bet a six-pack of root beer on the Dyer.

Hard dinghies have other advantages. Their initial cost is usually less than an inflatable, and they often last longer (our Dyer is more than 30 years old). They can be dragged over rocks and ledges that would rip the bottom out of an inflatable—important in a state like Maine where beaches are as scarce as clams in Aunt Minnie's

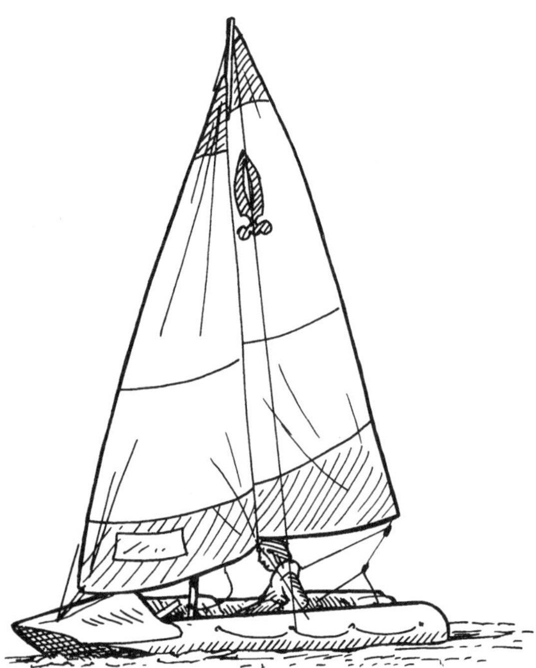

Sailing a Tinker.

chowder. And a beat-up old hard dinghy tied to the dock among a bunch of shiny new inflatables is practically guaranteed to be there when you return; I mean really... if you were a dinghy thief, which would you take?

For an increasing number of serious cruising boats, the answer to the dilemma of selecting a hard or soft dinghy has been to take both. This isn't as extravagant as it first appears. On our boat, the inflatable hauls provisions, supplies, and timid visitors who would be uncomfortable in the tippy Dyer. It also serves as a chase boat to fetch dinghy sailors whose enthusiasm for the downwind run exceeds their ability to sail back to windward. And if *Sultana*'s engine dies when the wind is calm, the inflatable does a yeoman's job as a yawl boat, pushing the old ketch along at a steady 4 knots.

The Dyer, on the other hand, is a lively sailer that keeps kids occupied for hours on end. It's the perfect boat for an early-morning row to work kinks out of shoulder joints. Having a dinghy *and* a tender allows part of the crew to go ashore without stranding the others. And on at least one occasion, having the dinghy available to give chase when the inflatable took off on its own was a lifesaver. Having both a hard dinghy and a soft tender is indeed the best of both worlds, but forced to choose, I would have to stifle my chronically conservative nature, bid a fond adieu to the dowdy Dyer, and go with the blow-up.

Scuba Diving and Snorkeling

When I first took up scuba diving—back when Lloyd Bridges' *Sea Hunt* was the hottest show on television—the undersea world was considered "the last frontier," populated by hordes of man-eating sharks, huge octopi with arms full of hideous suction cups, and slimy moray eels with rapier-like teeth. We who practiced this hazardous sport considered ourselves adventurers of the highest order—right up there with Marco Polo, mountain men, and astronauts. I remember sauntering out of the water in my ominous black wet suit with my face mask on my forehead and my diver's knife with its foot-long blade strapped to my leg—on the inside, just like Lloyd. The timid drew back in alarm, as if the Creature from the Black Lagoon had just waddled ashore on Coney Island, but one or two of stouter heart always ventured forth with the inevitable question: "See any sharks?"

"Only a couple," I would answer with practiced aplomb, "but small ones—about 20 feet—and I was able to drive 'em off with my knife."

Today scuba diving and snorkeling are enjoyed by millions of people the world over, secure in the knowledge that they are unlikely to be devoured by anything but a deep appreciation for the delicate beauty of nature under the sea. Sharks are a real threat in only a few isolated and easily avoided places in the world; and despite their fearsome visage, both octopi and moray eels are timid creatures, easily tamed and surprisingly affectionate once you get to know them. Scuba diving and snorkeling are no longer the provinces of the macho boor, thankfully, and little old ladies enjoy the sport right alongside young children.

Since I started, countless advances in equipment and technology have made diving safer and more enjoyable, and one of the most important was the inflatable boat. More and more waterfront areas once wide open to divers (as well as picnickers and beach lovers) are encircled by placards promising prosecution to anyone with the audacity to profane the sanctity of private property, and many state and local governments are banning scuba diving to, quite rightly, restrict the use of the dwindling supply of public waterfront to more tra-

Scuba diving.

ditional uses. In any case, the most interesting underwater scenery is accessible only by boat, and inflatables might well have been designed just for this purpose.

Scuba diving and, to a lesser degree, snorkeling are so much easier from an inflatable than from a conventional boat that a comparison seems unfair. Diving or snorkeling from canoes, dinghies, rowboats, and small motorboats is nearly impossible because of poor stability and the tendency of these boats to swamp or capsize. If a boat is large enough for a swimmer to get back aboard without dipping the rail (or worse), it is nearly always so high-sided that a boarding ladder or a swim platform is required. Good boarding ladders work well for snorkelers and swimmers, but scuba divers can be encumbered with more than 100 pounds of gear and equipment, which makes climbing a ladder difficult. A typical inflatable, on the other hand, has very little freeboard, and a diver or snorkeler can remove his gear while in the water, toss it aboard, and then clamber in after it. A big diving platform is probably best of all, but you need a big boat to go with it.

Diving, snorkeling, and even swimming can be dangerous from a conventional small boat because of their tendency to pound and hobbyhorse in any kind of a sea. Many swimmers have been injured and several have been killed trying to board a wildly pitching boat from the water. In contrast, when inflatables are not under power, they float on the surface of the water like an oil slick, with almost no tendency to pound even in a heavy sea. Even if they did pound a little, the consequences of being hit by a lightweight inflatable are far less severe than being conked on the head by a Boston Whaler or a Donzi.

Even the smallest inflatable boat (excluding play boats) makes a fine diving platform. Our little Redstart, the smallest Avon available when Susan and I bought it, would easily accommodate two divers and all their gear, although you did have to suit up before you launched. The Zodiac Mark II we bought next could handle six divers with ease. The Achilles we have today accommodates the four of us and all our gear, with plenty of room left for lunch and a cooler full of root beer. The bigger an inflatable gets, the better it is for diving, although a big RIB can be hard to get back aboard without a platform or a ladder. The 40-foot HBI with twin 200-hp outboards would be an ideal boat for carrying the whole dive club out to the Great Barrier Reef or the Blue Hole of Belize. My ideal dive boat is a 12- to 14-foot sportboat or RIB with a 25- to 40-hp outboard, transported on a trailer. Such a boat can easily carry four or more divers at planing speeds and opens up huge coastal and offshore areas to underwater exploration.

In most states where scuba diving is popular, divers are required to tow a float with a diver's flag. Light weight and low drag resistance allow the inflatable boat itself to serve as the float. Provided there isn't a lot of wind, even our big sportboat follows me obediently when I'm diving, responding to the lightest of tugs on its tether.

Motorboating

Another activity for which inflatables are ideal is just plain motorboating—which is best defined as just messing around in a boat. The inflatable version involves transporting your boat to some interesting body of water, launching, and then spending the day leisurely exploring all the little bays and coves and tributaries that attract your attention. In remote areas you will see wildlife and nature in a manner not possible from a road or trail. If you are a "birder," taking to the water

Motorboating.

opens a whole new world to you, and your life list will grow longer in short order.

In developed areas you can spend hours observing the back lawns of the mansions that line much of our suburban waterfront. You may notice that most of these palatial estates are devoid of people. It seems to be the nature of the super rich to be so occupied with becoming more so that they are seldom home. As you motor past their sumptuous but empty palaces, relax in blissful gratitude that you have managed to escape the burden of ostentatious wealth and have the time to cruise around in your rubber boat.

Inflatable boats of all categories lend themselves to motorboating, but sportboats and RIBs are ideal for it. With the help of launching wheels (see Chapter 5), a good-size inflatable can be launched in areas where launching a conventional motorboat would be out of the question. The shallow draft of inflatables allows exploration of the thinnest water. Their light weight makes it possible (but not always easy) to lift them over obstacles that would stop a conventional boat cold—a weir, fallen timber, or the occasional beaver dam. For those living in apartments and condominiums, small inflatables that can be transported without a trailer are particularly attractive.

Waterskiing.

Waterskiing

I don't like water-skiers much; they're noisy and they make a lot of waves zipping in and out of the moored boats as Susan and I try to enjoy our traditional evening libation. Only that contemptible device of the devil, the Jet Ski, can destroy the salubrious solitude of a quiet anchorage more quickly than a couple of kids with a powerboat and water skis. But sometimes, about halfway through my second cocktail, I find myself infected by the exuberance of the skiers. Sarah and Phillip are reaching the age where such raucous activities are attractive, and I'm not that old—yet. Our Achilles with its 25-hp outboard is, after all, a proven ski boat as long as it tows a single skier who doesn't expect too much. Perhaps with Sarah driving, Phillip doing lookout duty, and Susan standing by the VHF to activate the full medical evacuation capabilities of the Coast Guard; and if we start from shallow water; and if I get the skis to fit just right; and if Sarah promises to accelerate gently; . . . ah yes . . . perhaps some day . . . perhaps. . . .

But in the meantime, if you insist on joining the ranks of the raucous and profane, you'll find large RIBs ideal as ski boats. They are heavy enough to carry the power to pull any number of skiers, and they offer rapid acceleration with excellent visibility and maneuverability. Low freeboard and incredible stability make getting skiers in and out of the water a snap, and the hard deep-V hull offers control and planing performance that will equal or better conventional craft.

Any boat towing a skier should have the towline attached to a yoke or harness rather than to a single cleat, but this is particularly important when towing from an inflatable. The smaller the inflatable, the more important this becomes. The yoke keeps the pull of the skier on the boat's centerline, letting the boat track straight no matter how heavy the skier. Tie the tow rope to one side and the boat will tend to yaw to that side. The smaller the boat, the more pronounced this becomes. A small boat like our Achilles will simply run in circles around a skier sitting motionless in the water and wondering what was in the driver's last cup of tea.

If you already own a large sportboat or a small RIB with at least a 25-hp motor, there's no reason you can't enjoy occasional waterskiing. Just don't expect the bracing speeds and performance of the big RIBs. You should also remember that when towing a skier, the maneuverability of a fabric-bottom sportboat will be miserable, so give an extra wide berth to anchored boats with their curmudgeon skippers sipping martinis in the cockpit.

Fishing

Have you seen that bumper sticker that claims God doesn't deduct from your allotted total the time you spend fishing? Well, I have proof. My pal Harvey Darlymaple spends at least half his time fish-

Fishing.

ing, and he's already lived at least twice as long as folks expected after his wife caught him messing around with that new waitress down at the Rip Tide Lounge.

If Harvey fished from an inflatable boat, he might live even longer, because fishing from an inflatable can be pure pleasure. In a canoe or a small rowboat, much of your energy goes into seeing that the thing doesn't tip over, and you spend most of your time sitting on a hard and uncomfortable seat. In a blow-up boat the whole thing's a soft, comfortable seat, and if you feel like standing on the gunwales to cast, go right ahead—you couldn't turn the thing over if you tried.

Inflatable boats work well for all types of fishing, from a backpack trip to a beaver pond to offshore angling for blue-fin tuna. I can't think of any inflatable boat (with the possible exception of life rafts) that couldn't be used as some sort of fishing boat. The smallest soft tails are perfect for farm ponds, beaver ponds, and small streams. Sportboats are great on lakes and rivers; they make excellent bass boats and have the range to get you far back into the cypress swamps and bayous. And the big RIBs have the power, range, and seaworthiness to safely carry you far out to sea in search of saltwater game fish.

River Rafting

In the last few years the sport of whitewater rafting has gained a tremendous following in areas of the country where wild rivers are still available, notably the Rocky Mountain states, northern New England, and the Southeast. In the popular version of this exciting sport, one joins a party of eight or more like-minded adventurers under the care of a guide. Wearing life jackets, helmets, and knee pads, the entire group boards an inflatable raft that resembles a huge, poorly inflated soft-tail dinghy. Once aboard, they shove off for a terror-filled hour or so of hysterical screaming, repeated drenchings in ice-cold water, and bone-jarring leaps and plunges that would make breaking horses to saddle seem like a ride in the country. Miles downstream they emerge from the river with sodden clothing, shaky legs, and Cheshire-cat grins of pride and accomplishment. The majority even claim it was fun.

On a smaller scale, whitewater enthusiasts are taking inflatable boats into waters that were once the province of kayaks and decked canoes, finding that inflatables open up areas that are just too wild for the more traditional craft. Avon, Achilles, and several others make small whitewater riverboats designed for up to four paddlers, and inflatable kayaks work well in less intense rapids and rivers.

When using your inflatable boat in rapids, be aware that you're exposing it to dangers you won't encounter in more traditional uses. Fast-moving waters are often full of sharp rocks and snags just waiting to tear into an inflation chamber or rip the fabric bottom, and the water can be so turbid and murky that you can't see hazards until it's too late. Even on a slow-moving river, a single trip subjects your craft to more abrasion than a year or so of lake or ocean use because no matter how hard you try, you won't be able to avoid scraping against boulders and dragging across sandbars and rock-strewn bottoms. If the condition of your expensive inflatable is more important to you than the experience of exploring a wild river, either stay home or invest in a more specialized craft. But if you choose your water prudently and exercise reasonable care, there's no reason you can't use your sportboat or

River rafting.

soft tail in milder rivers and rapids. Just take along your emergency patch kit.

I have successfully taken inflatable dinghies and sportboats—loaded with Susan and the two kids—on tributaries of the St. John River in Canada, the northern reaches of the Connecticut in Vermont, the Kennebec River in Maine, and on several wild and desolate rivers in Central America.

My river technique is to launch the sportboat a bit underinflated so that the only hard part is the transom, which is protected by the stern tube extensions. I sit on the bow with a long paddle and steer while the kids and Susan sit on the side tubes with shorter paddles and propel the boat down the river backward. We must look rather comical from the shore, but it works. Together we have enjoyed some exciting jaunts, though admittedly on stretches of water that were tame and quiet (Class I or II) compared to what most river-rafting habitués would consider good water.

On a recent trip on the Rio Dulce in eastern Guatemala, we had further occasion to refine this technique. Tributaries of the Rio Dulce meander for miles through mountain canyons, tunnel through dense rain forest, and flow past native villages that have scarcely changed in a millennium. The traditional approach of using two autos—one upstream and one down—doesn't work in this wild and remote wilderness because there are few autos and fewer roads. If you want to go anywhere, you go by boat.

From the aptly named town of Fronteras, where the only bridge crosses the Rio Dulce, we would make a high-speed run to the mouth of the tributary we wished to explore. If the trip was longer, we hired a *cayuga*—a big outboard-powered dugout canoe the natives use as a taxi. Then we motored up the tributary as far as we could go—sometimes only a few hundred yards and other times 20 or 30 miles—until stopped by natural obstacles or the press of time. If we came upon small rapids with water too swift and shallow to motor through, we all piled out into the icy stream and "lined her up," using a technique developed to perfection by the French *voyageurs* in Canada. When we reached the headwaters or upstream as far as we could go, we stowed the outboard in the *up* position, broke out the paddles, and drifted back downstream with the current. The river we saw drifting down was always different from the one we saw motoring up—partly because of the different perspective, but mostly because of the wonderful silence.

What about a RIB? For the same reasons I wouldn't use a conventional aluminum or fiberglass skiff, I wouldn't use a RIB in whitewater or shallow rivers. RIBs are superb motorboats, but keeping one under control with paddles can be impossible. They won't respond to paddling, and without that response, you won't have the control you need to stay in the channel and avoid obstacles. Interestingly, the normally more durable hard bottoms are more likely than fabric bottoms to be holed when they hit a rock or boulder because they don't give. If you do punch a hole in the fabric bottom of a soft tail or sportboat, you can haul it onto a convenient ledge or sandbar and have it patched in a matter of minutes. It's quite another thing when you punch a hole in the bottom of your RIB.

Backpacking

I have occasionally strapped my little Redstart onto an aluminum pack frame, tied on a lunch bucket, a thermos of coffee, and my trusty fly rod, and struck out to try my limited fly-fishing skills against the wily brookies that inhabit the murky depths of a few remote beaver ponds known only to me, God, and the beaver. Backpacking may seem like the sort of activity that cries out for an inflatable boat, but there are a few reasons why I hesitate to recommend it to you. For one thing, at less than 40 pounds. the Redstart is light and easy to handle on a beach or the deck of a larger boat, but strap it onto a pack frame along with an appropriate pump, a paddle (forget the oars and floorboards), lunch, and the fly rod, you have a load worthy of a pack mule.

You can, of course, take along a companion to share the load, and the few times I've done this have worked out fine. While the Redstart makes a cozy platform for two fishermen, it's not uncomfortable once you come to understandings on who fishes on which side and that you can't cast together without snarling lines and tempers. However, the presence of another person destroys some of the magic inherent in the solitude that is the real reason for doing this in the first place. Furthermore, no matter who I take along, they always get snarkey when they find out they have to hike through the deep woods wearing a blindfold—I mean, a secret spot's a secret spot, right?

You might be tempted to carry a play boat, and I have met several intrepid outdoor types who have dragged these little boats miles back into the brush. Made from unreinforced PVC, they are lighter than the smallest "serious" inflatable; the energy saved in carrying the thing can be used to inflate it orally, obviating the need for a pump; and you won't have a major investment to worry about should it be torn asunder by an enraged bull beaver that mistakes the pictures of Mickey and Goofy for amorous competition. (It could happen folks. These toothy rodents are notorious for their bad eyesight and worse judgment, and they are plenty big enough to get your attention when they're mad.)

Despite the obvious advantages of low-priced unreinforced boats for backpacking, and despite the fact that hundreds of hikers use them, I have serious reservations about recommending them. Every remote pond or stream I've ever visited was chock full of snags, hidden rocks, and sticks lurking out of sight just beneath the surface of the tannin-rich water, and these hazards can rip soft plastic to shreds. If you want to try backpack boating with a play boat, do it with this risk in mind.

Today I don't do a lot of backpacking. The beaver ponds are still there and the trout are just as tasty, but the knees aren't quite what they used to be. However, faced with the decision of which boat to buy for backpacking, I would be tempted to try the inflatable kayak made by Sevylor called the Tahiti (an odd name if you know anything about Tahiti or the origin of kayaks). It's made from unreinforced PVC in the cheapo model (about 150 bucks) and PVC-coated polyester in the expensive version (about 500 bucks, neatly illustrating the economy of cheap fabrics). It weighs about 25 pounds in both versions, paddles well with one person, carries two as long as they're real friendly and not too big, and comes complete with paddles and pump.

The epitome of backpack boats, however, has to be the dandy little one-man inflatable catamaran made by Jack's Plastic Welding, Inc. of Aztec, New Mexico. Dubbed, appropriately enough, the Pack Cat, it is the only inflatable I know of designed for backpacking. The boat consists of two inflatable 12-inch tubes about 10 feet long connected by a metal frame with a seat slung between. It paddles well with a standard double-bladed kayak paddle, makes a fine fishing boat for backwoods streams and ponds, will handle whitewater up to Class IV, is safe and stable in ocean surf, and with PVC-coated 1,100-denier polyester fabric construction, is rugged enough to stand up to the abuse of an extended camping trip. But the best part of the Pack Cat is that it weighs less than 25 pounds, and will fit into a standard pack frame with enough room left over for camping gear and food. At a bit under $750, the Pack Cat is not inexpensive. It also comes in a slightly heavier two-person version priced just over $1,000.

Backpacking.

Surviving

Surviving the sinking of a ship or the downing of an aircraft at sea is the solitary activity appropriate to inflatable boats that participants indulge in with extreme reluctance. No one buys a life raft thinking he or she is going to use it, and most rafts live out their lives tucked away in their canisters or valises, never summoned forth as a survival craft in a disaster. That is not to say life rafts are never used. Far from it: hundreds if not thousands of happy travelers, anglers, pilots, and sailors are alive today because someone had the foresight to invest in a life raft (see illustration on page 18).

For small boats and planes, particularly those operating in latitudes where hypothermia is an immediate survival threat for a crewmember in the water, the one-person life raft is appropriate. The smallest, such as the Plastimo Solo, weigh less than 10 pounds and come in a package about the size of a standard flotation cushion, yet they contain all necessary features to make them true life rafts: rubberized fabric construction, automatic deploy-

The Grab Bag

One of the most important life-raft accessories isn't available from any supplier—the abandon-ship grab bag. Supplement every life raft with a bag containing everything the crew will need to survive for at least three days in reasonable comfort. Why only three days? Because the average rescue is effected in a matter of hours, especially in the popular areas where 90 percent of us do 90 percent of our boating. Also, three days' worth of supplies makes a fairly large package; much more, and the survival package would be bigger than the raft. If you aren't picked up right away, rations that allow "reasonable comfort" for three days will keep a person alive for up to a month when consumed at a minimum survival level. The trick is to recognize your situation early and go on emergency rationing before you eat up all the goodies in the first three days.

ment and inflation, a canopy for protection from the elements, a sea anchor, and water ballast for stability in rough conditions.

Larger boats and aircraft need larger survival craft. Four- and six-person life rafts are essentially larger versions of the one-person raft with additional features such as boarding ladders, flares, and room for survival rations. The largest inflatable life raft of interest to readers of this book will be the eight-person versions. Rafts larger than this are in the commercial category and primarily of interest to operators of charters boats and large fishing boats. Anything larger than an eight-person raft will be too heavy to be handled by the average yacht crew. If you need more than eight-person capacity, you will be better off with two smaller life rafts than with one big one even though the final cost will be higher.

There is another thing to keep in mind when considering what size you need. The US Coast Guard, US Sailing (formerly the US Yacht Racing Union), and the Offshore Racing Council (ORC) all agree that the minimum space requirement for a life raft is 4 square feet per person. This means a four-person raft is only required to have 16 square feet of floor space, not a lot of room unless you have a crew of very small people. Before you commit yourself to this minimum, spend an hour or two watching your favorite television shows with the entire crew confined to a circle that encloses 4 square feet for each member. If you're a masochistic reality freak and want to try something closer to the real thing, perform the same exercise on an outdoor trampoline on a rainy night—without the TV. Get two or three muscular volunteers to bounce the crew up and down while another volunteer douses everyone with buckets of ice water and yet another flings large quantities of warm vomit into the fray. You get the idea. Unless you're ready to redefine the concept of togetherness, you might do well to buy a raft at least one size larger than you need. But don't carry this too far; an underloaded raft can be more vulnerable to capsize in extreme conditions. Check the manufacturer's recommendations carefully.

THE STANDARD INFLATABLE AS A LIFE RAFT. Life rafts are a nuisance: they're expensive, cumbersome, and downright ugly, even when stowed in those neat plastic containers. What about using a conventional inflatable boat as a life raft? Won't a large soft tail or a sportboat do just as well as a dedicated life raft? Well, in keeping with a developing pattern of nebulous answers to such questions (my editor demands consistency), I can say, unequivocally, maybe.

If you are a commercial fisherman with a paid crew, or if you carry passengers for hire in any capacity, the answer is NO! plain and simple. The Coast Guard will insist that you carry approved, registered, and inspected life rafts. Likewise, if you race sailboats offshore, your sponsoring organization will insist that you have an authorized life raft. If you're thinking of borrowing your daughter's play boat from the swimming pool when you pilot your small plane to the Bahamas, forget it—even though no bureaucracy really gives a damn. To be effective as an emergency craft, a conventional boat must be carried inflated, logistically impossible in a small plane even were it advisable (which it isn't).

What about those of us who don't race, don't carry passengers for hire, don't have a paid crew, rarely sail or fly out of sight of land, and make up roughly 99.99 percent of the boating public? Rest assured that a conventional soft-tail dinghy or sportboat, or even a RIB, kayak, or riverboat, all make fine life rafts. They won't have a real life raft's inflatable canopy, water ballast system, or sea anchors. But in coastal waters, where rescue is likely within a few hours, a canopy isn't necessary. The inherent stability of an inflatable obviates the need for water ballast in anything less than storm conditions, and even if it does flip over, most inflatables work nearly as well upside down. If you need a sea anchor, you can rig one from a bucket or a sail bag, but you won't want one if you're anywhere near shore; you'll want to row, sail, paddle, or motor in that direction as rapidly as possible.

There are three provisos for using your conventional inflatable as a life raft. First, the boat must have an automatic inflating device or it must be carried inflated—either towed behind or stowed on deck where it can be launched quickly and easily—because if you ever need a life raft, it is unlikely you'll have time to blow it up. Second, you must have an adequate grab bag containing everything you would need in an emergency (see sidebar). And third, the inflatable must be large enough to carry the entire crew; you don't want your crew trying to decide who won't be coming along, especially since the obvious scapegoat for any disaster is nearly always the skipper.

By now perhaps you find yourself a bit overwhelmed by the array of inflatable boats offered and befuddled by the apparent absence of any boating activity not appropriate for an inflatable—Eskimo rolling is the only one I can think of. Take solace in the fact that I have omitted all nonboating activities. I've used my inflatable as a wildly uncontrollable toboggan and an impromptu swimming pool, the kids sleep in it like a camper, and the neighbor's cat has had two litters in it. Anyway, put up your feet and read on; we will try to clear the fog and perhaps have some fun along the way.

CHAPTER 4

Selecting a Boat

Most of us go about buying an inflatable boat in exactly the wrong way. We see a sleek and sultry new model at the boat show, and our eyes glaze over at glossy brochures that show the macho skipper surrounded by his scantily clad crew (some of the ads for the French boats will boil water). When we wake up we find we have whipped out the plastic, "ink stains have dried up on some line" (Glen Campbell), and we're bound to a new Bombablaster 15 with 50 horses on the stern—and to yet another one-eyed envelope in the mail. Nary a bikini-clad admirer is in sight. Impulsive buying is the hallmark of the American shopper, and it is the single largest reason that many suppliers of boats and boat gear do a significant part of their business at boat shows.

But you're too smart for that. You are first going to carefully analyze your needs, then you're going to inventory your wallet and bank accounts. Only after you know what you need and what you can comfortably afford to pay for it will you take a look at what is available. Start by asking yourself a few questions.

Do I Really Need an Inflatable?

There are a number of reasons *not* to buy an inflatable boat. As I've already pointed out, they're expensive. Inflatables usually cost more initially than an equivalent conventional boat, and because they as a rule don't last as long, they are even more expensive over the long term. When someone gets the time to do a first-class paint-and-varnish job on Sarah's 30-year-old Dyer, it will look like a new boat. There are plenty of even older small boats around in great condition, but a 30-year-old inflatable would be a real oddity. If you get half that many years out of a well-built and -maintained inflatable boat, consider yourself lucky. Ten years is a reasonable life expectancy for a good-quality inflatable used regularly, and full-time cruisers are usually happy if their inflatables last half that. The best of them won't stand up much longer to the stress and strain of daily use with even the best of care.

Inflatables require more care and maintenance than equivalent hard boats. Where Sarah's Dyer can be inverted on sawhorses behind the garage each winter, the Achilles must be carefully deflated, disassembled, powdered, packed into special bags, and stored in a cool, dry place. The Dyer can be left on a mooring for weeks or months in the summer, dragged ashore every so often to have the barnacles and sea grass removed from its bottom by the vigorous application of a paint scraper. Such treatment would destroy an inflatable in a season. If you aren't the type who takes meticulous care of your possessions, you may be better off with a hard craft.

Inflatables don't work as well for some activities as conventional boats. For example, inflatable kayaks are fine craft and can be heaps of fun, but if you're interested in serious paddling or competition, you won't be happy with an inflatable. If your idea of a thrill is a brisk row around the pond on a frosty-clear autumn morning in a responsive pulling boat, your first experience rowing an inflatable will make you want to bury your face and cry. Likewise, if you enjoy bass fishing on a casual and irregular basis (as I do), an inflatable sportboat will serve, but if you're a member of the army of bass-fishing fanatics who gladly drive from Moosehead to Okeechobee in pursuit of their finny prey, you're going to want one of those slick metal-flake Rangers with a live well and a casting chair at the bow. A blow-up boat just won't do the trick.

Okay, so now that you've given the matter careful consideration, you've decided (surprise, surprise) that it's an inflatable for you, but which one?

How Will I Use the Boat?

I know people who aren't interested in anything but fishing. They eat, sleep, and drink fishing, and when they buy a boat, it's a fishing boat. Others love scuba diving so much that they don't do anything else; they want a boat for that one activity. But most of us aren't what market analysts like to call "single-use buyers"; we want our new inflatable to fit a number of uses.

We might want to fish a remote beaver pond one weekend, explore a small stream to its source the next weekend, and do a little Class III whitewater work on the next, all of which can be handled by an inflatable kayak. Or suppose we want to do a little diving one weekend, have a picnic on a not-too-far-from-shore island the next, and take a buddy on a trout-fishing trip on a mountain lake the one after that; a small sportboat could be ideal.

Many small and medium-size inflatables (soft tails and sportboats) are purchased as yacht dinghies, but even these are multi-use craft that skipper and crew also use for snorkeling or fishing or even waterskiing. So those of you considering an inflatable as your next dinghy still need to consider what other activities you may want to pursue in your new boat.

The following chart illustrates the versatility of inflatable boats. Choose your favorite boating activity from the left-hand column, then choose the most appropriate boat by referring to the number of dots in the boxes. One dot indicates reasonable performance, two dots good performance, and three dots very good performance. If you engage in a variety of activities, add up the dots in the boxes to see which type of boat has the highest score.

ACTIVITY	PLAY BOAT	KAYAK OR CANOE	SOFT TAIL	SPORTBOAT TO 10 HP	SPORTBOAT 10 TO 25 HP	SPORTBOAT 25 TO 50 HP	RIB 10 TO 25 HP	RIB 25 TO 50 HP	RIB 50+ HP	RIVER-BOAT	LIFE RAFT
LIFESAVING			••	••	••	•	•	•	•	••	•••
SPLISHING & SPLASHING	•••	•••	•••								
BACKPACKING	•	•••	••								
YACHT TENDER		•	•••	•••							
EXPLORING BAYS AND HARBORS		••	•	••	••	•••	•••	•••	••		
EXPLORING COASTAL AREAS		•		•	•••	•••	••	•••	•••		
CAMPING AND BEACH CRUISING	•	•••		•	••	•••	•••	•••	••		
RIVER TRIPS - Class I	•	•••	••	••	••					•	
Class II		•••	•••	••	•					••	
Class III		•••	••	•	•					•••	
Class IV		••								•••	
Class V										•••	
SCUBA NEAR SHORE			•	••		•••	•••	•••	••	••	
SCUBA OFFSHORE					•••	••	•••	•••	•••		
WATERSKIING					••	••		••	•••		
FISHING STREAMS AND PONDS	•	••	•••	•••		•				•	
FISHING LAKES AND RIVERS		•	•	•••	••	•••	•••	••	•	••	
SALTWATER GAME					•••	••	•	••	•••		
DUCK HUNTING		•	•	•••	•	•••	••	•	•		
SHOWING OFF	•••	••			•••			••	•••		

Boat selection chart.

If you're an outdoorsperson who enjoys duck hunting in the fall, fishing on lakes and streams in the summer, and perhaps an occasional camping trip, a medium-range sportboat or RIB will be ideal for your needs. If you enjoy taking the kids to the beach and like to get off by yourself for some quiet fly fishing, a soft tail or a kayak might be just right. If you enjoy backpacking into remote streams and ponds but your second passion is waterskiing, your choice is tougher—either buy two boats or change your habits.

But hold on there; you're not ready to run out and spend your money just yet. You need to ask yourself a few more questions.

Where Will I Keep the Boat?

One of the most attractive features of inflatable boats has always been the ability to store them in a small space where they are out of the way yet accessible when you want to use them. The first life rafts aboard combat aircraft were lightweight and compact, but they had to be available quickly because in those days when a pilot needed his life raft, he needed it badly. With today's hectic lifestyles and our passion for immediate gratification, ready accessibility is only slightly less important. If a boat takes an hour or more of strenuous effort to assemble and inflate, I guarantee you won't use it as much as you think when you buy it.

Where will I keep it?

We buy inflatables as much for their utility as their compact storage, but the ability to deflate the thing and put it away in a closet is still an attractive feature, especially to those of us living in apartments and condominiums. Unfortunately the ease of deflating and storing a boat is inversely related to size and complexity. While a little unreinforced PVC play boat can be rolled up and stuffed in a drawer, a big RIB can't be deflated at all, for all practical purposes, and must be stored and transported on a trailer. We will give storage and transportation a closer look in Chapter 7, but for now suffice it to say that an appropriate storage space for your boat is critical, and you shouldn't buy a boat until you have this particular base covered.

How Much Do I Want to Spend?

Next to impulse buying, the biggest mistake the average boat buyer makes is spending far more than planned. It is incredible the excuses some of us use: "but honey, this great big boat is a much better value than that little thing"; "this one is just like Jacques Cousteau's"; "the big one will be safer"; "what if we decide to have kids?"; "with the bigger engine we can pull two skiers"; or the perennial favorite, "this sucker will blow that smart-ass Henry Wilson right out of the water."

The list of rationalizations goes on and on. If you're going to purchase wisely, you need to decide how much you want to spend and make that your absolute limit. The real danger—especially in these days of instant credit—lies in basing your decision on your ability to make the payments rather than the boat's suitability for your wants and needs. Do that and you can easily end up with a monstrosity you use once or twice a year. The rest of the time it takes up half the backyard or all the garage. Inflatable boats are expensive enough; don't spend any more than you have to.

Are you ready to buy? Not quite, but you are ready to start the process. Collect brochures from all the manufacturers you can. Pick them up from local dealers or send away to the addresses listed in the back of this book. You'll soon be swamped with glossy pamphlets, each containing a collage of fancy photos and glowing verbiage rhapsodizing the virtues of the subject product, which on careful reading won't say a thing. (This is known a "gobbledygook" in the advertising business.) The brochures should also contain a small amount of hard data ("actual factuals" in ad lingo). Concentrate on the actual factuals, ignore the gobbledygook, and block from your mind all images of macho hunks and bikini-clad young ladies.

Glean as much from the brochures as you can. Real information is well hidden by experts in obfuscation. Finding it is as tough as finding the clam in Aunt Minnie's fritters, but there is some there if you look for it. For example, brochures often tout construction details. And check the guarantee—better boats will have a better warranty.

If you have a specific question, ask the salesperson at your local dealership, but take everything salespeople say with a grain of salt. Some just don't know what they're talking about; others are egregious liars. An honest salesperson will respond with straightforward answers or get the information for you from the manufacturer. A bad salesperson will be evasive and misleading. A good test is to pretend you don't know a thing about inflatables (don't tell them you read this book) and ask a few questions about competing products. A bad salesperson will dump on the competition where a good salesperson will try to give you objective information that will steer you toward one product and away from less suitable alternatives.

Buying a Used Inflatable

Once you've determined the kind of boat that you want, it can make sense to look for a used one, but don't expect giveaway prices. While older conventional boats are deeply discounted, used inflatables in serviceable condition fetch prices not far below the new-boat price. The two reasons for this price stability are that the number of used inflatable boats available is limited and demand for them has remained high as more people recognize their advantages. People tend to hang on to inflatables—partly because they are more versatile than conventional boats and partly because a seldom-used inflatable stored away in the attic or a corner of the garage is far less "in the way" than an unwanted runabout. Another reason for scarcity is that inflatables haven't been around as long as regular boats and they don't last as long; an inflatable more than 10 years old is rare.

Don't let scarcity stop you from looking; it's still worthwhile to check the classified ads of your local papers and the boating section of your local want advertiser. *Soundings* magazine has an "inflatable" heading in its classified section with a dozen or so used inflatables under it every month.

Inspecting a Used Boat

If you get lucky and find a used boat at a reasonable price, there are a few steps you should take before you commit. Here's a checklist to help get you started.

- ☐ Overall appearance
- ☐ Fabric condition
- ☐ Tube seams
- ☐ Hard-bottom-to-tube seams
- ☐ Bottom seams
- ☐ Transom-to-tube seams
- ☐ Outboard bracket
- ☐ Bottom abrasion outside
- ☐ Bottom abrasion inside
- ☐ Valve condition
- ☐ Valve operation
- ☐ Valve-to-tube seams
- ☐ Oarlocks
- ☐ Floorboards
- ☐ Transom
- ☐ Steering cables
- ☐ Oars or paddles
- ☐ Pump
- ☐ Owner's manual
- ☐ Repair kit

Used-boat checklist.

Insist that the boat be inflated hard without the floorboards, engine, or any other paraphernalia installed. View the boat's overall condition. Does the fabric have a chalky look? That's perfectly normal on a Hypalon boat more than a year or two old, but if you're looking at a PVC boat, a warning flag should go up. PVC has a low tolerance for ozone and ultraviolet radiation; a chalky film on the surface of the fabric may indicate excessive exposure.

Be particularly suspicious of a boat that looks too good. An unscrupulous seller can improve a boat's looks by coating the fabric with a film of oil or petroleum jelly. Check the fabric for oiliness, and ask the owner if he has used a restorative on the fabric. Be especially alert for any surface treatment on PVC boats. More than one PVC inflatable has simply fallen apart after being treated with a silicone-based protectant such as Armor All. Even if the silicone doesn't make the boat's seams lose their grip, it will make future repairs more difficult.

Some manufacturers make both PVC and Hypalon boats, and it can be hard to tell which is which just by looking at them. When a manufacturer uses Hypalon, they call it Hypalon, but when they don't use Hypalon, they often try to hide the cheaper fabric behind a meaningless name. Since the original sales information may have called the material Strongan (Zodiac), 1100 Decitex (Bombard), or special fabric (Sevylor), the seller may not know what material is in the boat. Fortunately a simple test will tell you what the material is. Place a few drops of nail-polish remover (lacquer thinner and toluene also work) on the tube fabric in an inconspicuous spot. If the wetted area becomes sticky to the touch after a few seconds, you have a PVC boat; if it is unaffected by the solvent, the boat is Hypalon—it's as simple as that. It is important to test the tube fabric because some manufacturers made tubes from one fabric and the floors, dodgers, and other paraphernalia from another. You can reassure the owner that this test won't damage the fabric even if it does turn out to be PVC, but it may cause a slight stain—thus the recommendation to perform the test in an inconspicuous spot.

You can often spot a PVC sportboat by looking at the transom-to-hull attachment. Several manufacturers started bolting the transoms of their PVC boats when, despite their best efforts, they continued to have delamination problems. If the transom is fastened to the hull flange with bolts or screws, you can be pretty sure the hull fabric is PVC.

Next turn your attention to seams, paying particular attention to those on the main tubes. If there is any problem with the tube seams, it is likely that the boat is beyond repair. If the owner will permit it, go over all the tube seams with a mixture of water and dish soap (see Chapter 8), watching for bubbles that betray the presence of small leaks. Slow leaks in seams are difficult to find and more difficult to repair. Hypalon boats are more likely to leak at the seams than PVC boats, and older boats will generally leak more than newer ones—especially due to wicking. Small leaks shouldn't eliminate an older boat available at a good price. They just mean you'll have to top off the pressure more often—a small price to pay for an otherwise good boat.

Inspect the seams that hold the bottom fabric (or fiberglass or aluminum in the case of a RIB) to the tubes. Be on the lookout for abrasion on the outside of the joint and on the inside where the floorboards rub against the tubes. Abrasion here is both fairly common and difficult to repair. Check the transom attachment to the stern tubes and bottom. Some earlier PVC boats were notorious for the transom's separating from the tubes, a problem that can be impossible to fix. A separated transom is less common and easier to repair on Hypalon boats.

Turn your attention to the inflation valves—there should be one for each air chamber. Be sure they work smoothly and are airtight. Watch out for corrosion on metal parts, and check the seams where the valve attaches to the tube. Check the little diaphragm inside the valve. These are check valves to keep the air in the boat and they deteriorate quickly. This isn't a problem on boats currently in production because replacement diaphragms are readily available and easy to install, but a lot of boats were built by manufacturers that have gone out of business. Replacement parts can be impossible to find.

Next check the oarlocks. Oarlocks run the gamut from very simple to ridiculously complicated. Avon uses a patented oarlock that is little more than a block of solid neoprene with a hole in it for the oar to pass through. The only problem I've ever encountered with these simple oarlocks was a bizarre case where a dog had chewed one in half. Complicated oarlocks often have numerous small metal pieces prone to corrosion and loss, and you may be unable to locate replacement parts if either the manufacturer or the US distributor has gone out of business.

Check to make sure the wood is sound in all the wooden parts, which typically includes the floorboards, the transom, and probably the oars. Deteriorated or blistered varnish or paint is perfectly acceptable even though it may look terrible, as long as the wood is in good condition. Deteriorated varnish is easy to repair, but deteriorated wood is another matter. Most wood components in the major brands of inflatable boats are made from high-grade marine plywood and are very durable even after the varnish peels off, but extended exposure will eventually destroy even the best. While replacing floorboards or oars with new ones is no problem, they are expensive. Replacing a deteriorated transom is a job for a repair shop, and the cost can exceed the value of the boat.

The manual inflation pump needs to be in good condition. Pumps tend to receive a lot of abuse. Never rely on an electric pump as the primary inflation pump for the boat; you need a good-working manual pump aboard at all times. Make sure the nipple or barb that inserts into the inflation valve is in good condition and the correct one for the boat. These are usually a friction fit, and when they deteriorate to the point where they won't stay put, inflating becomes a frustrating two-person operation—one to pump and one to hold the nipple in the valve.

This is the time to check lifelines, seats and dodger, windshield, bags and cover, and all mechanical apparatus such as remote steering and engine controls. If the boat is a soft tail, give the outboard bracket a careful inspection. These are most often made from mild steel covered with neoprene or PVC, and once the integrity of the protective coating fails, the steel rusts away with astonishing rapidity. Just as astonishing is how much a replacement costs.

Finally, check to see that the emergency repair kit is in good condition, and make sure the boat comes with an owner's manual and repair instructions. Now you're ready to buy it, right? It depends.

GET IT SURVEYED. If you're considering a small boat and there isn't a lot of money involved, sure, go ahead and buy it. But if you're looking at something with an asking price in the thousands of dollars—say a big RIB on a trailer with a sizable outboard—haul it to a reputable inflatable-boat repair facility, preferably an authorized service center for that make of boat, and spend a couple of hundred bucks to have it surveyed before you make the final decision. It is possible for a boat that looks sound to be deteriorated beyond repair. The older the boat, the more essential the survey. Most repair centers will be happy to survey any boat and give you a detailed list of things it needs to bring it back to top condition. They will also give you an estimate of what the repairs will cost. You should ask for this even if you plan to do the repairs yourself since it can be an invaluable bargaining tool when dickering over the final price. If your prospective purchase passes this last step, give the lady your money and take your boat home.

Buying a New Inflatable

Okay, so you don't like the idea of a used boat. Or perhaps you can't find a used boat that measures up to your standards. Either way you're stuck with buying a new boat. The lining to that particular dark cloud is that the process is a lot easier. For one thing, you don't have to worry so much about the condition of the boat; you can assume a new boat is in perfect condition. If it isn't, any problems that arise should be covered by the warranty, which nicely introduces the only real danger in buying a new boat: if you're considering buying an off brand or a boat from a manufacturer you've never heard of, consider your choice carefully.

Buy a Name Brand

Consider the case of Charlie Schmuck (name changed to protect the innocent author) who bought a brand-new Bombablaster 15 (name changed to protect the guilty) right off the floor at the local boat show. It wasn't exactly the boat he wanted, but it was such a great deal that he couldn't refuse—half off the suggested retail price, a five-year unlimited warranty, and instant financing, plus a free beer cooler if he loaded the thing into his car himself.

The first thing poor Charlie discovered was that the foot pump that came as standard equipment was hopelessly inadequate: it took him more than half an hour of energetic pumping to inflate just the seat. A proper manual pump and an optional electric booster added an extra $122.50 to the price, plus shipping and handling. Well, perhaps he'd be better off with the electric pump anyway—it does save wear and tear on the sneakers.

Then he discovered that the manufacturer had misrepresented the compact qualities of the deflated boat. After it was inflated for the first time, there was no way even the great Houdini could ever have gotten the thing back into the storage bag. Fortunately this wasn't a big problem for Charlie because he had plenty of room.

Next Charlie discovered that despite the manufacturer's engine rating of up to 10 hp, his 9-hp Evinrude made his Bombablaster squat like a duck with a 20-pound anchor tied to its tail. Worse yet, when he opened the throttle, the bow of the boat rose in a terrifying manner to practically vertical and threatened to do a backward somersault. Charlie found he needed a long throttle extension so he could operate the boat from the bow, where his weight was just barely adequate to keep the bow in the water until the boat finally reached planing speed.

Charlie is an adaptable sort of guy and he learned to accommodate the idiosyncrasies of his new boat for the entire first season, though he claimed with a straight face that the boat was possessed by demons out to send his immortal soul into early retirement in the fiery pits. Then came the start of the second season. When Charlie unrolled his Bombablaster to inflate it for the first excursion of the year, he found to his dismay that the starboard seam connecting the tube to the floor had failed and the two were about to part company.

Next Charlie discovered. . . .

This was the last straw. Charlie fired off a lengthy but polite letter to the distributor, reminding them of the five-year warranty on seams and requesting information on where to send the boat for repairs. When after a month he got no answer, he called the number listed on the sales receipt. He got a recording announcing that the number had been disconnected. Charlie still has his boat, but he doesn't go out on the water much anymore, preferring these days to spend his leisure time on the golf course.

The story of Charlie and his Bombablaster is, unfortunately, far from uncommon. Inflatable-boat companies come and go with startling regularity. It is a highly competitive business, and only the strong survive to become reliable adult enterprises. Don't be seduced into complacency by the fact that a particular make of boat has been in business in Europe for 50 years or so and has a good reputation there. The responsibility for the boat rests primarily with the importer; if the company goes out of business, you will have little recourse to the overseas manufacturer. The message is clear: if you're going to spend a lot of money on a new inflatable boat, the safest course is to stick with a brand that you know from reputation or experience will be around for a while.

Local Dealer or Mail Order?

I'm a big believer in making major purchases from the biggest outfit I can find. The larger marine outfitters such as Boat/U.S. and West Marine now have retail outlets in most major population centers, they offer low prices, they stand behind everything they sell, and they employ knowledgeable people who actually seem to be interested in your problems. Their house brands can be excellent values since they are usually made under license by a major manufacturer. You get virtually the same boat as the manufacturer's brand-name boat, the same or a better warranty, and the same range of accessories and add-ons, but the price is often lower and the service often better.

Having said that, there is also a good argument for buying your boat from a local dealer. The local dealer provides more personal service than mail-order suppliers or chain stores, and the person servicing the boat is usually the same person you purchased the boat from in the first place. Local dealers are frequently more convenient, especially for small matters, replacement parts, and such things as periodic maintenance. Because of a one-on-one relationship with the distributor and/or the manufacturer, a good local dealer can run rings around most large stores and mail-order outlets when it comes to special service and personal problems.

The choice between a large supplier and a small local dealer is a tough call, one you must make for yourself. Since example can be the best illustration of an important point, I offer the following.

On a trip to the Florida Keys to indulge in a bit of scuba diving, fishing, and well-deserved relaxation with my family, I was faced with the dilemma of purchasing a new boat when our trusty (and heretofore reliable) Zodiac Mark II fell apart at the seams. It was a scary sight. We were towing the inflated boat on a trailer and had it loaded to the thwarts with scuba gear, camping equipment, and fishing tackle. The boat was in perfect condition when we left Marblehead, and although we had owned it for nearly 10 years, it looked brand new.

Just as we reached Virginia, tooling along at a conservative 60 mph on the interstate, I heard a loud flapping sound coming from behind. A gray blur in the rearview mirror signaled that the seam holding the bow dodger to the tubes had failed and the remains of the dodger whipped wildly in the slipstream. About 20 miles over the North Carolina line, one of the starboard handles, to which I had secured the tarpaulin cover, pulled off, and the tarp joined the dodger in its mad frenzy.

Another handle came off in Georgia. The transom began to peel away from the tubes in Jacksonville. As we neared the Keys, the port side deflated when the seam that secured the valve failed. By the time we pulled into our campground in Marathon, the boat was a disaster.

Fortunately Marathon is a major population center in the Keys where just about everything, including inflatable-boat repair, is available. So we unloaded all the junk from the boat, removed the floorboards, and hauled it to the Inflatable Boat Center of the Florida Keys. I reasoned that since all the damage was due to the failure of glue joints, it would be simply a matter of regluing the failed joints and we would be back in business. It might take a couple of days, but I was willing to pay extra for expedited repair. When I met owners Paul and Bobra (her real name—"My dad wanted a boy," she says with a good-natured smile), I was feeling optimistic. I was in for a shock.

Bobra is the expert on repairs, and she spent a half hour or so carefully inspecting the boat. "Well," she finally offered, a solemn look replacing the smile, "I have some bad news for you."

"Oh no," I said, thinking of the diving, snorkeling, and fishing I had planned for the next two weeks. "You won't be able to fix it by tomorrow?"

"Worse than that, I'm afraid."

"How much worse? Does that mean you can't fix it by the end of the week?" I could feel panic welling up and overcoming my typically calm and collected countenance.

"That means we can't fix it at all," she answered, with a quiet competency that told me my little boat was doomed. "I'm really sorry, but the repair would cost more than the boat is worth. And once you fix the failed seams, you won't get a week's use before the other seams fail. Just look at this." She effortlessly peeled off the starboard oarlock. "What you have here is a massive failure of the glue. We've seen several boats like this and we've had to stop trying to fix them. It's simply not a good service to our customers."

I was flabbergasted and a little suspicious that they might be trying to take advantage of my

plight to sell me a new boat. "What if I take it to someone else?" I asked.

"I'll be glad to supply you the names of several people who will be happy to give you a temporary patch job, but you'll be wasting your money."

A little incredulous and a lot angry, I drove back to the campground to break the bad news to Susan and the kids. We had driven more than 1,500 miles for a boating vacation and our boat had fallen to pieces. After a brief war council, I got on the phone to the major catalog houses to try to order a new boat. All were sympathetic and tried to help, but because of the logistics and an intervening weekend, the quickest delivery any could offer was four or five days—nearly half of our remaining vacation. This would have been excellent service under normal circumstances, but it wasn't good enough to help in our case.

Late that afternoon we were back at the Inflatable Boat Center talking to Paul about a new boat. By early the next afternoon we were sitting in a brand-new bright-red 12-foot Achilles sportboat with our faithful Mariner 25 kicking us at top speed toward Sombrero Light Reef and some of the best snorkeling we've ever experienced this side of the Yucatán. In the space of 24 hours Paul had helped us decide what boat we needed, agreed on a price that was competitive with the mail-order houses, ordered the boat delivered from the distributor by UPS overnight at his expense, helped us with the registration, arranged for the exchange of an aluminum floorboard damaged in shipping (he had a new one sent to our house in Marblehead), given us extensive instructions in how to inflate, deflate, and care for our new boat, and told us where we would find the best diving and fishing. When we arrived to pick up the new boat (we gave the old one to a missionary headed for South America who was happy to get it in any condition), we also found the name of our sailboat lettered on the side.

"How much for the paint job?" I asked, both surprised and pleased that Bobra had found time to do this last little thing for us.

"No charge," she said, flashing a smile wide enough to tell the world that here was a business that wanted satisfied customers and was willing to work for them.

CHAPTER 5

Outboards, Oars, and Other Options

No matter what type of inflatable craft you end up with, it is likely you will want to augment it with a few optional extras to expand the enjoyment and utility of your boat. There is a plethora of gadgetry and flangery available that will tempt you to part with yet another portion of the unused balance on the old Visa card. Let's run through a few of the more popular options to make sure you really need a battery-operated echo sounder for your new kayak before you hand over the plastic.

Outboard Motors

When I bought my old Zodiac Mark II about a dozen years ago, my relationship with inflatables was limited to my trusty Avon soft tail and childhood adventures with a war-surplus life raft. I had no experience with outboard motors, at least not on inflatables. In fact I was downright disdainful of these noisy and cantankerous despoilers of salubrious silence and solitude. I firmly believed that if the Great Skipper had wanted us to have outboards, He would have issued us one. To attribute to mere coincidence the fact that we are born with the same number of arms as there are oars on a skiff seemed to me to be beyond credulity. I have since modified this fundamentalist attitude toward outboards and now accept them as a necessary evil—like politicians and bureaucrats, who also foul the air with noxious fumes and make more noise than their functions require.

The Mark II was my first inflatable large enough for a serious motor, and I was impressed by Zodiac's claim that it could handle a 40-hp outboard. Although I wasn't that knowledgeable about outboards, 40 horses seemed like a lot for a 14-foot boat weighing less than 200 pounds. I ended up selecting a 25-hp Mariner because I intended to use the boat for fishing and would be hauling it all over New England. At about 100 pounds, the 25-horse was the largest motor I could lift into the back of the truck unassisted without blowing hernias into everything south of my belt buckle.

This unscientific approach to selecting an outboard proved serendipitous the very first time I used it. Susan and I hauled our new boat to an uncrowded launching ramp on a little lake in New Hampshire where we could take our time getting used to it. We managed to assemble the floorboards and to inflate the thing without doing any permanent damage to our boat or our relationship. We launched the inflated boat and mounted the motor as directed by the instruction manual. I climbed aboard and chauvinistically announced that it might be better if I went alone for the first trial run.

The motor started with the second yank and sat purring on the transom. I slipped it into gear, immediately pleased with how well we put-putted across the lake with the throttle at idle. After about a hundred yards, I felt more confident and advanced the throttle a quarter of a turn. What I didn't know was that this particular motor goes from idle to full throttle with a half turn of the grip, so I was at half throttle. The light boat leapt forward like a racehorse out of the gate, catching me completely by surprise and toppling me backward toward the stern. I grasped tighter to the one thing I had a grip on, twisting the throttle into the full-open position.

Now I don't like to brag, but among my friends I'm known for my ability to remain cool in the face of adversity—the greater the adversity, the cooler I get. This time I got so cool that I froze at the helm and sat staring in rigid perplexity as the jagged rocks on the opposite shore sped toward me and my new boat at about 25 knots. Three-quarters of the way across the lake, I regained enough composure to realize that if I didn't do something soon, there wouldn't be anything left to do. I turned the motor to steer the boat away from the rocks. But in the confusion of trying to follow unfamiliar assembly and inflation instructions, I had neglected to

inflate the keel, so I was about to learn another lesson about inflatable boats: without a keel, they don't steer worth a damn. In fact, they don't steer at all. When I turned the motor, the boat obediently turned to point the way I wanted to go, but without the lateral resistance of a keel, the now sideways boat continued traveling in the original direction. When it didn't respond to my efforts to steer it away from the rocks, I reacted instinctively by turning the motor even more—"hard to starboard" in nautical parlance. This sent the boat into a violent spin—like a dog chasing its tail—while it continued at full speed toward the rocks.

At some point the combination of adrenaline and rapid-fire synapses got a message through to my befuddled brain: "It's the throttle, stupid." I reached up with my left hand and yanked the kill switch. Now the only significant difference between hitting rocks and shutting off the motor while operating an inflatable at full throttle is that the boat isn't totally destroyed. The boat stopped—instantly and completely—but I didn't. The rapid deceleration ripped the tiller from my hand and threw me flat on my face in the bow where I lay stunned for about a quarter of a second before being drenched by lake water. This was to prove (blissfully) the last lesson of the day: when an inflatable boat stops suddenly, the waves from the wake overtake the boat and will, in extreme circumstances, climb over the transom and swamp the boat.

I lay there dazed and bruised and soaking wet. When I lifted my groggy head enough to look over the gunwales toward the launching ramp, I could just make out the figure of Susan jumping up and down and waving her arms like a cheerleader at a winning football game. It slowly dawned on me that she thought the entire performance was just for her amusement.

What then, you might ask, was so serendipitous about my selection of a 25-hp motor? Well, can you imagine what would have happened if I had bought a 40-hp outboard? I certainly would have made it all the way to the rocks, and you, dear reader, would have been spared yet another personal anecdote. But this little story (which, like those preceding, is practically true) does illustrate how important it is to take the manufacturers' claims of horsepower capability with a large grain of salt. When you read that a 14-foot 200-pound inflatable can be operated with a 40-hp outboard, that means that *with a fully loaded boat and calm conditions*, the boat and crew can survive full-throttle operation.

All inflatable boats operated with outboard motors are enormously sensitive to load. When I'm alone in our 12-foot Achilles (with the same 25-hp outboard), I can operate at full power only in ideal conditions—a flat calm day with plenty of room. Even then it is an exhilarating and somewhat unnerving experience. The boat leaps onto the plane almost immediately and skims across the surface of the water much like a crop duster skims the top of a corn field. In fact, it's the closest thing to flying I've ever experienced.

Loaded with two scuba divers and their gear, and a picnic cooler full of lunch and root beer, the same boat will wallow and complain before reluctantly climbing onto the plane and proceeding at a pace that is adequate but less than exhilarating—about half the speed it reaches when I operate it alone. The boat will plane with up to six adult passengers, but with this much weight, it is a laborious and painful experience for the little boat, and it doesn't like it one bit.

When you buy a new inflatable boat with an outboard, it is important to give adequate thought to matching the two. Let's take a quick run-through of the categories and consider how each responds to outboards.

Play Boats

Several manufacturers of unreinforced PVC boats sell optional outboard brackets, but PVC boats built without reinforcing fabric can't be inflated stiff enough to allow efficient powering with even the smallest motor. If you try to inflate a play boat with enough pressure to keep it rigid, it just gets bigger (especially on a warm day) in exactly the same way that a balloon grows larger when you put more air into it. If you are considering a play boat with an outboard, try it before you buy it. I'm sure the experience will change your mind and you will either buy a more substantial boat or do without the outboard.

Kayaks

One of the best things about inflatable kayaks is they don't need outboards. Even if installing one were possible (which, to my knowledge, it isn't), it would be like putting a scuba tank on a catfish.

Soft Tails

Because soft tails are so miserable to row, more owners are fitting them with floorboards and motor brackets, and they operate quite well set up this way. The limiting factor is their inability to plane regardless of the size of the outboard. The motor is also in a rather precarious position. Only the smallest outboards are appropriate for a soft tail, and the boat must be equipped with floorboards. Two or three horsepower is the maximum, and some of the smallest soft tails, much like the play boats, don't operate well with even the smallest outboard. If you put a larger motor on your soft tail, it will make more noise and churn up more water, but it won't go a bit faster or handle a bit better.

ELECTRIC OUTBOARDS. The little electric outboards sold as trolling motors in fishing-supply outlets are becoming popular with owners of soft tails. Compact enough to fit handily on most standard outboard brackets, they weigh only a few pounds. At less than a horsepower they won't move you fast or into a heavy sea or wind, but they will move you across the pond in normal conditions. And they do it cleanly and quietly, so you can devote your full attention to watching birds or catching trout.

Electric trolling motors have been around for about 30 years, but until recently they required a large and heavy lead-acid battery that was both cumbersome and dangerous aboard a small inflatable. This changed with the introduction of deep-cycle gel-cell batteries. These are smaller than deep-cycle lead-acid batteries of equivalent amperage (although they're still a bit heavy), and they are spill-proof, working just fine upside down. They can be submerged or even dropped overboard without ill effects, provided they are retrieved and dried in a timely fashion. Like any deep-cycle battery, gel-cell batteries can be discharged and recharged hundreds of times without suffering damage—treatment that would quickly destroy a lead-acid auto battery. The gel cell makes electric outboards ideal for use on a soft tail inflatable, provided you have a floorboard to support the weight of the battery.

We must add two caveats before we move on. Manufacturers can't seem to resist the temptation to overstate the power of their trolling motors, so view horsepower ratings with suspicion. Some use the current draw at start-up as the basis for calculating power. This may overstate the actual horsepower by as much as double because it measurers the power required by the motor to get going instead of the amount of work it will do once it is running smoothly under load. The best approach is to use horsepower ratings as a comparison between motors from the same manufacturer only and ignore the horsepower comparison between brands.

The second warning has to do with the tendency of gel-cell batteries to deliver a consistent level of power for a long period, then discharge rapidly. A gel-cell battery fitted with a voltmeter will show a full 13 to 14 volts right up to the time it stops working, where a lead-acid battery will show a gradual discharge. The danger is in using all your juice to motor across the lake to get to where the big ones are jumping, then finding yourself, after a long and tiring day, rowing back against the wind because you've drained your battery. You could take two batteries, of course, but they are expensive and heavy. It may be better to row across in the morning and use the motor to get back in the evening.

Similarly, on a stream or river always try to work upstream from where you launch, using the motor to work against the current. When the battery is dead, you can use the current to get back to the car. By the way, if you find yourself in a situation where the current or wind is too much for your little electric and you can't make headway, don't despair; just lock the motor in position, let it run, and break out the oars. With the motor running, the boat will row a lot easier—it's like having a second oarsman.

Sportboats

Sportboats were the first inflatables designed for outboard power. A hard transom provides a rigid platform for mounting the motor, and the stern tubes (the fat little tubes that extend past the transom) provide the reserve buoyancy to accommodate heavy motors. But the most important development was the incorporation of a keel to provide the lateral resistance essential for directional stability. Without a keel, an inflatable with an outboard will spin around like a windblown leaf.

While you *can* row a sportboat—the small ones actually row better than soft tails—once they get much over 10 feet, an outboard becomes mandatory. A small sportboat operates quite well with a 4- or 6-hp motor, and even the largest will reach planing speed with only 10 or 12 hp, provided you don't expect it to carry the local chapter of the Isaac Walton League across Lake Superior for the annual fish fry and moose roast.

Manufacturers may claim that motors up to 50 hp can be mounted on their largest sportboats, but consider how your boat will be loaded and used before spending your money. If you're a waterskier or plan to take groups of scuba divers and their gear for long trips, the largest outboard may be useful, but if you just want to go fast in a lightly loaded boat, a motor of about half the maximum rated horsepower will save you a pot full of money and aggravation. (Troubles with outboards, as with boats in general, increase geometrically with size.) When selecting an outboard, use information provided by the manufacturer and the salesperson only as guides. If possible, don't buy the boat until you have taken a demonstrator for a test spin. If the dealer doesn't have a demonstrator, he should be willing, nay eager, to provide you with the names of owners who have bought boats similar to the one you're considering. Call them. You'll find most people are candid and honest about their boats, and you might even find someone willing to take you for a ride.

ACTIVITY	OUTBOARD	PLAY BOAT	KAYAK OR CANOE	SOFT TAIL	SPORTBOAT TO 10 FT.	SPORTBOAT 10 TO 12 FT.	SPORTBOAT 12 TO 15 FT.	RIB TO 10 FT.	RIB 10 TO 12 FT.	RIB 12 TO 14 FT.	RIB 14 TO 16 FT.	RIB OVER 16 FT.	RIVER-BOAT
SPLISHING & SPLASHING	Forget the outboards, they simply take all the fun out of it.												
BACKPACKING	If you're fool enough to try to backpack an outboard, you may as well take about 50 HP.												
YACHT TENDER	MIN HP MAX HP			1.5 3	3 10	5 15	10 30	5 10	9 20	15 35	25 70	40 100+	2.5 10
EXPLORING BAYS AND HARBORS	MIN HP MAX HP			1.5 3	3 10	5 15	10 30	5 10	9 20	15 35	25 50	40 50	5 10
EXPLORING COASTAL AREAS	MIN HP MAX HP				3 10	10 25	10 30	10 25	9 20	15 35	25 50	40 50	5 10
CAMPING AND BEACH CRUISING	MIN HP MAX HP				3 10	10 25	10 30	9 20	10 25	15 35	25 50	40 50	5 10
RIVER TRIPS - Class I	MIN HP MAX HP			1.5 3	3 10	10 25							5 10
Class II	MIN HP MAX HP			1.5 3	3 10	10 25							5 10
Class III and above	Outboards neither needed nor recommended.												
SCUBA NEAR SHORE	MIN HP MAX HP			1.5 3	3 10	10 25	10 30	9 20	10 25	15 35	25 50	40 50	
SCUBA OFFSHORE	MIN HP MAX HP					10 25	10 30	9 20	10 25	15 35	10 30	40 100+	
WATERSKIING	MIN HP MAX HP									30 35	25 70	60 100+	
FISHING STREAMS AND PONDS	MIN HP MAX HP			1.5 3	3 10	5 15	10 25						2.5 10
FISHING LAKES AND RIVERS	MIN HP MAX HP			1.5 3	3 10	5 15	10 25	5 10	9 20	30 35	25 50	40 50	5 10
SALTWATER GAME	MIN HP MAX HP						25 30			25 25	25 70	40 100+	
DUCK HUNTING	MIN HP MAX HP			1.5 3	3 10	5 15	10 30	5 10	9 20	15 25	25 40	40 50	5 10
SHOWING OFF	MIN HP The art of showing off requires biggest and heaviest outboard you can manage to fit on your boat. The louder the noise and the bigger the wake, the more attention you will get.												

Selecting an outboard.

RIBs

Due to their deep-V hull designs, small RIBs row as well as aluminum or fiberglass skiffs of equal size. Even so, the vast majority are fitted with an outboard; I have only seen one or two in regular use without one. RIBs are designed as motorboats, and they have excess reserve buoyancy in the stern to compensate for the added weight of the outboard. This is usually built into the hull rather than dependent on stern tube extensions (as with the sportboats). Without an engine, the stern of a RIB will float unusually high, which doesn't affect the rowing characteristics that much but does look a little strange with the stern tubes sticking out like tail fins on a '59 Caddy.

Once you get beyond the smallest RIBs, an outboard ceases to be an option. It becomes a matter of selecting the proper motor configuration, horsepower, and propeller combination. Follow the recommendations of the manufacturer, but view the maximum recommended horsepower with suspicion. Large RIBs often require long-shaft motors.

When you get serious about horsepower and start talking in numbers over 100, it may make sense to consider two smaller outboards rather than one big one. For example, twin 50s on the transom of a big RIB will run more efficiently than a single 100. You get more thrust because the props are more effective off the centerline; you can trim and steer with asymmetrical thrust; and you have the added safety of redundant engines, so if one of them decides to blow its doohickey out its gizmo while you're trolling for marlin in the Gulf Stream, the other one will get you home.

The accompanying chart (page 42) is a good starting point for matching boat and motor(s), but the array of available power options is well beyond the scope of this book. RIBs are even more sensitive to power loading than other inflatables, so it is doubly important that you try various boat and motor combinations before you buy. Talk to your dealer and collect all the brochures and pamphlets you can get your hands on. You may find useful information in a powerboat text such as *Boat Handling Under Power* by John Mellor (Sheridan House, 1993), and if this is your first boat, *Getting Started in Powerboating,* Second Edition (International Marine, 1995) will be a big help. The main thing is to take your time. If you're thinking about buying a big RIB, you're thinking about spending a lot of money. You want to get it right the first time.

Tiller Extensions

The first sportboats on the market (like my Zodiac Mark II) were very good designs, but as the market heated up, many manufacturers committed two egregious sins they should have resisted. They reduced the diameter of the main inflation tubes by an average of about 2 inches, and they moved the transom aft, reducing the size of the extension tubes by about 25 percent. They committed these atrocities not to save money but to gain internal volume so their salespeople could say "our boat holds more than their boat." The trade-off was in flotation at the stern, so when a heavy motor (like my Mariner) is placed on the transom of one of these newer boats (like my Achilles), it squats in the water like a constipated goose straining for relief.

Aside from looking funny, this creates some serious problems. The lack of adequate flotation means that scuppers that are supposed to make the boat self-bailing are forced underwater, making the boat self-swamping instead. If I park the boat and forget to replace the drain plug, it will fill with water in about 15 minutes. The little flapper valve designed to prevent this backflow doesn't work—never has, never will.

This squatting also makes the boat work harder to reach planing speed. When you first accelerate, the stern sinks even farther and the bow rises to the point where the boat seems to want to flip over backward. Everything not tied down—the

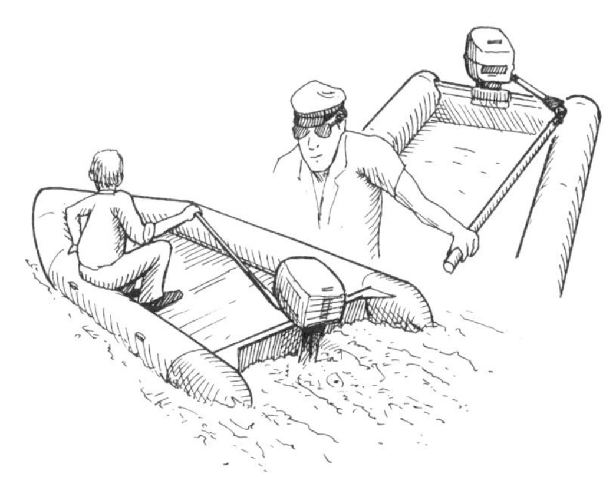

Tiller extensions.

gas tank, root-beer cooler, scuba gear, and all the passengers—comes sliding aft to pile up against the transom, adding weight in the stern and making things worse.

When I called Achilles to discuss this little problem, they denied that there was a problem. When I insisted I wasn't imagining things, they suggested that I adjust the trim of the motor and mount hydrofoils on the motor's anticavitation plate. The fins helped a little, but the motor needs to be trimmed for *operating* on plane, not for reaching it. What the boat needs is more flotation in the stern. I don't mean to pick on Achilles; most other manufacturers have done the same thing. The exception seems to be Avon, which may help to explain why they lead the pack in sales despite their hefty price tags.

What's all this got to do with tiller extensions? A lot. Any tail-heavy boat will benefit from the addition of a tiller extension. This moves the weight of the operator forward where it helps keep the bow down during initial acceleration, letting the boat reach planing speed more quickly and comfortably.

You can buy fancy tiller extensions from most boating-supply houses. Some are articulated (no, Gracie, that doesn't mean they speak well) and have telescoping handles. West Marine sells a dandy called the HelmsMate for about 40 bucks. You can also fabricate an extension in about two minutes from a scrap of PVC drain pipe and a hose clamp. I use the drain-pipe kind—a crude but cost-effective method of getting the beef into the bow.

There are a few small but significant problems with tiller extensions. They move the operator away from the engine, so while the operator can control the throttle with the extension (on most outboards), the clutch and transmission controls are out of reach. The potential for embarrassment is high. An operator arriving at the dock going a bit too fast dissolves into a blur of arms and legs as he scrambles aft to get the thing into reverse before the boat joins the poker game in the bait shack.

Hydrofoils.

A second problem deals with Euclidean geometry. The swing of a tiller is a section of a circle with the pivot point of the motor as the apex, the extremes of the tiller movement as the legs of the angle, and the end of the tiller as the arc. Any high-school student in Germany or Japan (and a precious few in the USA) can tell you that as you increase the radius of the circle, which is what you do when you install a tiller extension, without increasing the arc (limited by your reach), the angle at the apex reduces in proportion to the length of the legs. Thus, when you swing a 1-foot-long tiller through a 1-foot arc, the motor will turn about 57 degrees, but when you swing a 3-foot tiller through a 1-foot arc, the motor turns only slightly more than 19 degrees. This isn't a big problem until you slow down to pull up to that same dock; then it's "uh-oh, here he comes again."

An articulated tiller extension solves the Euclidean problem by changing the question from geometry to trigonometry, but lest we become Pythagorean, let's just say articulated tiller extensions work fine on motors up to about 10 hp. On high-power high-speed boats, however, they can be scary and even dangerous. If you have a big boat, wheel steering is a better choice.

Wheel Steering

As already mentioned, some boats can actually be dangerous when fitted with a powerful outboard operated from the stern. Their bows rise excessively as they try to accelerate up onto plane, and if the wind catches them just right, they can flip over backward. Wheel steering allows the operator to drive the boat from a more forward position, where the weight helps balance the boat and hold the bow down. Keeping the weight forward also improves handling and the comfort of the ride when the boat is operated on anything but a smooth surface. Most small sportboats, all large ones, and all but the smallest RIBs could benefit from the addition of wheel steering.

Wheel steering moves the operator's weight forward.

Improved forward visibility makes high-speed operation safer with wheel steering, and long trips are less tiring when you are on a comfortable seat behind a steering wheel instead of perched on the side tube gripping the tiller. Less appreciated benefits are throttle and shift controls independent of the steering, making their operation easier and more convenient, and (my personal favorite) making accidental acceleration less likely.

Besides the cost (about $350 and up), there are several other disadvantages to wheel steering. For one thing, a steering wheel in a small sportboat or RIB looks kind of silly—like the owner is trying too hard. The steering apparatus and necessary seat take up a lot of already scarce room. Wheel steering can be awkward and complicated to install (it is usually installed on large boats and RIBs at the factory or by the dealer). But the biggest problem with a steering wheel on a small inflatable is that it eliminates the ability to deflate and store the thing out of the way between uses, making operation from a trailer nearly mandatory.

Oars and Paddles

The discussion of oars and paddles as options may seem frivolous if you labor under the reasonable expectation that your new inflatable will come equipped with adequate means of manual propulsion, but alas, this is seldom the case. Many a boat needing a good pair of oars comes with a set that is woefully inadequate; others that need oars come equipped with paddles; and a great many that require paddles come equipped with delicate imitations made from thin aluminum and flimsy plastic. A few of the top brands still come with a decent set of wooden oars as standard equipment, but even these are often too short to row the boat efficiently. Short or flimsy oars may be provided for penurious reasons—they do it to save money—but usually it is to save space. The oars that come with the boat are often sized to fit into the storage bag.

Large sportboats and RIBs often don't have oarlocks; they're equipped instead with a tiny paddle. The theory is that modern outboards are so reliable that oars aren't necessary, and indeed many outboards do see heavy use under adverse conditions for years without a single failure. However, if your motor does quit (even the best is bound to stop sooner or later) and you need a paddle, you're going to need a good one, not some comical imitation made from aluminum tubing and plastic. If you buy a boat that isn't equipped with oarlocks, one of your first additions should be at least one and preferably two stout wooden canoe paddles with handles long enough for you to actually move the boat with them. Canoeists know this type as a stern paddle. If you operate your boat in waters that could be hazardous in an unpowered boat, you would be even wiser to equip any boat smaller than a big RIB with a set of Avon-style oarlocks and a decent pair of oars.

At least those inflatables meant to be paddled—kayaks, for example—will come with the proper equipment, right? Afraid not. A serious paddler is about as likely to be happy with the paddle that comes with an inflatable kayak as a pool shark is with the cue that comes with the table.

Selecting a proper paddle requires a little thought. Inflatable kayaks require double-bladed paddles. Single-blade canoe paddles don't work because the J-stroke used by the stern paddler to control the direction in a traditional canoe is ineffective in an inflatable. The increased drag and lack of sustained forward momentum of inflatables means that by the time the paddler gets to the J portion of the stroke, the boat has practically stopped. The stern paddler in an inflatable must switch sides with every stroke, which is tiring with a single-blade paddle and may slop a lot of water into the boat. The double-bladed paddle needs to be longer than one for a conventional canoe or kayak. Inflatable boats are beamier than conventional craft, and the longer shaft gives the paddler added reach for comfortable paddling.

The size and shape of the blade is also important. If your paddling is on lakes or the ocean where you will depend on the force of the paddle to move the boat, a paddle with a large blade surface area will work better. For rivers and streams where the current is sufficient to move the boat and directional stability and steering are more important than power, a smaller surface area works better. Likewise a rectangular-shaped blade with a radical curve or hook will usually work better in open water, while a pear- or teardrop-shaped paddle with a straight blade will work better in moving water where the backstroke and drawstroke can be more important than the forestroke.

You must determine the actual size and shape of the paddle that is just right for you by trial and error. Such diverse considerations as your physical size, weight, upper-body strength, and budget (good paddles range from about $60 up) are as important as the size and type of your boat and where and how you plan to use it. Your best bet is to search out a shop specializing in whitewater sports that will let you try different paddles until you find one you like.

Selecting a paddle for a riverboat is a bit easier than for a kayak. Here a sturdy wooden single-blade canoe paddle with a broad, straight blade and a blunt tip is best for nearly all situations. The riverboat paddler uses the blade to push off from rocks, fend off snags, and pole across gravel bars as much as to propel the boat, and a simple wooden paddle stands up to this rough treatment best. And at about $25 apiece, cracking or losing a paddle isn't such a heartbreaker. You need a paddle for every member of the crew, of course, but take along at least one extra.

Launching Wheels

If your inflatable is larger than a soft tail or small sportboat, and you plan to use it by yourself where there is no launching ramp, a good set of launching wheels will ease getting it into the water. There are several versions. One type mounts on the transom and folds up out of the way (more or less) when not in use. Another looks something like a four-wheeled baggage cart and carries the boat on its side. Yet a third type mounts to the transom only when the boat is being launched, then is removed and stored away while the boat is in use.

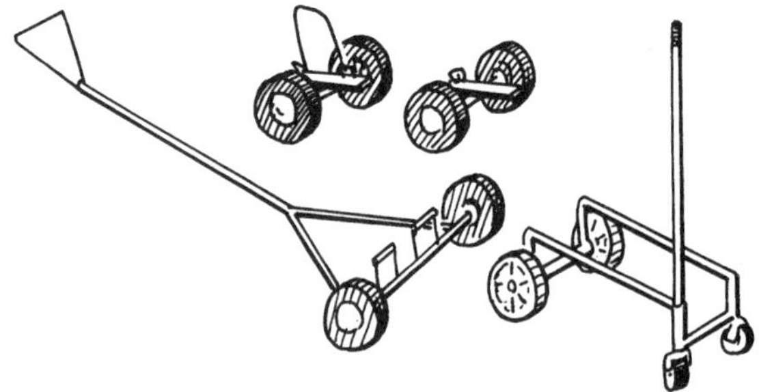

Launch wheels.

Each has advantages and disadvantages. Permanently mounted wheels are handy and always available but necessarily small, and they tend to be flimsy and break easily. The dolly is by far the easiest to use for dry storage, but it is bulky, must be used with the outboard removed, and doesn't work well on beach sand. The type that bolts temporarily to the transom is the most rugged and the best for launching from a beach, but someone has to get in the water to mount and remove it, and most are too big to take with the boat. One of the slickest systems is the Wheel-A-Weigh (available from West Marine and other places that sell inflatable accessories); it has permanently mounted brackets that allow the wheels to be flipped up on the transom or easily removed, depending on your immediate need.

Which launching wheels you should choose (if any) depends on the size and weight of your boat and where you intend to launch it.

Air Pumps

One of the most critical (and obvious) pieces of ancillary equipment for every inflatable boat is an air pump. We are all issued two perfectly good air pumps at birth, and perhaps your lungs will be all you need for a small toy boat for the kids to use at the beach. Even the smallest boat, however, requires a lot of air and will leave you red-faced and exhausted after a half hour of huffing and puffing. A rudimentary pump for anything larger than a small beach ball is a worthwhile investment.

Almost all well-made inflatable boats (and some of the not-so-well-made ones) come with an equally well-made manual pump as standard equipment. The majority of these work on the bellows principle and are operated by stepping on them in a vigorous manner. When set to music, this is called the *Inflatable-Boat Two-Step* or, for Scott Joplin/ Bobby Short fans, the *Blow-It-Up Rag*. Bellows-type pumps are adequate for all but the largest boats.

The number of stomps required to get your boat launched is directly proportional to the size of the boat and the size of the pump. My old Zodiac was a 1,300-stomp boat. The newer Achilles, because of smaller tubes, can be inflated hard in less than 800 stomps. The pump I use with the Achilles also serves as a handy pressure gauge: when I can stand on the pump full of air without forcing any more into the boat, I have 3¾ pounds per square inch (psi) in the tubes—just about right for this boat.

Another type of manual pump is a cylindrical device that looks much like a bicycle pump on steroids. These work on the piston principle. The operator stands on flanges at the base and moves the handle up and down. Piston pumps move a lot of air and they offer better exercise for the arms and lower back than do the stompers, but they aren't as much fun to watch someone operate. They choreograph better with Led Zeppelin, or maybe the Stones, and that never was my thing.

Bicycle pumps and other manual tire pumps don't work well for inflating boats, by the way. They are designed to move small quantities of air under high pressure—up to about 85 psi or higher. Your inflatable boat requires just the opposite: a large quantity of air at a low pressure—3 or 4 psi max. Even if you did adapt the inflation valve so you could use a tire pump, you would expire from exhaustion, or old age, before you got the boat inflated. Likewise, the little 12-volt compressors that plug into your cigarette lighter or clip onto your battery terminals won't work either. They don't move enough air.

You could use a tank-type compressor, either a small one like you have in your wood shop to blow out dust, or a big one like your local gas station has to run air ratchets and inflate tires. If you do inflate your boat with one of these, watch the pressure very carefully; you can quickly damage your boat by putting too much air into it.

The problems with manual pumps are that they require a lot of burned calories and they take a long time to do the job. If you're lazy with a frantic desire to get things done in a hurry (who isn't?), consider an electric pump. An electric pump will blow up even the largest boat in a fraction of the time without raising a single bead of sweat. Several models are available, but they all work about the same way. The one I've used with my last three inflatable boats is nothing more than a modified 12-volt vacuum cleaner. I clip the two electrical leads onto the car's battery, hold the exhaust over the inflation valve, and relax for 10 minutes or so. (For inflating the boat at home, the exhaust port of a household vacuum cleaner or a shop vacuum will work just fine.) Most inflation pumps also work in reverse, deflating the boat for storage more completely and quicker than the conventional method of alternately folding the boat and sitting on the largest bubbles.

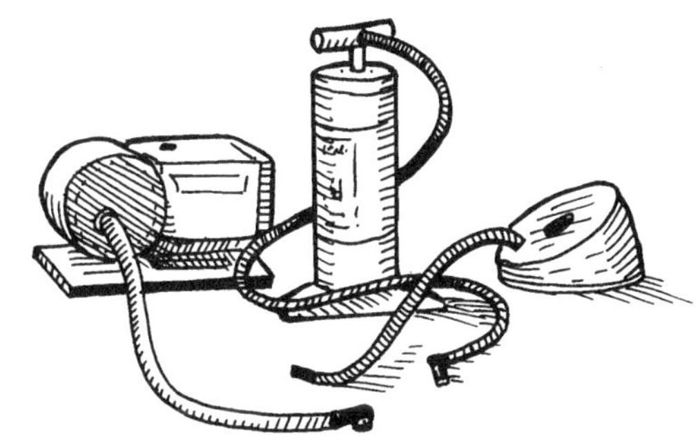

Air pumps.

Electric pumps suffer from two common failings (hey, nothing's perfect—excepting perhaps Beethoven's Fifth Symphony and Susan's linguine in clam sauce). Without electricity they are as functional as a Democratic reform program with a Republican budget. And they won't inflate your boat to operating pressure. This means that after you fill the boat with the electric pump, you must top it off to optimum pressure with a manual pump. You use an electric pump with, not instead of, your manual pump.

Other Options

Hydrofoil kits, boarding ladders, navigation lights, Bimini tops, inflatable seats, fishing-rod holders, and (believe it or not) a pressure water system with a shower are just a few of the options that will tempt you to part with your hard-earned money when you visit your local inflatable dealer. Whether these options are frivolous, useful, or downright

Other options.

necessary will depend on you, your boat, and how you intend to use it. The dealer where you buy your boat will have a long list of extras, and the big marine mail-order houses all have an impressive list of options in their catalogs. With the facetious exceptions of oars and outboards and a few other "extras" like the gas tank, it is important to remember that options are . . . well, optional. You don't really need them to enjoy your new boat, and many times your life will be simpler, your boating more carefree, and your Visa balance smaller without them. Consider your option purchases carefully and check the quality of the product before you buy it. Some add-ons on the market are so flimsy and poorly made (molded-plastic launch wheels come instantly to mind) that they would look ludicrous on your quality-built Avon or Caribe.

As for me, I don't need any more options; my boat is fixed up just the way I want it. But browsing through the International Watercraft catalog the other day, I couldn't help but think that the Bimini top they sell would be a nice addition. It would fit just aft of the hot tub—at the end of the shuffleboard deck—and keep the rain off the entertainment center.

CHAPTER 6

Operating an Inflatable

The operation of inflatable boats differs somewhat from the operation of more traditional craft, and there are considerable differences in the way different types of inflatables are operated. It behooves us to spend a little time on this subject. And because the most important operational consideration is always safety, let's get this particular hot dog off the spit and onto the bun where we can get a good bite out of it first.

Safety

A recent issue of the Seven Seas Cruising Association monthly bulletin reported the compelling and tragic story of two people returning in their dinghy to their anchored yacht just as a mild offshore storm arrived. Their outboard motor stopped running when they were less than a hundred yards from their destination, and because they had no other way to propel their boat, they were quickly blown out to sea. Despite a heroic rescue effort, not a trace of the dinghy or the occupants was ever found.

This dramatic tragedy illustrates the necessity for paddles or oars in a motor-driven craft, but just as important, it illustrates how rapidly and unexpectedly misfortune can strike, and how misfortune not dealt with swiftly and efficiently can lead to irreversible consequence. Operating any kind of boat places you in a hostile environment and subjects you to countless dangers. You must anticipate those dangers and be prepared to deal with them when they arise.

I'm going to skip the usual litany of general safety considerations here—not because they aren't important but because you've heard them all before. Avoid sunburn is one example. Don't swim with sharks is another. But some safety issues bear repeating. When it comes to life jackets, running lights, and alcohol and drugs, these are simply too important to pass over.

Life Jackets

Current Coast Guard regulations call for all boats less than 16 feet long to carry at least one Type I, II, III, or V PFD (personal flotation device) for every person on board. Boats 16 feet to less than 26 feet long require one Type I, II, III, or V PFD for each person on board, plus one Type IV throwable device. Type V PFDs combine foam flotation with an inflatable bladder, but note that "pure" inflatable vests have not yet received Coast Guard approval. Except for Type V, wearing the PFDs isn't required; you just have to have them "readily accessible" on your boat. Some states, however, require children under a specified age to *wear* an approved PFD when aboard (check the laws in your state). The Coast Guard takes PFD requirements very seriously, and every encounter will begin with their request to see the proper type and number of PFDs.

If you have a regular runabout or motorboat, stuffing the required PFDs into the forepeak may be fine, but fast inflatables are lighter and bounce higher when they hit a wake, wave, or obstruction, so the chances of someone being thrown from the boat are greater. If you operate your inflatable boat at high speed farther from shore than a comfortable swim, everyone aboard should be *wearing* well-fitted and comfortable life jackets.

TYPES OF PFDS. The Coast Guard categorizes PFDs into five types. *Type I* is a heavy-duty offshore vest with a minimum of 22 pounds of buoyancy. Type I vests might be appropriate for a big RIB operated at high speed in rough conditions, but they are bulky and uncomfortable to wear.

Type II are called *near-shore vests* and have a minimum of 15.5 pounds of buoyancy. A neck support is supposed to hold the head of an unconscious victim out of the water. They are lighter than Type I, but they are still bulky and quite uncomfortable to wear. Nevertheless, they are the type boatowners most often carry to satisfy Coast Guard requirements. Type IIs, because they support the head above water, are the only choice for small children and larger kids who can't swim.

They come in a variety of sizes for children according to body weight, and their cost is low enough that mom and dad won't balk at buying a new one when it's needed. Children should never be allowed aboard an inflatable without an appropriate life vest.

Type III vests have the same buoyancy as Type IIs, but without the neck support. They are lightweight, reasonably comfortable, and inexpensive, making them the best bet for about 90 percent of inflatable-boat owners. There are also Type IIIs tailored for kids by body weight, the usual choice for older kids who can swim.

Type IV PFDs aren't vests. They are what the Coast Guard calls throwable devices—cushions, life rings, and horseshoe buoys with the proper Coast Guard label. Cushions are required to have at least 18 pounds of flotation (16.5 pounds for a ring, 20 for a horseshoe). They are great to sit on, but don't ever depend on one to save your life in a boating accident.

Type V is a collective category established to satisfy the special needs of specific water sports such as waterskiing and kayaking. If you use your inflatable kayak in whitewater, or if you are considering entering your big RIB in offshore muscle-boat races, you will find a Type V vest designed just for you. For the most part they are lightweight, comfortable, safe (some are impact tested to 100 mph), and often even stylish. Type Vs are expensive, however, and depending on the device and how you're using it, the Coast Guard may not count it against their minimum requirements.

The thing to watch out for when buying a vest is the filling. Avoid polyethylene foam—used only in the cheapest vests—because it's stiff. Kapok (shudder) is still an approved filling and likewise should be avoided. Kapok can become so water saturated that it may actually pull you under. Look for vests filled with Airex or Aquafoam; both are light, soft, and comfortable, and they are, of course, more expensive.

My personal favorite is an Aquafoam-filled Type III fishing vest made by Sterns called the Sans-Souci (not impact tested). I like it because it's comfortable and it has lots of pockets, which I usually fill with enough junk to sink a small coastal freighter. Susan says it gives me a rugged look like a real sportsman. The next time she invites me out to dinner at the Ritz Carleton, I think I'll wear it just to surprise her. The only trick will be finding a tie that compliments day-glow orange.

Lights and Other Required Safety Gear

Operating a boat at night without proper lights isn't just dumb; it's also against the law. Make sure you have proper lighting aboard any time there is even a slight chance you will be caught out after dark. Current Coast Guard regulations call for all power vessels under 12 meters in length operating in inland waters after dark to display 112½-degree red (port) and green (starboard) sidelights visible from a distance of 1 mile in clear weather, and an all-around white light visible from a distance of 2 miles. Oar- or paddle-driven vessels must have a flashlight or other white light that can be shown in time to prevent collision.

Running lights need not be complicated. For years I have used the little battery-operated flashlight-style running lights with suction-cup bottoms. The suction cups usually don't work, so someone aboard ends up holding the lights, which is only a minor inconvenience. If you will be out after dark, it is also a good idea to have a flashlight aboard. Take two just in case, and don't forget the extra batteries.

The only other equipment you need is a sound signal—a horn (although it is not actually required equipment for boats under 12 meters)—and three red flares for boats operated at night. The flares may be handheld, meteor, or parachute type, and they must be Coast Guard approved (it will say so right on the label). They must also have a current expiration date; expired flares, no matter how good their condition, don't count.

Alcohol and Drugs

Safety statistics are unanimous in their condemnation of alcohol and drugs as the cause of well over half of all fatal marine accidents, so the most obvious concession to safety is to resolve never to operate a boat while drinking. Wait until the anchor is down or you are safely ashore before popping open the brewskies, and if you've had a few while waiting for the big ones to bite, find a shady spot on shore and take a nap before you fire her up and head back to the lodge.

Fortunately most of the people smart enough to read this book are smart enough not to operate complex machinery while loaded or stoned. But the next time you see the Sheriff's Department launch towing grappling hooks down the middle of the lake or you watch while they peel some poor slob off the breakwater, you can be certain alcohol or dope was involved and be reminded that there are still a lot of really stupid people around.

Sinking

The idea of floating around on a cold and dark ocean full of creatures with teeth and tentacles in a boat that is little more than a bag of air can be a pretty scary thing. What about the danger of sinking? People unfamiliar with inflatable boats have a common phobia of the boat springing a leak and deflating. But in more than 20 years of messing around with rubber boats of all shapes and sizes, I've never even heard of one sinking. Sure they deflate, delaminate, disintegrate, swamp, and self-destruct, but they don't sink. Everything larger than a play boat has multiple air chambers, and it would be very unusual for more than one of them to be punctured at one time. Even should the unlikely occur, a completely deflated boat will retain enough flotation to keep the occupants afloat. So stop worrying about sinking; it just won't happen. But don't use this as an excuse not to wear your life jacket.

DEFLATION. While it is practically impossible for your inflatable to sink, it is possible to have a tube deflate and create a dangerous situation. For example, an iron spike protruding from a piece of flotsam (Boston Harbor is full of old dock timbers floating just below the surface) can rip a gash in a side tube in a flash. The tube will collapse in seconds and the boat will most likely swamp. Remember that inflatable boats (excluding play boats) have at least two and as many as six inflation chambers. They also have considerable reserve buoyancy even when deflated, so you aren't about to sink.

As with any marine emergency, the first thing to do is to get a hold on your emotions. Get your passengers under control, get everyone into life vests, and shut down the motor if there is one. The biggest danger is panic, and you don't want anyone trying to swim for it or otherwise indulging in hysterics. Once everyone has been reassured that they aren't going to drown or be eaten by large aquatic creatures, you can assess the situation and take appropriate action.

Ninety percent of the time, nearby boaters will immediately come to your assistance. If you have a handheld radio (see sidebar), you can summon help. In most popular boating areas, a mayday call on VHF channel 16 will have you surrounded by rescuers within minutes; boaters are like that. But let's assume you're on your own and must take care of the situation without outside help.

If a bow tube has collapsed, folding it back into the boat can often make the boat watertight and maneuverable if somewhat abbreviated and cumbersome. In some boats you may even be able to operate the motor at slow speed; if not, you will need to row or paddle to safety. However you propel the boat, head without delay to the closest shore and worry about getting to your planned destination later.

The collapse of a side tube is generally more critical than the collapse of a bow tube, especially in sportboats with outboards, because the weight of the engine may tend to capsize the boat. If the outboard is lightweight, you might be able to make the boat watertight by lifting the collapsed tube and holding it vertical, then bailing the water from the boat. Another trick is to lash anything that will float—empty water jugs, spare life jackets, inflatable seats, picnic coolers, and the gas tank (even a full gas tank will float)—to the collapsed tube. This lightens the boat and helps keep it on an even keel. Making any headway in this situation is difficult, and unless you are in immediate danger—adrift in a shipping lane in the fog perhaps, or being blown out to sea by an offshore wind—you are probably better off sitting tight and waiting for rescue.

In a truly critical situation with a large, heavy motor mounted on the transom, you may have to ditch the outboard and gas tank and any other heavy gear on the boat. Without the motor you will be able to make some progress by paddling; rowing is nearly always impossible with a collapsed side tube.

If you do drop the outboard, and if you have time, rig a buoy so you can return and salvage it later. In shallow water the gas tank left attached to the engine can serve as a buoy (if the fuel line is long enough); just make sure to close the fuel shut-off valve and the tank vent. In deeper water a plastic soda bottle tied to the motor with a length of fishing line will suffice.

Handheld VHF Radios

A remarkable result of the miniaturization phenomenon is the availability of inexpensive portable VHF radios hardly bigger than a pack of cigarettes. The popular ICOM IC-M9, for example, weighs less than 11 ounces and is small enough to carry in a shirt pocket (although it will be more comfortable on your belt). Of course tiny radios don't have anything directly to do with inflatable boats, but they are so useful that every boater, canoeist, or kayaker should know about them.

Several dozen channels of the VHF spectrum are reserved for marine use, and you as an operator of an inflatable boat are authorized by an act of Congress to use them. Most of the channels are dedicated to certain functions. Drawbridges operate on channel 13, emergencies and hailing go on channels 16 and 9, and the Coast Guard uses channel 22A. Pleasure boaters chat on channel 68 and several others reserved just for that purpose. It takes a little getting used to, but it's not as hard as it sounds.

VHF marine operation is under the control of both the Coast Guard and the Federal Communications Commission. You need a license to operate on the marine bands, but you don't have to take a test; just send in the form that comes with your radio and a check for $115. The license is a station license, by the way, that gives you the right to operate only from the boat for which the license is issued. If you already have a license for your big boat, it will cover the use of a handheld in your dinghy.

If you are being blown offshore and you don't have an anchor, tie the outboard onto the painter and use it. If the painter is too short, use the lifelines to add length. You can even use the fuel line if you need it.

If you have a catastrophic side-tube collapse in southern waters, it can be a good idea to get everyone out of the boat and into the water holding onto the lifelines, especially if there are a lot of people in the boat. This has the added effect of reducing windage if an unfavorable breeze is blowing, and even a nonswimmer can help kick the boat to shore. But even in warm waters this technique should be viewed as a last resort because hypothermia sets in very quickly. In my favorite cruising grounds in Maine and the Canadian Maritimes, it is unthinkable. Hypothermia is a major hazard, and your first concern should be to keep everyone warm and dry.

Deflation of a tube on a RIB is usually more of a nuisance than a danger because most RIBs have enough reserve buoyancy in the rigid hull to allow restricted operation of the outboard even with the tubes completely deflated—provided the boat isn't overloaded. A few will function reasonably well without any tubes at all.

As you can see, there are about as many ways of dealing with emergencies in an inflatable boat as there are emergencies. The most important thing in any emergency is to keep your head—you'll surely find a use for it before the day is out.

Rowing and Paddling

Inflatable kayaks and canoes don't paddle as well as their hard-shelled cousins, and soft tails and sportboats don't row as well as a skiff or dinghy. This isn't to say that rowing or paddling these boats can't be a lot of fun—it can—but there are ways to make it easier and even more enjoyable.

Blow It Up Hard

For every boat larger than a play boat, get in the habit of inflating it as hard as you can with the standard foot pump. Don't worry about damaging your boat by putting too much air into it; quality boats will withstand pressures above what you can generate with a manual pump. Some boats come with a pressure gauge, but they generally aren't necessary. The maximum pressure attainable with a standard foot pump is likely to be very close to the optimum operating pressure (with the Achilles I must jump up and down on the bellows for the last few pumps). Your boat should feel hard to the touch and bouncy when you jump on the gunwales; any sponginess or softness means you need more air. It is amazing how much more responsive a properly inflated boat is compared to the same boat underinflated just ½ psi.

When you blow up your boat on a hot beach or launching ramp, putting it in the water cools the air and reduces the volume. After the boat has been in the water for a few minutes, top off the air pressure. Coming the other way, if you drag your boat up onto the hot sand for a day in the sun, bleed off enough air to reduce the pressure by about 25 percent. The pressure in a fully inflated boat can double when you take it from cold water to hot sand. No, your boat won't explode, but the additional stress on the seams can shorten its life.

Use the Floorboards

Soft tails and sportboats row and paddle more efficiently with floorboards installed. Most sportboats come with floorboards, but you may have to pay extra for them if you buy a soft tail. Floorboards aren't available on some lower-priced boats made from unreinforced PVC (such as the Sevylor Caravelle, which has an inflatable floor), but that doesn't deter my friend and sometimes co-conspirator Douglas Alvord one little bit. He has developed a simple plywood floorboard and seat combination that almost anyone could duplicate. It won't make the Sevylor (or any other soft tail) into a good rower, but it will make it row better. So with Douglas's kind permission, I include his design here for anyone with a do-it-yourself bent.

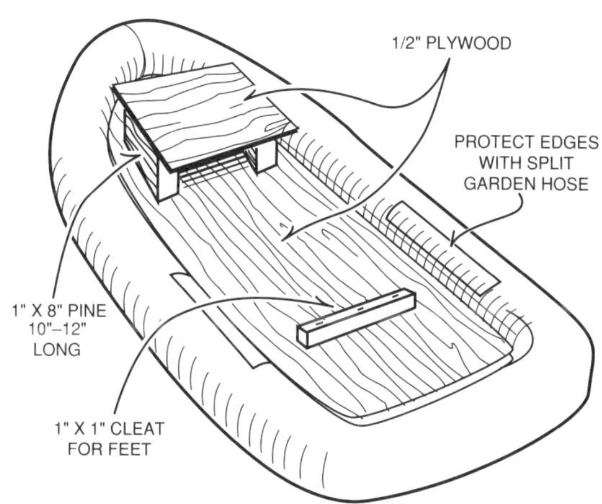

Douglas's floorboards.

Avoid Wind and Current

When your destination is upwind or upcurrent, finding sheltered water and rowing to a position upstream (or upwind) of your destination is usually smarter than trying to buck the current. For example, if you're fishing a river and find yourself on the opposite shore with a heavy current between you and your camp, instead of heading into the current on a straight line toward your destination, paddle or row upstream a ways. Stay close to shore where the flow is lighter; you may even find counter-currents and eddies flowing in your direction. When you are about twice the river's width upstream, row straight across; the current will carry you back down to your camp. This strategy works equally well against a strong headwind.

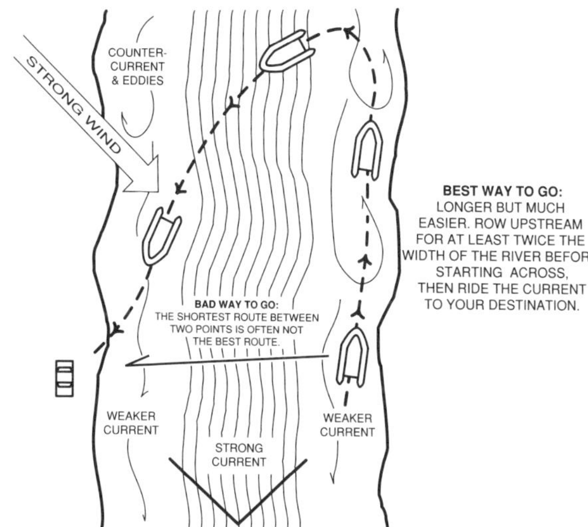

Sheltering from current or wind to get upstream or upwind.

Inflatable Kayaks

Kneeling on the bottom with my butt on the aft thwart, and using a long stroke that starts about midships and terminates with a light J-stroke just aft of the bang plate, I can paddle my old Mad River Voyager (a fiberglass canoe) all day. When I tried this in an inflatable kayak, I was exhausted after half an hour. It's better to sit up straight on the seat and use the arm and shoulder muscles to take short, strong strokes—with no J-stroke at the end. The J-stroke is ineffective; paddle on alternate sides of an inflatable to keep it tracking straight. This slops a lot of water into the boat with a canoe paddle, so use a double-bladed kayak paddle.

Riverboats

Riverboats and soft tails are equally dreary to row or paddle in calm water, but put them in moving water and they're in their element. The absence of a keel plus the wide beam makes a riverboat difficult for a single paddler to handle because it wants to change direction with every stroke. However, two paddlers (or more) sitting on opposite sides can make the thing go anywhere they want it to. It will go sideways or backward as well as forward. And when there arises a lack of consensus on the proper direction befitting the circumstances, as is bound to happen, the boat will spin on its axis like a merry-go-round.

If you must row a soft tail or riverboat, don't take long, sweeping strokes as in a traditional skiff. Place your seat as near to amidships as possible, sit with your back straight and knees together, lower your oar blades until the handles are about 45 degrees to the water (much deeper than with a conventional boat), and jerk the oars toward your chest. Let your arms and back provide 90 percent of the power. Don't expect any glide. Get the oars back into the water as soon as you can and repeat the stroke as quickly as possible. This chop-and-jerk technique looks just as awkward as it sounds, but it is definitely the best way to row a soft tail. Once you develop the proper cadence and the necessary muscles, it is surprisingly effective.

Sportboats and RIBs

Rowing a sportboat is a bit more rewarding than rowing a soft tail, and sportboats also paddle pretty well. The difference is the keel (inflatable or otherwise), which keeps a sportboat going in the direction it is pointed rather than skidding off sideways with each stroke of the oars or paddle. For the same reason they don't blow off sideways as fast in a stiff breeze.

Big sportboats and a lot of RIBs will row better with oars longer than those supplied with the boat. You can buy a pair of solid wood oars for under fifty bucks, but before you do, make sure they will work with your oarlocks. Standard oars work fine with Avon oarlocks. You'll need to drill a ⅜-inch hole in each oar to use them on an Achilles. Most Zodiacs need a special saddle and stud (available from International Watercraft) attached to each oar. On some brands of boats, the oarlocks are so complicated or so flimsy that you're better off changing to Avon-style oarlocks or just using paddles.

With two or more people aboard, paddling a sportboat or a RIB can be more efficient than rowing. The paddlers sit on the tubes on opposite sides of the boat and dig in. Two energetic paddlers with decent paddles can move a sportboat right along. This is the only way to go for a big RIB not equipped with oarlocks. A kayak paddle won't work: the wide beam forces the paddler to move from side to side with each stroke, which is tiring and inefficient, and the angle is wrong for the blades to bite the water properly. If you're going to paddle, don't rely on that silly little thing that came with the boat. Throw it away and buy a decent pair of canoe paddles.

When using a sportboat in rapids, always deflate the keel so you can use a drawstroke to move the boat sideways. The boat won't slip and slide like a riverboat or soft tail, but there will be a definite improvement in lateral maneuverability.

Poling

An underrated method of moving a boat through shallow water is *poling*—the way southern folks have moved their pirogues down the bayous for centuries. Poling is almost as easy as it looks. The operator simply stands in the stern and pushes the boat through the water with a long pole. The only trick is steering by shifting your weight and twisting with your feet while pushing on the pole. It takes a little practice, but most everyone will have the hang of it after half an hour.

The mistake most beginners make is using a pole that is too short. Any straight stick will do, but it should be at least two to three times the length of the boat, flexible, and stout enough to withstand a healthy shove. The ideal wood for a pushpole is hickory. Bamboo is also great. Oak is a bit heavy. Avoid pine and poplar.

Poling works with any kind of inflatable but is particularly useful for moving soft tails and riverboats upstream. A skilled poler can push a boat through Class II rapids.

For fishing in shallow water, the pole has another benefit. When you want to stop in a promising spot, just shove the pole into the bottom and secure the boat to it. This keeps the pole out of the way while you cast and keeps the boat anchored until you're ready to move on.

Sailing

My sailing experience in inflatable boats is limited to a few happy hours as a passenger in a Tinker Tramp. The Tinker is the only production inflatable I'm aware of currently offering a sailing rig. I was very impressed with how well the Tinker sailed, and with the quality of the engineering and construction of the components. I was also impressed with the price of the sail package: it adds more than $700 to the base price.

Several years ago there was another sailing inflatable on the market called the Breeze. It was technically interesting because it featured a three-piece folding floor and unreinforced plastic tubes. The boat itself was inexpensive (less than $800), and the sailing kit cost about half as much as the one for the Tinker, using lee boards instead of the Tramp's daggerboard. Alas, the Breeze is gone with the wind, but you might find one on the used market. My advice? Try it before you buy it, and don't pay a lot.

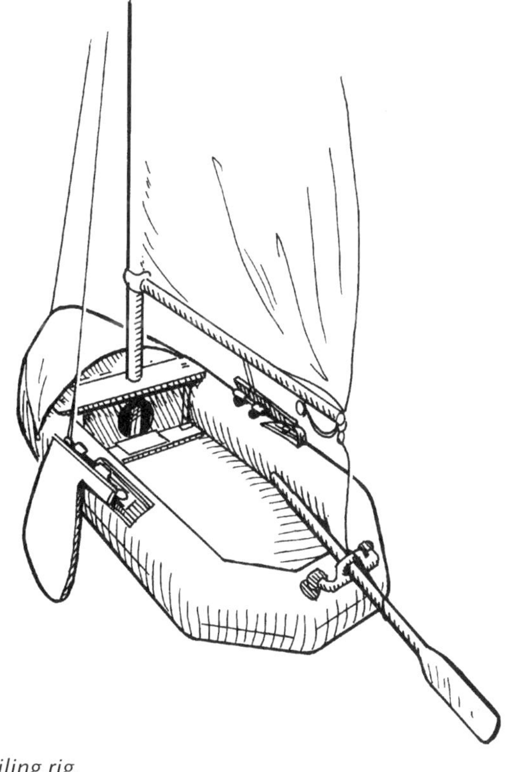

Sailing rig.

Many years ago Avon offered a terrific little sailing kit for their popular Redcrest dinghy. They didn't sell many because it was overpriced, so you aren't likely to find one on the used market, but with just enough changes to avoid infringement problems (I hope), the rig is illustrated here. It is simple and straightforward, and anyone a touch handy should be able to make a reasonable facsimile out of plywood and other readily available materials. If you adapt this design to your inflatable, send along a photo and let me know how it works.

Powering

We've already covered many of the unique characteristics of inflatable boats under power, but we missed a few, and a few others bear repeating. I have also included a few tricks here that will help you maximize your enjoyment of your inflatable powerboat.

Play Boats and Soft Tails

Don't try to use an outboard on any boat made from unreinforced plastic, regardless of what the dealer or the manufacturer tells you; it simply doesn't work. A small outboard can add utility to a soft tail if the boat is inflated hard and has a good set of floorboards, but don't expect a lot of performance regardless of the boat's size. Use only the smallest and lightest motors available because soft tails don't have reserve flotation in the stern. Electric trolling motors work well (see Chapter 5).

Remember that directional stability is nonexistent in boats without keels. Anticipate turns well ahead of time. Drawstroking from the bow can help with the turns.

Sportboats and RIBs

One of the most important considerations for operating a sportboat or RIB (beyond the critical matching of boat and motor, which we've already discussed) is trim and weight distribution. Strapping the gas tank and all heavy cargo into the bow and keeping your passengers seated as far forward as possible will usually facilitate planing and make the ride more comfortable. Wheel steering (Chapter 5) should be considered as a means of better weight distribution on larger boats.

Trim can be as important as load. The trim setting adjusts the angle of the outboard to the transom, and it is accomplished in different ways on different motors. Small motors usually have a series of holes for a pin that holds the motor at a selected fixed angle. Large motors have electric or hydraulic trim that can be adjusted underway. Start with the trim setting in the lowest position and raise it gradually until you get the most comfortable ride. The lowest setting is often the best for inflatables.

When you mount the engine to the transom, think about how you will use the boat. If usually the only passenger will be the driver sitting near the stern, you may want to mount the motor a bit off-center away from the driver. The slightly asymmetrical thrust of the off-center engine will help compensate for the added drag on the driver's side caused by the driver's weight. Adjusting the motor's trim tab will help to keep the boat tracking straight.

HEAVY WEATHER. Nearly all sportboats and many RIBs are wet. When you operate one in windy or rough conditions, expect a great deal of crew-soaking spray to be blown into the boat. Their light weight makes them tend to pound in anything other than smooth water; the smaller and faster the boat, the worse the pounding. This combination of pounding and spray flying into the cockpit can turn a pleasant excursion into a trip through hell should the weather turn unexpectedly foul. Fortunately you can take steps to make conditions bearable, if not comfortable.

When your boat starts to pound, you can of course slow down, and at times this is the only thing that will help. Unfortunately, slowing the boat below planing speed often multiplies the amount of spray that comes aboard. Changing direction slightly can reduce or eliminate pounding without forcing you to slow below planing speed. If you are heading into waves a foot or more high, attacking them at an angle of about 45 degrees offers optimum comfort. Going downwind, a course 10 to 15 degrees off the wind will usually be more comfortable than motoring directly downwind.

Another way to counter pounding is to get as much weight into the bow as you can without making the boat bow heavy. Move all heavy gear forward and tie it down. Encourage passengers to sit as far forward as possible. Shifting weight forward—and lashing it there—is particularly important when motoring into the wind; a strong gust under the bow can flip a stern-heavy inflatable.

Steps to reduce pounding can increase the amount of spray coming aboard. A bow-heavy boat will generate more spray, and quartering the waves (crossing them at a 45-degree angle) can increase the amount of water coming over the weather (upwind) side. Shifting the load to the leeward side so that the downwind tube is deeper in the water frequently helps. The downwind tube then provides most of the lift and flotation, thus generating most of the spray, which will be blown away from the boat. The higher-riding windward tube acts as a spray shield, deflecting most of the windward spray before it is blown into the boat and leaving skipper and crew dry and happy (sort of).

REALLY HEAVY WEATHER. Every so often even the most careful skipper can be caught offshore or in the middle of the lake when the bottom drops out of the barometer and the wind starts blowing the tops off waves the way a beer drinker blows the heads off fresh draft. Waves build to 3 or 4 feet with astonishing rapidity. If you try to race home at planing speed, you'll find yourself flying off the tops of waves and landing with a crash in the troughs. Big RIBs can handle punishment like this, but most other inflatables can't. The first thing to do is slow down and collect your wits.

Get everybody aboard into life jackets (and rain gear if it's available), and get them off the side tubes and seats and onto the floor. A sudden storm in open water can be really scary to anyone experiencing one for the first time. Reassure your passengers that they are perfectly safe and that inflatables are the world's most seaworthy boats for their size. If there is lightning around, explain to your passengers that inflatables don't have enough mass to attract lightning, which makes the chances of being hit about the same as being run over by a camel.

Once everyone is settled, find a speed at which the boat maintains its heading without pounding or jumping off the tops of the waves. Into the wind, staying just below planing speed and quartering the waves, is often the most comfortable. The boat will want to slide down the back of the wave and turn sideways—broach—at the bottom of the trough; the slide is harmless, but keep the boat tracking and don't ever let it broach, even if you have to give it full power to start up the face of the next wave.

Going downwind it is frequently possible to motor along at the same speed as the waves by taking them at a slight angle. You can sometimes ride on the crest of a wave for several hundred yards before sliding off and moving to the next one. The boat's tendency to surf on the front of a wave you are overtaking is more dangerous than sliding down the backside going the other way; a breaking following sea can quickly swamp a boat that broaches in the trough. It is doubly important to avoid broaching and to keep the boat moving up the face of the next wave.

Your immediate objective should be to get the boat into sheltered or calm water; worry about getting home or back to the car after the storm passes. Head for the sheltered side of the lake, or try to duck behind an island or peninsula for protection. Never try to land on a beach where waves are breaking. Surf conditions always look better than they really are from a seaward perspective because you only see the smooth backsides of the waves. If you see waves breaking on a beach or shore, head in the opposite direction even if it means going back out to sea or back to the middle of the lake.

If you're not in danger of washing ashore, hitting obstructions, or being run down by other traffic, the best thing to do might be nothing at all. It is perfectly acceptable to simply shut down the outboard, make yourself and your passengers as comfortable as possible, and let the boat drift while you wait for the weather to improve. This is called *lying a-hull* in nautical jargon. If you resort to this tactic, console yourself and reassure your passengers with the fact that you are safer in your stable inflatable than you would be in any other type of boat of the same size. While lying a-hull, if you are being blown toward a hazard or away from your ultimate destination, a jury-rigged sea anchor will slow your drift.

SEA ANCHORS. The simplest make-do sea anchor is a bait bucket (or any kind of bucket with a bail) tied to the bow painter. Another good one can be made from a pair of trousers with the legs knotted and a couple of sticks (break a fishing rod if you need to) tied in a cross and secured to the waistband to keep the waist open. If someone has to drop his drawers to stop the boat from drifting, get the fattest person aboard to volunteer. It's the size of the waist that's important—the bigger the better; the length of the leg doesn't matter at all.

Sea anchors.

Always rig a sea anchor from the bow using the longest piece of line you have aboard. Rigging it from the bow keeps the boat pointed into the wind, which reduces windage and greatly improves your ride. Weight it with a piece of chain or a small anchor to keep it below the wave action.

Don't drop your regular anchor during a storm unless you are at risk of being washed onto a lee shore, carried out to sea, or blown into some other immediate danger. If you do drop your anchor just to "park" and it sets properly (which is unlikely in storm conditions), the jerking of the anchor line in the waves will be extremely uncomfortable and could damage your boat.

No book can suggest strategies for all sea conditions and all types of boats. The important thing to remember is that if you are being beaten senseless by the waves and soaked to the skin with rain and spray, don't sit there like a martyr. Try different speeds, different angles of attack, and different load configurations until you find the one that works best. Even if you don't end up keeping dry, you'll at least stay busy, your passengers will think you know what you're doing, and maybe you can forget for a while just how miserable you are.

Towing the Inflatable

Inflatable boats used as dinghies are often towed behind the mother ship. This practice is normally safe and acceptable, but there's a nick in the ax blade, as my Grandpappy used to say. There are circumstances when towing should be avoided at all costs, so let's get those out of the way first before we discuss towing technique.

Several years ago, on a weekend trip from Marblehead to Plymouth Harbor, we were sailing across Massachusetts Bay in a steady southeast wind and 10-foot seas. The Dyer was on the stern davits and the Zodiac trailed behind on a double tether. *Sultana* likes this kind of weather. Her bow rode high on each crest before crashing into the trough and sending sheets of spray 50 feet to either side, giving us an exhilarating if somewhat unnerving ride.

Suddenly the boat shook, and then there was a loud crash. At first I thought we had hit something or perhaps lost a shroud, but a second and a third crash followed in quick succession. The boat shook with each impact as if we were being bombarded by cannon balls.

The problem turned out to be the Zodiac. As *Sultana* reared up on a wave, the inflatable was sliding forward down the face of the previous wave. When the crest passed beneath the stern, the inflatable rode up and smashed into the bottom of the Dyer with enough force to cause me to worry about losing both. Had the Dyer not interfered, the inflatable would have been thrown into the cockpit.

On another occasion, this one a trip from Puerto Cortez, Honduras, to Punta Gorda, Belize, we were trailing the Achilles on a long tether. Winds were light but we had a heavy following swell cresting at about 15 feet. We were sailing along at a comfortable 5 knots when I looked off to starboard and saw the dinghy alongside. It had caught a wave and was surfing past *Sultana*. It sped ahead until the end of its tether it brought it up short and snapped it around like a frantic squirrel-chasing dog reaching the end of its leash. As Sultana regained the lead, the Achilles slid back astern like a piece of flotsam until the tether snapped it around once more. In a few minutes here it came again.

In both instances the inflatable was appropriately rigged for towing, and we left port in calm conditions for a relatively short passage. But we had violated the first rule of towing inflatables:

Rule 1: Never tow an inflatable dinghy in anything but protected waters. The open sea changes quickly, and when it does, it may be too late to get the dinghy on board. More than one mariner has been forced to cut loose an inflatable when it swamped in an unexpected storm and created a hazard to the mother ship. Also, towing a fabric-bottomed inflatable is a lot like dragging a small sea anchor even when the boat isn't swamped, generating enough drag to take as much as a full knot off your boat speed.

Calling this Rule 1 suggests at least a Rule 2, so while we're at it, let's list them all.

Rule 2: Except for short hauls in flat calm conditions, never tow the dinghy with the outboard, gas tank, or other heavy objects aboard. The added weight significantly increases both the drag on the mother ship and the stress on the tow rings. An unexpected squall can flip a towed inflatable, so never carry anything in it you can't afford to lose.

Rule 3: Always tow with a bridle (see illustration, page 60) attached to properly installed tow rings. Many inflatable dinghies have a large handle installed at the point of the bow, but never use this for towing. For one thing, you shouldn't tow from a single point, and for another, these handles are typically attached with only a strip or two of fabric or seam tape and will eventually tear out.

Rule 4: Never tow at planing speed. This puts too much stress on an inflatable dinghy. The ideal towing speed, determined by experimentation, allows the dinghy to ride comfortably on the crest of the *second* wave in the wake. If you want to go faster, get the dinghy aboard first.

Rule 5: Except for short distances at slow speeds, never tow a soft tail or any other inflatable that is not self-bailing. An inflatable only partly filled with water creates tremendous drag that can easily cause damage. Most soft tails are so light and easy to handle that there's seldom any reason to tow them anyway.

Tow Rings

Some inflatables come with a good set of D-type tow rings as standard equipment. Others come with flimsy or inadequate tow rings. Still others come with no tow rings at all. If the inflatable you are buying is among these last two groups and it will be frequently towed, have the dealer remove any flimsy tow rings and install a set of heavy-duty D-rings—35 mm or larger for soft tails and 50 mm or larger for sportboats and small RIBs. Or buy a set from International Watercraft and install them yourself. They come attached to backing pads you bond to your boat with special two-part glue. Follow these instructions:

1. With the boat inflated hard, locate the correct position of each tow ring (see illustration) and clean the area thoroughly with solvent—acetone or toluene for Hypalon boats, and methyl ethyl ketone (MEK) for PVC boats. Wipe the area with Interlux #202 to remove silicones, then outline the mounting pad with a felt-tipped pen.
2. Deflate the boat, then scuff the outlined area and the back of the mounting pad with 80-grit sandpaper.
3. Mix an adequate quantity of the right glue (see Chapter 9) for the fabric (Hypalon or PVC) in your boat and apply it evenly to both surfaces.
4. Let the first coat of glue set until it is dry to the touch—about 10 to 30 minutes—then apply a second coat and let that set until it is tack free. The difference between tack free and dry is hard to explain. After 30 minutes the first coat will be dry. After about 3 to 5 minutes the second coat will be tack free—no longer sticky but retaining a rubbery quality.
5. *Very carefully* place the D-ring pad in position and press hard. The glue will bond instantly on contact, so if you get it wrong, you'll have to rip it off and start over.
6. Because of the D-ring pad's irregular surface, you can't use a roller to apply pressure, at least not from the top. The solution is to place the tube with the D-ring attached face down on a bag of sand or lead birdshot and roll it from the back. Better yet, pound the bond with a block of wood and a hammer. (See Chapter 9 for additional gluing and patching instructions.)
7. Let the glue cure for at least two days.
8. Install a bridle and painter as shown on page 60, using eye splices. Some people rig a small stainless or bronze block on the painter for the bridle to pass through, but in my experience this block tends to bang around. A nylon thimble does the job just as well and is easier to handle and easier on your decks. The important thing is for the painter to slide on the bridle without restrictions to equalize the stress on the two towing points, which greatly improves

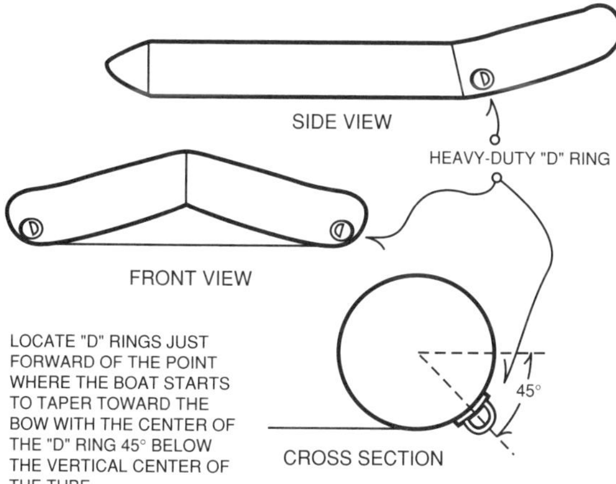

Locating tow rings.

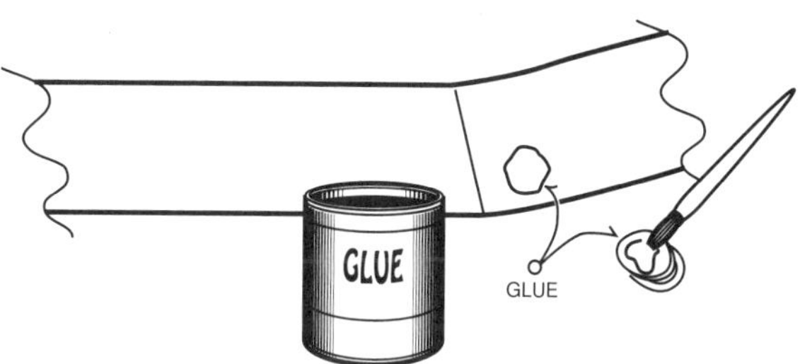

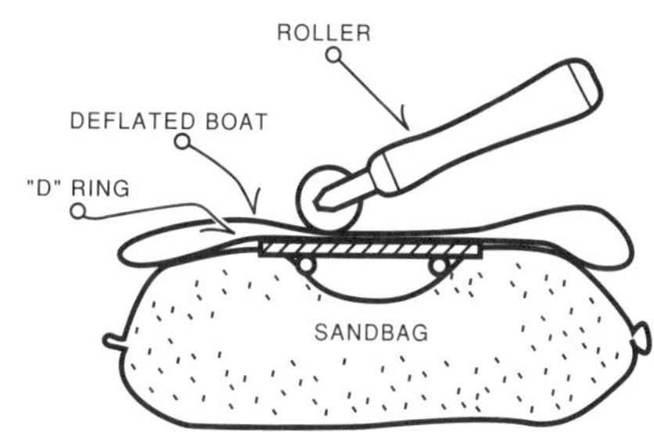

Installing tow rings.

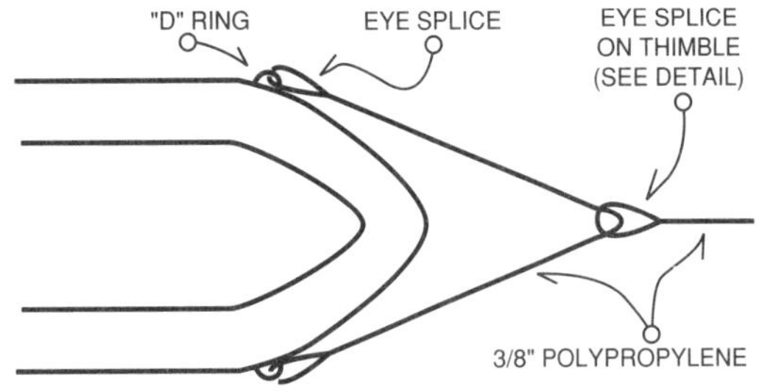

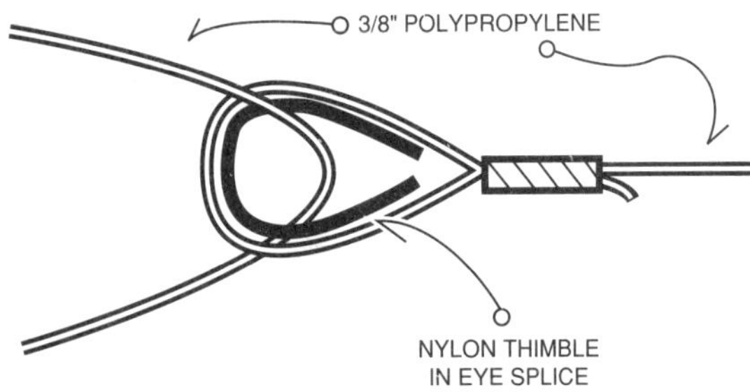

Installing bridle and painter.

tracking. I long used ½-inch nylon rope for both bridle and painter, but recently I switched to ½-inch polypropylene because it floats and keeps itself clear of *Sultana's* prop. Yellow is the easiest color to see.

Towing Technique

One of the things I really love about cruising in the Caribbean is watching how full-time cruisers do things. Cruisers are a fiercely independent, self-reliant, and resourceful group, and they are forever trying new techniques. Nowhere are their attempts more visible than in the various ways they tow and otherwise manage their inflatable dinghies.

Some pull the bow up onto the stern pulpit and lash it so that only the stern tubes are in the water when the boat is towed. Others lash the stern up so that only the bow is in the water. Both methods dramatically reduce wetted surface and drag, and keep the dinghy under control in all but the worst sea conditions. The only drawback is that considerable chafe can occur where the dinghy rests on the mother ship.

A double bridle is another popular way of towing an inflatable dinghy, especially a large one. Pass the end of a line attached to one stern cleat through the bridle of the dinghy and secure it to the mother ship's other stern cleat. I use this method for long tows under power—such as motoring down the Intracoastal Waterway—because it keeps the inflatable under positive control about 20 feet astern. The painter tied slightly slack serves as a lazy safety line.

The double bridle is also an excellent way for powerboats to tow a relatively heavy dinghy. If the dinghy is towed on a double bridle just far enough aft to ride on the second wave of the wake, it will remain under positive control and won't try to charge the mother ship.

When towing a sportboat under sail, I usually forgo the double bridle in favor of a single 100-foot towline tied to the painter (with double bowlines) and secured to the lee stern cleat. This sacrifices control in favor of keeping the dinghy far enough astern to keep it out of trouble during short tacks and other maneuvers. Should it catch a following sea and start to surf, keeping the towline on the downwind side encourages the dinghy to sail into the lee of the mother ship instead of crashing into the stern and flustering the captain, frightening the passengers, and otherwise riling up the crewmembers.

The Ultimate Bridle

Let's digress into a hypothetical situation for just a moment. Suppose you were head of the refreshments committee for the annual Lions Club picnic and bull roast out on Mystery Island. Further suppose you had four half kegs of draft beer, five cases of soft drinks, 200 pounds of ice, 50 pounds of steaks, 10 pounds of hot dogs (your humble author loves hot dogs), 15 bags of charcoal, and a jar of Aunt Minnie's special horseradish piccalilli stowed on board your trusty inflatable, and you want to tow the whole thing the 3½ miles across Marblehead Harbor to the island. We just said we shouldn't tow a loaded dinghy, and certainly not one overloaded to this extreme—the D-rings would pop like corks out of shook-up bottles of warm champagne. But to load all that stuff into the mother ship and then back into the dinghy when we reach the island is a lot of work. What to do? What to do?

This is a job for . . . ta-dum . . . ta-dum . . . Super

Bridle. Simply take a ½-inch rope roughly three times the length of your dinghy and reeve it through the towing rings, slip 3- or 4-foot lengths of garden hose over both ends to prevent chafe, then lead the bridle under the boat and tie both ends securely to eyebolts in the transom or to the outboard's carry handle. Now when you tow the dinghy—slowly and carefully and praying for no powerboat wakes—all the towing forces will be transferred to the transom, which is strong enough (we hope) to carry the load.

Use Super Bridle only under extreme conditions, such as the semi-emergency hypothesized above. It is also useful for towing an inflatable that has undersized tow rings, or one that doesn't have any tow rings at all. In the latter case, simply reeve the bridle through the bow handle, side handles, or lifelines before securing the ends to the transom. If it doesn't have any of these things (some RIBs are completely bare of attachments), rig a hackamore hitch (see illustration) on the bow, secure the ends of the bridle to the stern with bowlines looped over the stern tubes—protected with sections of hose over the line—and tow her away.

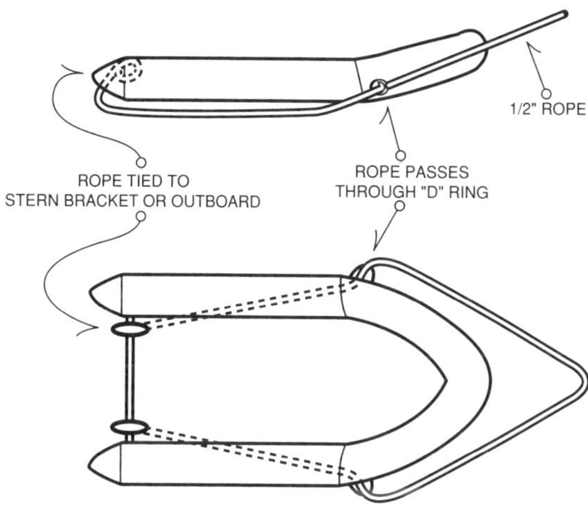

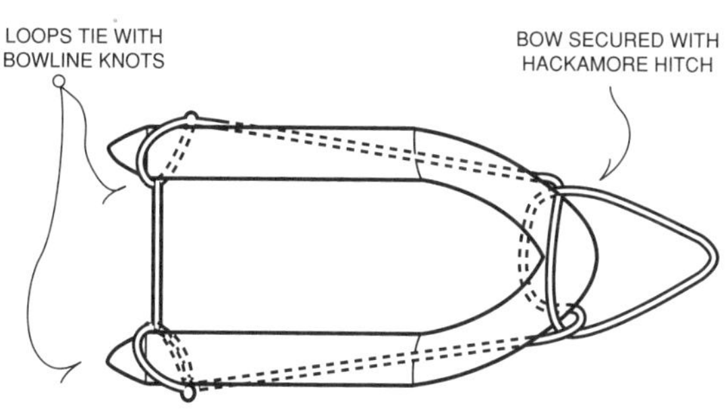

Super Bridle.

Stowing the Inflatable Dinghy on Deck

Under some circumstances towing is fine, but when you venture onto the open ocean or you want to run your powerboat at planing speeds or you wish to make the best possible time in your sailboat, you simply have to get the dinghy out of the water and onto (or into) the mother ship. There are several ways to do this, and as with most things nautical, the bigger the dinghy, the more difficult it becomes.

The easiest inflatables to stow are soft tails and roll-up sportboats. To stow our little Avon Redstart, Susan and I simply hauled it on deck, let the air out, rolled it up, stuffed it into its canvas bag, and stuck it in the lazarette. There it remained, out of sight and out of mind, until we needed it. The Achilles we have now is too big to stuff into anything (as was its Zodiac predecessor). A boat this size needs to be carefully deflated and folded, preferably on shore. It packs into two bags—one for the boat and one for the floorboards—that must be carried on deck. There is no question of stowing the boat below; the bags are just too big and cumbersome.

How about stowing the inflated boat on deck? That is hardly necessary with a soft tail and usually not advisable since it will catch and hold rainwater, even when stowed upside down (if the floorboards aren't installed). If the soft tail is doubling as a life raft, it must be stowed inflated to be ready to launch in an emergency, and it will need a tight-fitting cover to keep it dry. Otherwise, carry your soft tail deflated.

Small sportboats, and even large ones if the mother ship is big enough, can be made to stow on deck quite nicely. The most common routine on sailboats is to invert the dinghy forward of the mainmast and lash it, bow forward, to the deck. This often takes up the entire foredeck, which makes sail handling difficult and necessitates headsails cut high enough to clear the dinghy as the boat tacks. A roller-reefing jib minimizes the problem.

On sailboats over 40 feet, the inflated dinghy is often stowed just aft of the mainmast. It is usually inverted and lashed to the handrails. Once the mother ship reaches 60 feet or so, deck space can usually be found to store the dinghy upright on chocks. Amidships storage allows the use of the main halyard or the topping lift and boom to hoist the dinghy aboard. Unfortunately midship storage also blocks forward visibility from the cockpit and restricts airflow through the main deck hatches (and often blocks the Charley Noble).

The dinghy on a large powerboat is most often carried upright in chocks on the foredeck, with the motor and gas tank installed and the dinghy protected by a tight-fitting cover. Smaller power craft and boats without a flying bridge can carry an inflatable in the same manner but on the cabin top. Either arrangement generally requires a dedicated derrick or davit for launching and retrieving the dinghy.

Powerboats with swim platforms on the stern can take advantage of a pair of neat little gadgets called Weaver Snap Davits. These consist of two rings you glue to one side of your inflatable and two snaps you fasten to the trailing edge of the platform. To use the davits, pull your inflatable abeam the swim platform, clip the rings into the snaps, remove the outboard, oars, and everything else, and lift the dinghy out of the water using the davits as pivots. Lash the boat flat against the transom. You can also simply hoist the boat sideways onto the platform and lash it down, but the snap davits make the process a little easier.

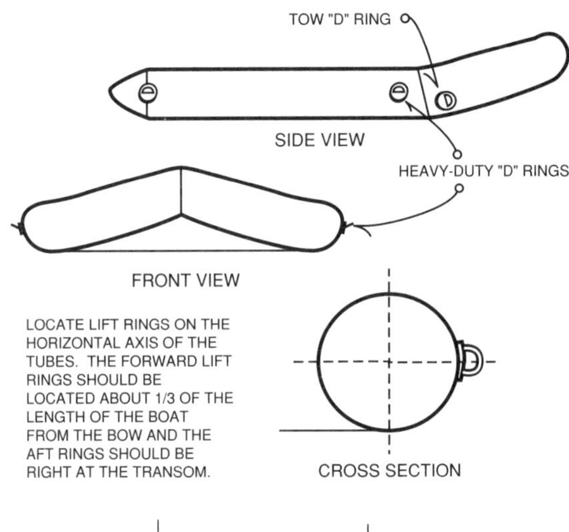

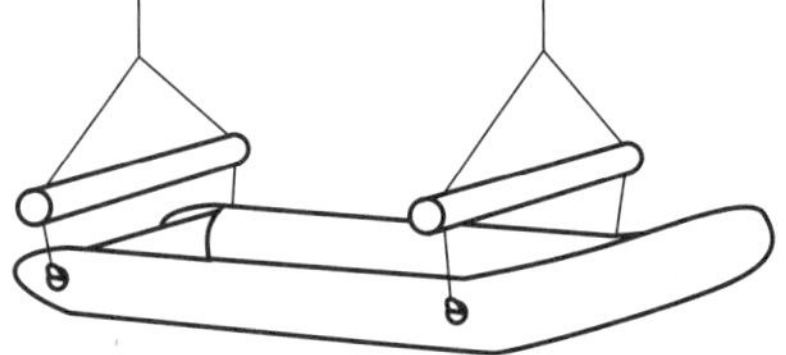

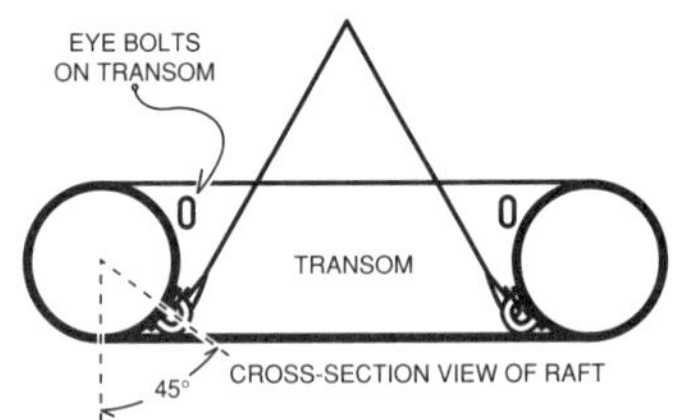

Lift rings and yoke.

Davits

What about swinging your inflatable dinghy from conventional stern davits? If your boat will carry a hard dinghy this way, it will carry an equivalent inflatable equally well. The most important consideration will be the attachment points for the lifting harness. Many cruisers lift the bow with the towing bridle and attach a yoke to a pair of eyebolts through the transom to lift the stern. The eyebolts in the stern are okay, but using the towing bridle places vertical loads on D-rings that have been installed to be pulled horizontally. A better arrangement is to install a separate pair of heavy-duty D-rings oriented for lifting. The best arrangement is a set of four lift rings. Whereas the towing bridle should be attached to the tow rings with eye splices, attach the davit yokes to the lift rings with snap shackles so they can be easily removed.

You will need to take steps to protect the fabric of an inflatable on davits from chafe. The lift rings need to be installed as low as possible on the side tubes, but above the rub strake. The low mounting point takes advantage of the much stronger shear strength of the lift-ring bond, and it better supports the weight of the boat. The lift-yoke crosspiece should be slightly wider than the beam of the dinghy so the snap shackles will be held away from the fabric. An alternative that works very well is to place the rings on the inside of the tubes and forget the yokes.

The dinghy is usually tied to the davit uprights to keep it from swinging. Prevent chafe where it rubs by permanently installing chafe pads on the uprights (short sections of canvas fire hose lashed with parachute cord work well). If there is any contact where the lift-yoke crosspieces rest on the inflation tubes, these should also be protected with chafe pads.

Stowing the RIB Dinghy

A big drawback to using a RIB as a dinghy is that you can't deflate the thing for storage when making a passage. But because of the RIB's better performance under power, its ability to handle larger engines, and the added durability of the hard bottom, more are being used for dinghies anyway. A small RIB makes an excellent dinghy, but when it comes time to make a passage, a RIB can be a real pain in the transom.

Like any other dinghy, a RIB can be towed, but because of its lack of drag compared to a fabric-bottomed dinghy, it has the same tendency to surf on a following sea as a hard dinghy. If you must tow your RIB, it might be advisable to rig a small drogue to trail off the stern to slow it down a bit.

The ideal place to carry a RIB on a large yacht is on a pair of stern davits, where it will ride like any other inflatable. Make sure you remove the drain plugs: I saw an Avon filled with rainwater rip one of the davits right off a big cruising yacht in Beaufort, South Carolina—blunt testimony to the rugged construction of the Avon but kind of tough on the big boat. RIBs can also be carried on deck in the same manner as fabric-bottomed boats.

If I didn't have a boat big enough to accommodate a fully inflated RIB, I would forget about it as a dinghy, but *you* might find the other advantages of a RIB offset the stowage problem. Resist the temptation to deflate the tubes; you won't save that much room and the tubes are much more subject to damage when deflated. When a RIB—or any inflatable, for that matter—is to be stowed for more than a day or so, it is excellent practice to bleed off a bit of pressure so that the boat is still firm to the touch but not hard.

Inflatables as Towboats

If you have a sportboat or a RIB with a medium-size outboard, you will be astonished at how powerful it is as a towboat. I've seen a 9-foot Caribe with a 10-hp motor pull an adult water-skier. On those rare occasions (although not as rare as I'd like) when the old *Sultana* finds herself hard aground on a mud bar or reef, the Achilles with its 25 hp has always snatched her off before she sustained damage beyond a few scratches in her bottom paint. *Sultana* weighs in at over 35,000 pounds; the Achilles with two crew weighs less than 600 pounds.

Although an inflatable makes a dandy towboat, it isn't as easy to tow with one as it is with a hard boat. There are a few tricks to learn.

Tow with a Bridle

No matter how light your towing job, always rig a bridle. A bridle distributes the load of the tow so that it is shared equally by each side of the boat, which allows you to make turns while towing with an inflatable. My towing bridle is usually nothing more than a 15-foot length of ⅝-inch Dacron rope tied to both aft handles with bowlines. I tie the towline to the bridle with another bowline so it is free to slide back and forth. If you plan to do a lot

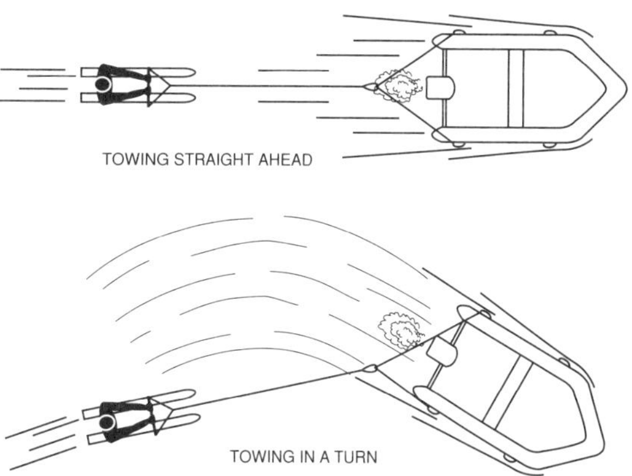

Towing with a bridle.

of towing, waterskiing perhaps, install a pair of eyebolts on the transom as far apart as you can get them. Handles aren't intended for towing, and with continued use they are bound to be damaged.

Don't Tow—Push

One of my earliest nautical memories as a child on Chesapeake Bay is of yawl boats pushing big bugeyes and skipjacks into the mouth of the Choptank River, returning from a day of "drudging" oysters. There aren't nearly as many skipjacks as there used to be, and the oysters have pretty much been drudged, but using a little boat to push around a big one is still an effective way to move boats around in an anchorage or harbor.

In a confined area it is usually easier to push a boat than to pull it. Using a hard boat as a yawl boat requires several large fenders to protect both boats from impact and abrasion. The pneumatic nature of an inflatable allows the entire hull to act as a fender, so you don't have to worry about putting scratches in the hull of the boat being moved. Inflatables make dandy yawl boats.

To push with an inflatable, simply lay the bow somewhere against the big boat and shove it with the dinghy. Pushing is tricky and requires a skillful hand on the throttle and tiller, especially if you need to use full power, but it is a skill worth learning. As you increase power, the inflatable will tend to yaw; a gradual increase of the throttle and careful control of the tiller is required. A boat being pushed from the stern will tend to run away from your inflatable as soon as you reduce power even a little because of the inflatable's tendency to stop quickly. This can be startling if you aren't expecting it. To stop a boat you are pushing, zip around and push from the other side. This is more effective than trying to back with a line attached—and more fun.

It makes a lot of sense to practice pushing techniques before you really need to use them. Spend an afternoon pushing a big boat around a part of the harbor where the audience isn't too big. Then when you really need to do it, people watching won't think you're practicing a new Keystone Cops routine.

One other thing. Don't ever try to push a water-skier. I've tried it several times, and they tend to fall under the boat and get all scrambled up in the prop.

Pushing a water-skier.

Towing Alongside

When you have a long distance to tow, the best method is to lash the inflatable alongside the big boat, get the engine running at optimum speed, then use the big boat's rudder to steer your course. If you are towing a powerboat with tiny rudders (they need propwash to have much of a turning moment) or with outboards or outdrives, you will likely have to steer with the inflatable's outboard. In any case, the trick to doing this successfully is to lash the inflatable so that the outboard is aft of the stern of the big boat. If you simply lash the boats side-by-side, you won't be able to maintain directional stability (nautical jargon meaning you won't be able to steer the damned thing).

Using Dacron lines, tie the dinghy bow and stern to the big boat. Rig a spring line from the bow

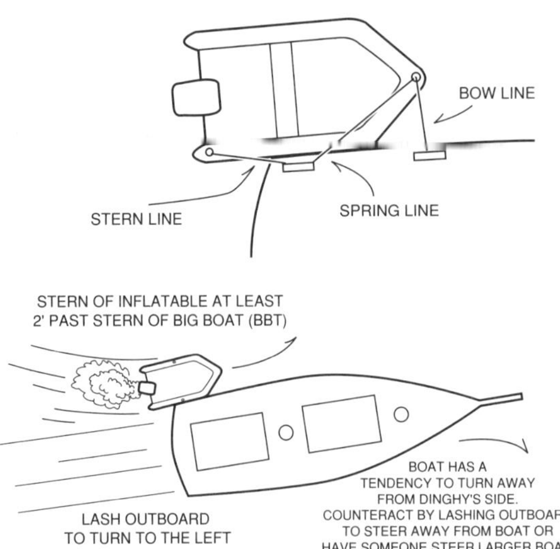

Towing with the dinghy lashed alongside.

of the inflatable to the stern cleat of the big boat. Adjust and tension the lines to pull the boats tightly together and to position the inflatable so it protrudes at least 2 feet past the stern of the big boat. The farther astern, the better your control will be. To counter the tendency of the big boat to turn toward the opposite side due to asymmetrical thrust, lock or lash the outboard so it is trying to turn the dinghy slightly away from the big boat—10 degrees is usually about right.

I once used this technique in very rough conditions to move a stalled 38-foot powerboat from halfway to Monhegan Island, Maine, to the safety of Boothbay Harbor (about 10 miles), so I know it works. I've never tried it on water-skiers, but if it didn't do anything else, it would at least keep them out of the prop.

Anchoring

Sellers of accessories for inflatable boats often offer special anchors. You should be wary of some of these. One example is a mushroom-shaped device that is completely covered with plastic and comes in 8- and 10-pound versions. Another is a folding grapnel made of galvanized cast iron that comes in sizes from about 3 to about 10 pounds. Both are well made, but their effectiveness in holding your boat is secondary to their ease of stowage. The mushroom stows nicely and the plastic keeps it from scratching your floorboards, but it is practically useless for anchoring. The grapnel also stows easily, and it holds well in bottoms covered with large rocks, cobbles, or tree stumps, but it doesn't hold at all in sand or mud. Grapnels are handy when fishing from a kayak or soft tail, but I don't recommend them for anything larger.

The best anchor for all inflatables, effective in nearly all anchoring situations, is a small Danforth on 150 feet of nylon line with about 10 feet of galvanized chain between the anchor and the line. The sizes of all the components of your anchoring system are important. An anchor too small for your boat will be ineffective, perhaps even dangerous. An anchor too big will be a nuisance to stow. Anchor line needs to be up to the potential loads, but not so large that benefits of the nylon's elasticity are lost. The size of anchor and line you need also depends on how and where you use your boat, but the accompanying chart gives the recommended sizes for most applications and is a good place to start.

BOAT	LINE LENGTH	LINE SIZE	CHAIN LENGTH	CHAIN SIZE	ANCHOR TYPE	ANCHOR SIZE
PLAYBOATS	N/R	N/R	N/R	N/R	N/R	N/R
CANOES & KAYAKS	100 FEET	1/4 INCH	N/R	N/R	FOLDING GRAPNEL	3-5 POUNDS
SOFT TAILS IN RIVERS & STREAMS	100 FEET	1/4 INCH	N/R	N/R	FOLDING GRAPNEL	5-7 POUNDS
SOFT TAILS IN LAKES & OCEAN	150 FEET	1/4 INCH	6 FEET	3/16 INCH	DANFORTH	5-7 POUNDS
SMALL SPORTBOATS	150 FEET	1/4 INCH	10 FEET	3/16 INCH	DANFORTH	5-10 POUNDS
MEDIUM SPORTBOATS W/SMALL RIBS	150 FEET	1/4 INCH	10 FEET	3/16 INCH	DANFORTH	8-12 POUNDS
LARGE SPORTBOATS W/ MEDIUM RIBS	150 FEET	3/8 INCH	8 FEET	1/4 INCH	DANFORTH	10-15 POUNDS
LARGE RIBS IN LAKES & OCEAN	200 FEET	3/8 INCH	12 FEET	1/4 INCH	DANFORTH OR PLOW	12-20 POUNDS
LIFE RAFTS	N/R	N/R	N/R	N/R	N/R	N/R
RIVERBOATS	N/R	N/R	N/R	N/R	N/R	N/R

Anchor recommendations.

Never toss your anchor; it will tangle in the chain and line and fail to hold the bottom. Lower it gradually but steadily straight down until you feel it hit bottom, let the boat drift back a few feet, then pay out at least three times as much line as the water depth. For example, if you are in 20 feet of water, let out a minimum of 60 feet of anchor line. Actually the more line you have out the better, but changes in wind and tide will swing your boat in a circle around the anchor. In this example you would need a clear radius of 120 feet.

To make sure your boat stays put, get in the habit of setting your anchor every time you drop it. Let out the proper amount of line, then put your motor in reverse and try to pull the anchor out. If the boat stops cold when you reach the end of the line, your anchor is set. If it doesn't, pick up the anchor and try again. When there is a wind or a current, you don't need the motor; just let the boat drift to the end of the line, then give it a sharp yank to make sure the anchor has a grip on the bottom.

The Amazing Trefethen Offshore Anchoring System

Occasionally we come across a place where we would like to go ashore but are precluded from beaching the boat because the combination of sharp rocks and wave action would quickly damage or destroy it. This is when we resort to an offshore anchoring system we have developed over the years that is both effective and simple.

The entire system consists of 300 feet of ⅜-inch nylon rope, 10 feet of ¼-inch chain, an 8 pound Danforth anchor, and some miscellaneous hardware. Attach the chain to the anchor with a conventional shackle. Pass the line through a 2-inch × ¼-inch stainless steel ring (available from any marine supply) and position the ring at the center of the line (at the 150-foot mark). Double and seize the line to secure the ring in this location. Pass one end of the line through the fixed eye of a conventional snap shackle, then splice the two bitter ends together to form one gigantic loop. We wind this doubled anchor line onto a plastic extension cord caddie and stow it with the anchor and chain in a mesh dive bag.

The final component is a second snap shackle spliced onto the end of the boat's 10-foot painter. To use this system, clip the free-running snap

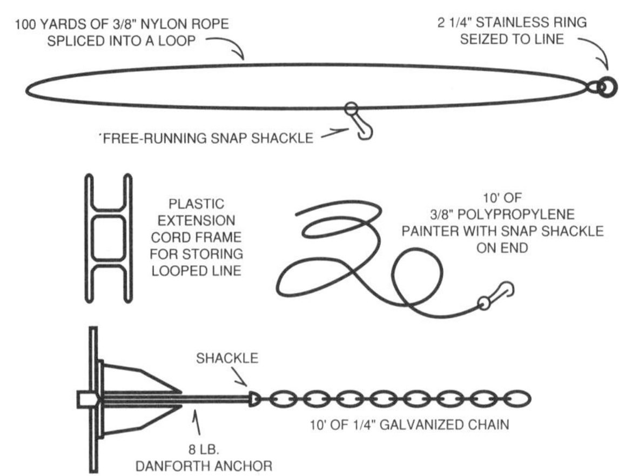

Offshore anchoring system components.

shackle on the loop to the end link of the anchor chain, and clip the painter snap shackle to the ring. Drop and set the anchor 30 or 40 yards from the shore and let the line run out as you land the boat. After you unload, it is a simple matter to pull the boat offshore by pulling the loop through the free-running snap shackle until it is stopped by the ring. Secure the onshore end to any handy object—a large rock or tree stump—and the boat will ride safely at anchor until it is retrieved by pulling the loop in the opposite direction.

This system works particularly well on rocky shores, but we also use it on sand beaches or clam

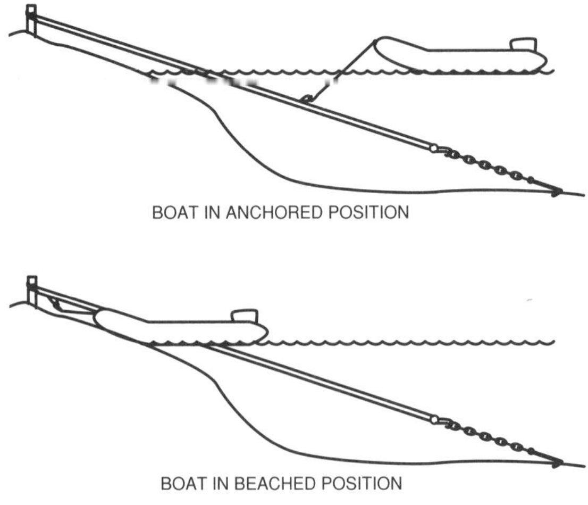

Anchoring system in use.

flats where the surf is too heavy to safely land the boat or a falling tide would strand it. It always works, and we quite literally wouldn't leave home without it.

Security

An unfortunate aspect of today's boating scene is that maritime crime is increasing nearly everywhere, and there are fewer and fewer places where you can leave your shiny new inflatable tied to a dock with any assurance that it will be there when you get back. In the Caribbean, dinghy theft is epidemic, and in some areas, like Charlotte Amalie Harbor in the US Virgin Islands, to leave your dinghy unattended for even a few moments is to practically ensure that it will be gone when you return.

Nighttime Security

The favorite MO (method of operation—remember *Dragnet*?) of dinghy thieves operating at night, especially in the Caribbean, is to slip up to a yacht in the wee hours of the morning, cut the painter with a sharp knife, then let the dinghy drift away until it can be recovered with relative impunity. They then tow the dinghy to a dark spot to strip it and probably vandalize or destroy it. Dinghy thieves are hardly ever interested in the dinghy; inflatables are too easy to spot and hard to fence (*Dragnet* again). What they really want is the outboard motor.

The first step toward ensuring the dinghy you tie up at dusk is still there at dawn is to remove the outboard, gas tank, oars, and all other removables to reduce the boat's appeal. Unfortunately, removing the outboard isn't always practical. Our 25-hp Mariner weighs more than 100 pounds and must be hoisted aboard with the main boom—a task too complicated to do on a routine nightly basis. The next best thing is to get the boat out of the water, which is, surprisingly, easier than removing the outboard.

The easiest way to get a dinghy out of the water is with stern davits. A boat underway should never carry her dinghy on davits with the outboard mounted, but as a matter of practice, many cruising sailors hoist dinghy and motor for overnight storage. I've never seen any problems arising from this technique.

An increasingly popular way of securing an inflatable out of the water for the night involves using the main halyard and a sling or harness to hoist the dinghy and outboard alongside the mother ship. The dinghy will need lift points attached the same as for davits. Attach a four-point sling to these points, shackle the halyard to the sling, hoist the dinghy a foot or so clear of the water, and secure it for the night, resting against the mother ship. On *Sultana* it's no effort at all for Sarah and Phillip to secure the Achilles for the night this way, using the halyard winch to do the heavy work.

Lifting the dinghy out of the water for security, either with davits or a halyard, has the added benefit of keeping the bottom clear of marine growth. Since the bottom is allowed to dry out every night, grass, barnacles, and other creatures that like to live on dinghy bottoms never get established.

In high-risk areas the dinghy and motor should be secured with a cable and padlock even when lifted clear of the water. Recently in the Rio Dulce, the yacht *Adios II* lost her brand-new Caribe with an equally brand new 10-hp outboard (the previous dinghy had been stolen in Venezuela) when thieves lowered the dinghy from its davits and made off without a trace while the crew slept below. In a similar incident, thieves boarded

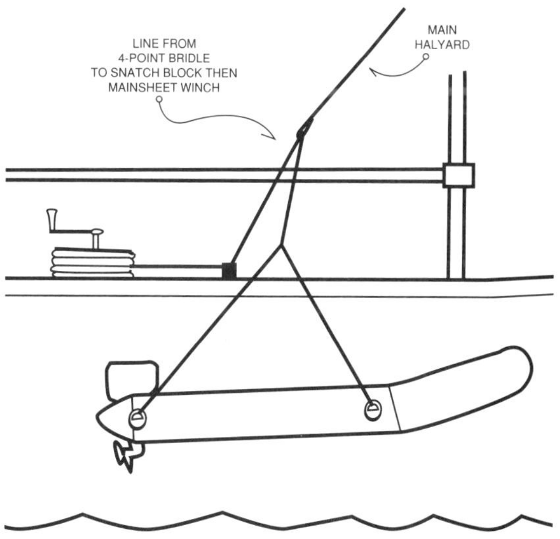

Broadside hoist.

Tacit of Lymington but failed in their attempt to steal an outboard that, fortunately, was secured to the shrouds with an inexpensive bicycle lock.

Daytime Security

Dinghies stolen in the daytime are most often taken from public docks while their owners are shopping or otherwise occupied in town. Dinghies are taken from docks by professional thieves, of course, but in the Caribbean and many other places, they are also taken by joy-riding youngsters. On Isla de Utila off the north coast of Honduras, I returned to find the Achilles full of nine rambunctious children, all about 8 to 10 years old, studiously trying to pry open the lock. I expected them to run away when I approached, but instead they all started clamoring for a ride. We had a pleasant if somewhat noisy trip around the harbor and were all good buddies afterward, but I always made sure the dinghy was locked to something solid.

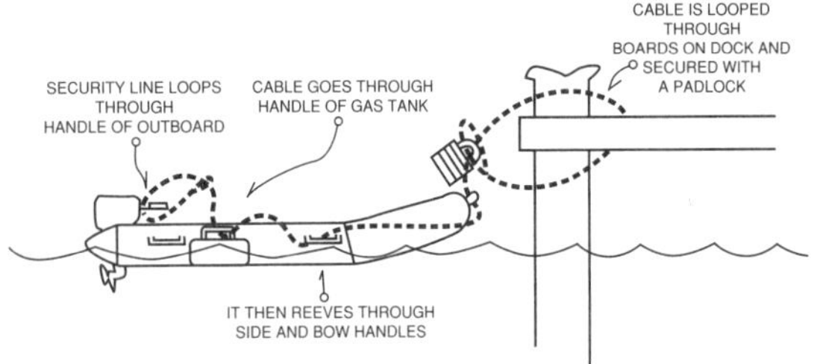

Using a security cable.

Many cruising sailors use chain as large as ⅜ inch to secure their dinghies to public docks, but chain has a terrible tendency to ding up both the floorboards and the mother ship, and it clangs and clanks and always gets rusty—even when it's galvanized. A piece of rigging wire with 4-inch loops on each end works much better. West Marine made mine from 3⁄16-inch 7 × 19 flexible stainless cable, forming the loops with swaged sleeves. It cost about 10 bucks. To use it, I pass one loop through the handle of the outboard, then pass the second loop through the first. Next I pass the second loop through the handle of the gas tank and anything else I want to remain in the boat (I once had a bag of garbage stolen from the dinghy in Mexico), then through the bow handle of the boat and onto the dock, where it is secured with a padlock.

This arrangement works extremely well, but at about 1½ times the length of the boat, my cable is occasionally too short to reach the dock over a raft of dinghies. My next one (if this one ever wears out, which is unlikely) will be about twice the length of the dinghy and will be made from 7 × 7 vinyl-coated stainless lifeline wire.

CHAPTER 7

Storage, Trailers, and Tarpaulins

Boat storage falls generally under two broad categories: winter (or off-season) storage and in-season storage when the boat is not in use. Off-season storage is more of a concern to those of us in the frigid North where winter winds blow cold and where snowblowers come out when the sandals and suntan oil get stored away.

Winter Storage

Storage problems increase geometrically with the size of the craft. A small PVC play boat can be stored quite nicely in the bottom drawer of a cabinet. A soft tail or an inflatable kayak needs a bit more storage space—perhaps the bottom of a hall closet. A deflated sportboat will be out of the way in a corner of the basement, but a large RIB on a trailer can easily take up both bays of a two-car garage. An unwritten corollary to Newton's third law of motion (stuff at rest tends to stay at rest) states that stuff at rest expands to fill all space available for stuff to rest in, so finding storage for even the smallest boat for the off season is likely to require some forethought.

Play Boats

Unreinforced PVC boats are unquestionably the easiest to store because they are also the smallest and most compact, but this doesn't mean you don't have to use care. The big dangers to PVC are sunlight and heat, both of which a boat stored near a window in a garage or attic might encounter. Ultraviolet radiation from the sun can quickly degrade the material to the point where it seriously damages the boat. Heat has some equally bad effects. PVC already has a high degree of "memory" that leaves a boat folded for any length of time with permanent wrinkles where the material was creased, and even mild amounts of heat significantly increase this memory. And if any pressure is applied to the material while it is more than warm to the touch, the material will flow and the boat will be distorted, sometimes to the point of being unusable.

Freezing temperatures can also damage unreinforced PVC. The cold doesn't actually harm the plastic but makes it inflexible, even brittle if temperatures are low enough. The danger comes when you try to unfold or move the boat when it is cold. The material cracks into a tear, sometimes causing catastrophic damage. The fabric can also be lacerated by the ice that forms if any water is left trapped in the folds or air chambers of a stored boat.

Soft Tails, Kayaks, and Small Sportboats

Nearly all new inflatable boats come with an instruction book that outlines the manufacturer's concept of ideal storage for their product. Most suggest storing soft tails and sportboats in a dark place where the humidity is low and the temperature remains a constant 48° F. So if you happen to have a large wine cellar and are willing to part with a few cases of your prized Bordeaux or amontillado (send them over to my place and I'll keep an eye on them for you), you have the perfect spot for your inflatable boat during the off season.

Alas, many of us don't have a wine cellar, and those who do may fear that the smell of rubber boat will contaminate the Dom Perignon. We must search for another, less suitable alternative. A basement or garage that can accommodate a partially inflated boat will do nicely even without climate control, and an attic isn't bad if it's insulated and ventilated to prevent heat build-up. Self-storage facilities, sprouting up in urban areas like mushrooms after a summer rain, are an increasingly popular option for storing large sportboats and RIBs on trailers.

FOLDING FOR STORAGE. Storing your boat partially inflated may be inconsistent with why you bought the thing in the first place. If you are going to deflate your boat for storage, carefully follow the manufacturer's instructions for collapsing and folding the boat. They have determined the best way to fold their boats into the smallest possible package without damaging the fabric. Most boats come with storage bags, one for the boat and another for the floorboards. Following the instructions in the owner's manual is the best way to get a deflated boat back into the bag. In case you don't have the manual, here are basic instructions that will work for most boats:

1. Deflate the boat enough to remove all floorboards, oarlocks, and anything else that can be removed, then reinflate it stiff but not hard.
2. Wash the inflated boat with soap and water (Chapter 8), then vacuum the entire boat, paying special attention to the area under the floorboards. If you don't have a wet-vac, let the boat dry first. When you have removed all traces of abrasive dirt and grit that tend to collect there, dry the whole boat with a chamois or a towel. While you're at it, scrub the floorboards and everything else that could stand a cleaning.
3. Deflate the boat. Most will self-deflate when the valves are open because the weight of the fabric is sufficient to force out the air, but this takes a little time. Attempts to expedite the process by jumping up and down on the tubes are usually only marginally effective. If you're in a hurry, speed things up by sucking the air out, using either the suction port on your inflator or the suction side of a vacuum cleaner.

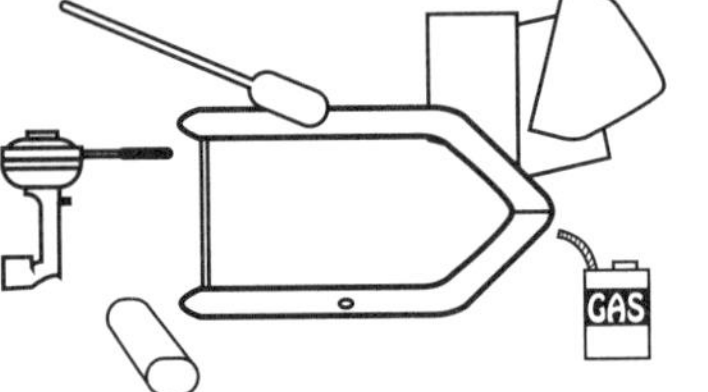

1. DISASSEMBLE BOAT

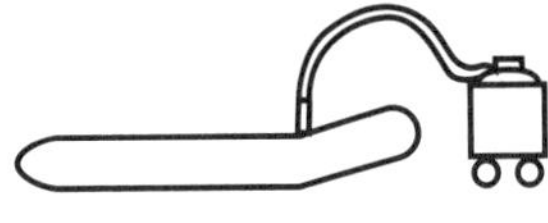
2. VACUUM BOAT

3. DEFLATE BOAT

4. DRAIN WATER

5. SPRINKLE WITH TALCUM POWDER

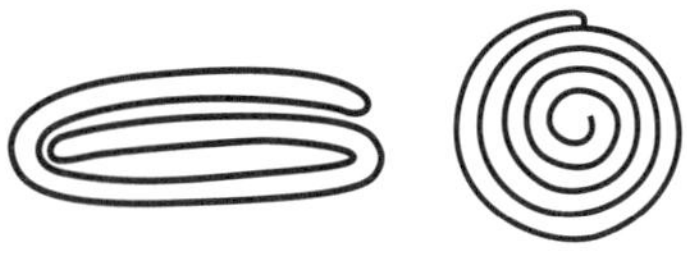
6. WITH SOFT TAILS, FOLD IN THIRDS OR ROLL UP

7. SPORTBOATS: FOLD TRANSOM FORWARD AND COLLAPSE TUBES ONTO TRANSOM

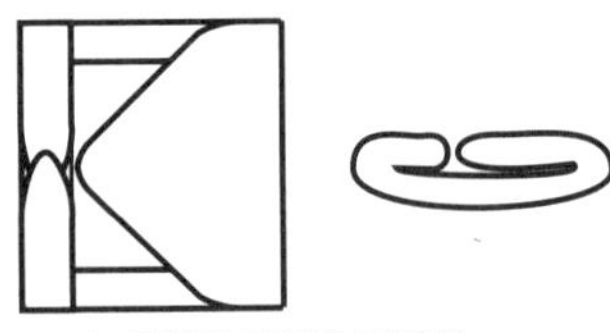
8. FOLD BOW BACK

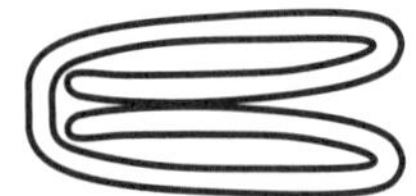
9. FOLD TRANSOM ONTO BOW

10. TIE BOAT WITH NYLON STRAPS

Folding an inflatable boat.

4. Make sure all water is drained from air chambers. Water is introduced into the chambers when a boat inflated with warm, humid air is launched into cool water, which causes the moisture in the air to condense. This condensed moisture won't evaporate and doesn't drain easily, so at the end of the season there can be a surprising amount of water in the tubes of a boat that has been deflated after each use. Inflatable keels are vulnerable to additional water incursion through the inflation valve from water that accumulates in the bilge. If the stored boat could be subjected to freezing temperatures, all water must be drained from the air chambers to prevent ice damage. The easiest method is to position the boat so the open inflation valve is at the lowest point of the air chamber, and the water will drain out.
5. Coat the boat with a liberal dusting of talcum powder (see sidebar).
6. Fold a soft tail into thirds or roll it up.
7. If yours is a sportboat, fold the transom forward onto the floor fabric and side tubes. Collapse the stern tube extensions onto the transom.
8. Fold the bow back into the center of the boat on top of the side tubes.
9. Fold the stern (or transom) forward onto the folded bow. Most boats fold nicely into quarters, but smaller boats may do better in thirds; experimentation will reveal the most appropriate pattern for your boat. It is an excellent idea to vary the pattern, folding your boat into quarters one time and into thirds the next to avoid repeated folding at the same spots. Some sportboats, particularly roll-ups, lend themselves to rolling rather than folding.
10. Before you put it into its bag, secure the bundled boat by tying it with flat straps of nylon webbing. Don't use rope because it will chafe through the fabric more quickly than webbing. Fasten the straps with reef knots; buckles, particularly metal buckles, can pinch the fabric and cause leaks.

Talcum Powder

In the days when war-surplus life rafts reigned supreme, it was standard procedure to coat the entire boat with talcum powder every time it was stored away. The natural rubber surfaces of early boats tended to fuse when left in contact with another rubber surface, unavoidable when boats are rolled or folded for storage, and the talc helped prevent this surface bonding. Today's inflatable materials are far less likely to fuse, but dusting your boat with talcum powder is still a good practice even though it's no longer required or even recommended by most manufacturers.

A liberal dusting of baby powder on all exterior surfaces of your boat has several important effects: the powder acts as a dry lubricant to help prevent abrasion between surfaces that rub together when the boat is moved about; it absorbs moisture that may have penetrated the fabric; and using a brand that contains a mild fungicide stops mildew from getting established while you aren't looking. A less important but pleasant side effect of using talcum—especially scented baby powder—is that your boat won't smell like the inside of an old boot when you unroll it for the first time next season. The next time you're at Costco, Sam's, or Kmart, buy an industrial-size bucket of baby powder, then use it on your boat every time you put it away. If there's any left over, you might sprinkle some on the baby's bum—it can't do the little tyke any harm.

Big Sportboats and RIBs

If you have a large sportboat or a RIB that you transport on a trailer, it may be best to leave it on the trailer during the off season, provided you can get it into a garage or shed. You have to store the trailer anyway, so you won't save any floor space deflating the boat. Thoroughly clean the boat, then fit it with a snug cover made from canvas. The cover keeps the boat clean and removes the temptation to use it as a handy storage bin for the odds and ends that clog every garage ever built.

Sportboats stored on trailers for the winter should have the floorboards removed, and remove the motor from the transom of both RIBs and sportboats whenever possible. The trailer for a sportboat should be fitted with long bolsters (sometimes called *bunk boards*) rather then rollers. A trailer-stored boat needs enough air in it to ensure that the tubes won't drape over the sides and chafe against the trailer, but in no case should a boat be stored inflated hard. Nearly all boats lose air over time, so it's important to check the pressure periodically—about once a month is usually enough—and add air if required. Remember that cold air pumped into a boat will expand when it warms, and a boat inflated with warm air will soften when temperatures cool.

Most sportboat and RIB manufacturers recommend storing their boats inflated enough to hold their shape without being hard. Deflated sportboats stored in a bag are prone to wear at folds and where the fabric bears on the boat's hard parts. Deflated side tubes of RIBs are particularly subject to damage from chafe because they can't be rolled up and stuffed into a protective bag. Disassembling boats can also lead to the misplacement or loss of small bits and parts. Whenever space allows, you will be well advised to store your boat assembled and softly inflated.

Outdoor Storage

The best advice on storing your inflatable boat outdoors for the winter is don't. It's cold out there and your prized Metzler or Calypso will get rained and snowed and blowed upon with relentless regularity by all the frigid forces Mother Nature can muster. Much better to keep her inside where she will be nice and warm and cozy—in a spare bedroom perhaps, or in the living room behind the couch, or in the basement, or the garage, or in the worst case even in the chicken house if the rooster doesn't mind.

Ah yes, but the sad reality is that as much as we love our rubber boats, we don't want them cluttering up the house in the off season. Those of us lucky enough to own a two-car garage may also be lucky enough to own two cars. We converted the basement to a rec room. And we tore down the chicken house 25 years ago when the price of a Frank Perdue roaster got to be less than the price of a bag of chicken feed. The only place left to store the old Bombablaster is in a corner of the backyard behind the barbecue pit under the flowering crab. So be it. Let's get on with it and make the best of a bad deal.

Storing your inflatable outdoors on a trailer is all right provided the trailer is blocked off the ground and the boat is properly supported and protected from all the nasty things Mother Nature will try to do to it. You should remove the outboard motor and gas tank and store them separately, but if you have to store the motor on the transom, leave it in the *down* position. In either case have the motor winterized in accordance with the manufacturer's instructions. Protect the boat with a tight-fitting canvas cover.

Once your boat is covered and parked where you want it, support the axles of the trailer with cinder blocks or bricks so it is level from side to side and the weight is off the wheels (see illustration, page 73). Remove the plugs from the transom drains and block the tongue of the trailer so the boat tilts about 5 degrees toward the rear. This rearward slant will cause any water that does find its way into your boat to drain right out. To make sure, fold back the cover and toss in a few buckets of fresh water. If your boat doesn't have transom drains or some other way of evacuating water from the boat, don't store it outside.

The last step in your outdoor storage plan is to buy a rectangular tarp at least 4 feet longer and wider than the dimensions of your boat and trailer combination. Common blue plastic tarps are okay and will last a season or so, but a good canvas tarp is better and may outlast the boat. Rig the tarp over your boat and trailer like an old-fashioned Boy Scout pup tent. It can be supported by a line between two trees or by using tent poles and pegs. The important things are that there is plenty of room all around the boat, the tarp extends past the covered boat and trailer at least 2 feet all around, there is plenty of air circulation, and the tarp isn't attached in any way to the trailer or the boat.

In-Season Storage

There are two ways to store an inflatable boat during the season: inflated and deflated. Play boats, soft tails, and kayaks are usually stored deflated because they are easy to reinflate and they are often transported in the trunk of an automobile, in the lazarette of a yacht, or on the frame of a backpack. Some small sportboats—especially the roll-ups—are also easily inflated prior to each use. Even large sportboats are often deflated between uses so they can be carried in a van, a station wagon, or a utility vehicle. I know an apartment dweller who kept his Avon sportboat and 15-hp outboard in the closet of his third-floor walk-up. He used the boat on trips all over New England, transporting it in an

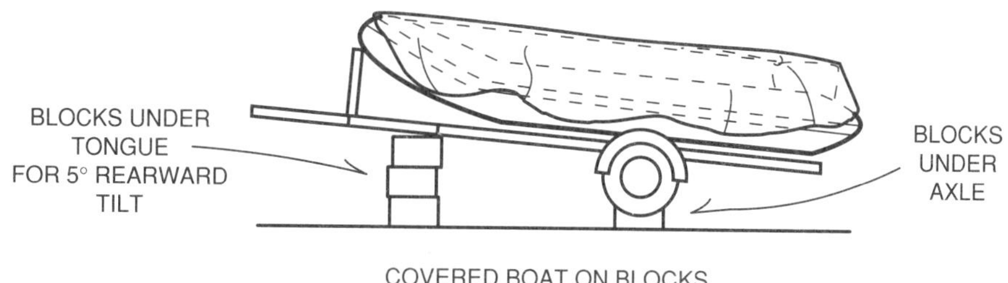

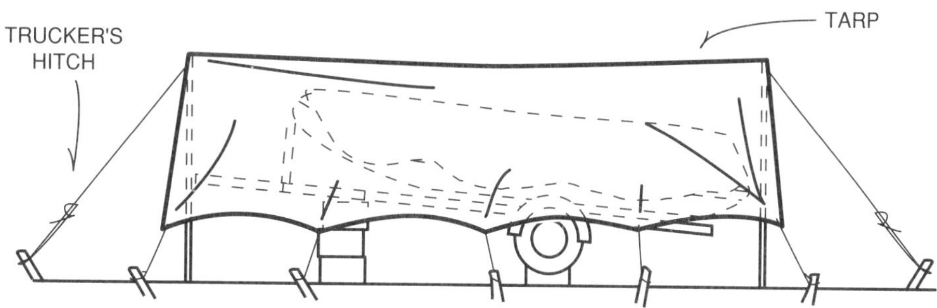

Covered boat and trailer under tarp.

antique Ford Bronco. The boat and associated paraphernalia weighed nearly 300 pounds and engulfed the entire back of the vehicle, and it took two people half an hour to prepare the boat for the water. But my friend considered this a small price to pay for the fun of owning a high-speed motorboat without the hassle and expense of mooring, launch, or storage fees.

Launching

Transporting a boat deflated can increase wear and tear on the fabric due to the abrasion associated with loading and unloading the deflated boat and with getting the inflated boat to the water without a trailer. This problem is minor with soft tails, roll-ups, and small sportboats, but larger boats are heavy, and there is an irresistible temptation to drag them to the launch area.

It is important to store and transport deflated boats in their protective bags. You should also carry a heavy drop cloth to put under the boat while you're inflating it on the parking lot or launch ramp. If you must drag your boat, put it on the doubled drop cloth, then drag the cloth to the water. It's far better to destroy a drop cloth than the bottom of your boat.

Instead of dragging your boat, you could fit it with launch wheels. These facilitate launching larger boats from a beach or a ramp and were discussed in Chapter 5. Another alternative is keeping your boat inflated and transporting it on a trailer, an option we will shortly discuss in detail.

In-the-Water Storage

As a general rule, avoid leaving an inflatable boat in the water for extended periods, and never leave a PVC boat in the water without protecting it from ultraviolet radiation. Occasionally, however, there can be good reasons to leave a boat in the water for a week or so, and some boats stay in the water for the entire season regardless of how inadvisable it might be. Large boats that are awkward to launch and retrieve might be left on a mooring or at a dock, for instance. And many cruising sailors habitually tow their inflatable dinghies behind the yacht, removing them from the water only when it's time to make a long passage.

There are good reasons for not leaving an inflatable in the water. Wooden components become saturated, and even the best plywood will delaminate over time. Marine organisms set up housekeeping on the bottom of an unprotected boat. All sorts of mosses and grasses attach themselves to both Hypalon and PVC with amazing tenacity, and barnacles find the bottom fabric of an inflatable an irresistible place to build their little calcium castles. Fabric-bottomed inflatables are particularly susceptible to resultant damage, and even brief exposure in warm salt water—a few days or a week—is plenty of time for these organisms to become established. Boats kept in the water are also more vulnerable to theft and vandalism than are dry-stored boats.

If you must leave your inflatable in the water for more than a couple of days, make sure it is protected from the elements by a good cover, protect the bottom with an appropriate anti-fouling paint (Chapter 8), and secure it against theft with a cable and lock. Any time you get a chance to carry your boat up on the beach to dry out for a few hours (longer is better), do it.

Trailers

If you buy a large sportboat or RIB, you will likely prefer to keep it on a trailer—if not year-round, then at least for the boating season. A trailer accommodates a larger boat than you can carry in the back of car or small truck, and it greatly reduces the hassle of getting the boat into the water. A trailer fitted with rollers works fine for a RIB, but for a fabric-bottomed inflatable the rollers must be replaced with bolsters. Any large boat will be significantly easier to launch if the trailer has a tilt feature for sliding the boat into the water.

A boat trailer is not required, however. I've seen several inflatable boats transported on standard garden trailers, and for years I carried my fully inflated soft tail tied on the top of my old Jeep. It

wasn't that I was too lazy too deflate it. Carrying it on the roof left more room in the Jeep. It also lent the whole rig a jaunty, outdoorsy sort of look that was somehow a lot more important then.

If you use a trailer, make sure it is appropriate for the size of your boat; you don't want to haul a heavy boat around on a trailer that's too small. Follow the manufacturer's maximum weight recommendation, keeping the size of the trailer as small as possible. Small trailers can be detached from the towing vehicle and easily rolled across a beach or down a steep bank by hand. Some lightweight trailers quite adequate for smaller boats are available economically in kit form.

A good trick to remember when launching your inflatable on a beach is to let some air out of the tires of the trailer (or the launch wheels) so they will roll across the beach without sinking into the soft sand. Don't forget to reinflate the tires at the nearest gas station at the end of the day. Better yet, buy a tire inflator for your scuba regulator (available in any good dive shop) and use the air left in your tank after a dive to reinflate the tires. You'll also need a pressure gauge; scuba tanks can hold up to 3,000 psi of air pressure, a bit much for the 50 psi trailer tires typically require.

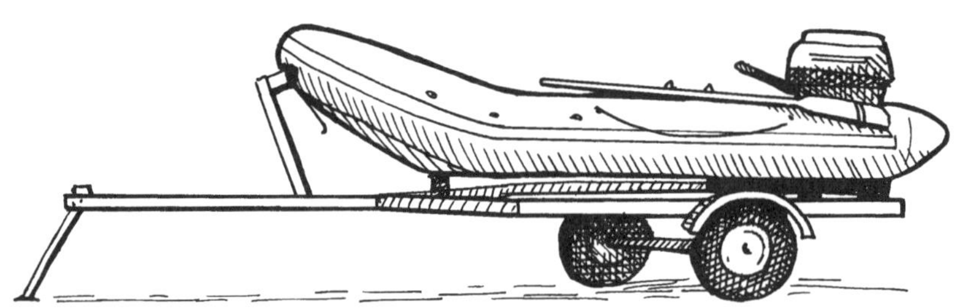

Boat on trailer.

If you buy a trailer for your inflatable, remember these simple rules:

- Buy the smallest trailer that will comfortably carry your boat and all its gear. Nearly everyone I know with a trailer-mounted boat carries stuff in it—picnic coolers, scuba gear, etc.—although most manufacturers say you shouldn't. If you do haul stuff in your boat, try to keep the weight to a minimum and lash down everything that can shift around. If you're driving a long distance, leaving the gas tanks empty until you get there saves considerable weight.
- Get a heavy-duty trailer with heavy-duty springs and extra-heavy-duty galvanizing. Don't even look at a trailer that isn't galvanized even if you only use your boat in fresh water. If you're interested in a kit, the Calkins Z-14 (available from West Marine) comes with galvanized parts and will carry up to 500 pounds. If you want a garden trailer to do double duty, you're on your own.
- Try to talk the dealer into replacing the standard wheels with wheels a size or two larger. These will give your boat a smoother ride, last longer, and make it easier to launch on sand. If you buy the trailer as part of a package, you'll have a little more leverage to extract this concession. While you're at it, buy a spare tire and wheel and bolt it to the tongue.
- Install a pair of Bearing Buddies before you ever use the trailer. These special fittings keep water out of the hubs and bearings to prolong their life.
- Except for the smallest boats, get a trailer that tilts to make launch and recovery easier.
- Equip your trailer with a set of Fulton boat guides with Dry Launch replacement lights mounted on top of them. I've never seen standard trailer lights last more than two or three dunkings in salt water (more in fresh water, but not many), and guide-mounted lights stay dry during launch. Guides also keep everything in view to facilitate both towing and launching; you can't see an empty small trailer behind a pickup without them.
- For any inflatable except a RIB, have the rollers removed and bolsters or bunk boards installed. Make sure the bolsters are long enough to support the entire length of the boat, including the transom, which probably means throwing away the stock bolsters and making your own out of pressure-treated 2 × 4s covered with at least two layers of indoor-outdoor carpeting.

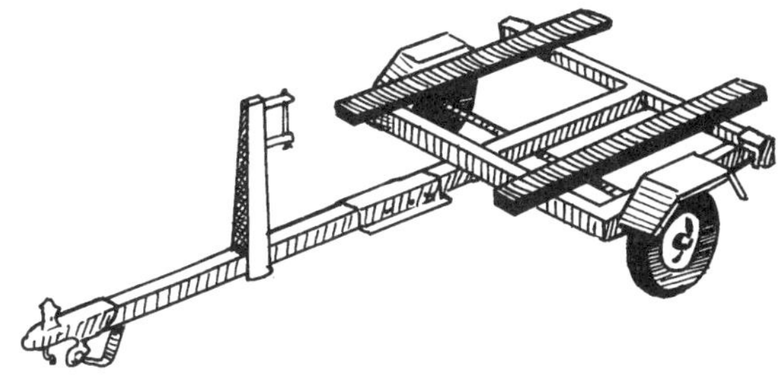

Bolsters.

Covers

I highly recommended covers for all boats, but they are particularly important for UV-vulnerable PVC boats. Inflatables transported on trailers should also be fitted with covers; otherwise, the accumulation of road grit can cause severe abrasion problems, especially in boats with floorboards. Most dealers offer covers tailored specifically for the boats they sell. Mail-order houses sell generic covers. Since the latter are made to fit a range of boats, they may not fit your boat very well, but they still do an adequate job if a more suitable alternative isn't available.

Boat covers require some sort of support to keep the center from sagging and collecting rainwater, leaves, and other detritus. The simplest is a line from a bow fitting (if you have one) or from the winch stanchion on the trailer to the carrying handle of the outboard, pulled taut with a trucker's hitch (see sidebar). Installing the cover (or even a simple tarpaulin) over the line forms a ridge that makes rain run right off.

A more secure, permanent, and aesthetic way to eliminate the center sag in a cover is to install open-ended pockets for transverse bows. The pockets should be permanently installed in the cover

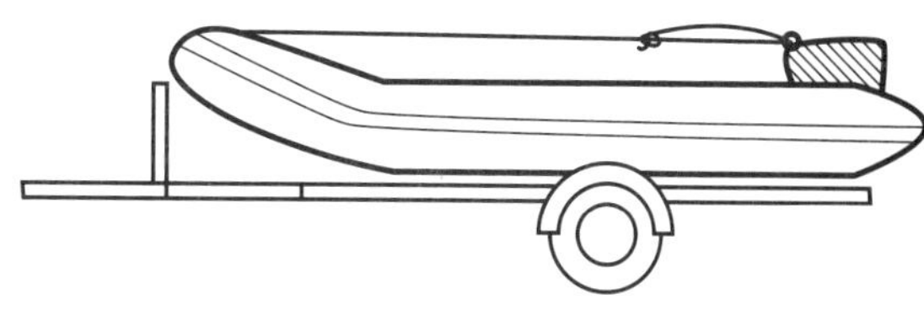

Cover support.

Trucker's Hitch

The *trucker's hitch,* formerly called the *mule skinner's hitch*, is one of the most useful knots for inflatable-boat owners. Besides being used to tighten a cover support (as shown), it is the best knot for tying a boat onto a trailer, for pulling tarps and covers tight, for lashing gear and duffel in the bottom of a boat for a rough passage, for securing a boat between pilings to avoid chafe, for hauling a boat onto a trailer when you don't have a winch, and for about a hundred other uses that will pop up every time you use your boat. Any time you need a taut line, this is the knot to use. It isn't the easiest knot to master, but it's not as hard as it looks either. Here's a simple way to do it.

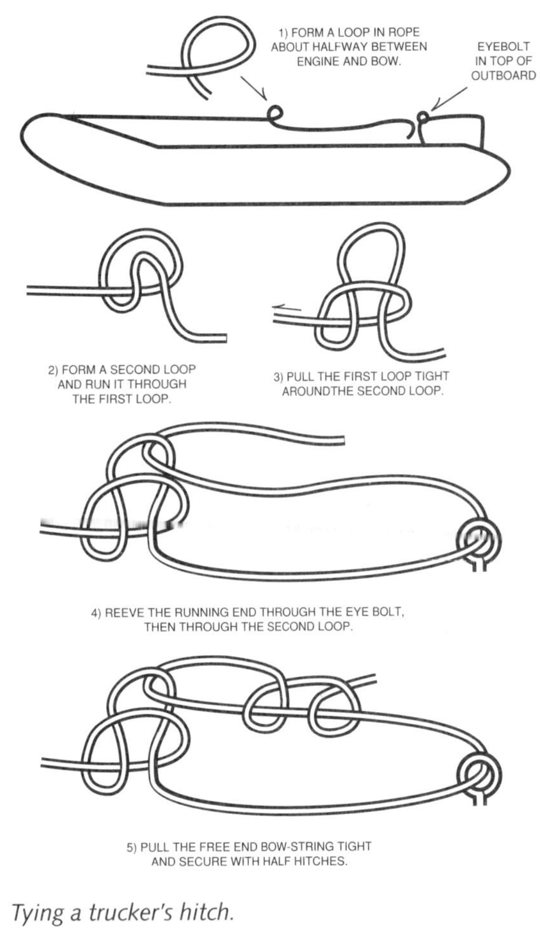

Tying a trucker's hitch.

and need to be about 2 feet apart. Make the bows from ½-inch PVC pipe cut about 5 feet long (more or less, depending on the width of your boat). When you're ready to cover the boat, simply slide the pipe battens into their loops and spring the ends into the sides of the boat to form bows, somewhat like the bows on a covered wagon. Chafe isn't really a problem with the smooth pipe, but if it makes you feel better, put chafe pads between the pipes and the fabric. If you want to be really uptown, put caps on the raw ends.

Plastic covers are better for occasional use than nothing, but they encourage moisture to condense. Mildew will get established on your boat in short order if you leave a plastic cover on for any length of time. Plastic tarps are best secured to the trailer with bungee cords, but no matter how many cords you use, there will still be loose folds flapping in the wind. Leave the ends open enough for air to circulate and don't be too fussy about keeping the sides tight; good air circulation is one of the best ways to fight mildew. Just make sure the tarp is tight enough to exclude raccoons, squirrels, and the family cat, all of which like to use loosely covered inflatable boats as nurseries.

When using bungee cords, always secure the hooks to the tarp and the trailer. Never attach the hooks to the boat because they are bound to dig into the plastic and cause chafe. Protect contact points with chafe pads.

Covers made from canvas, either synthetic or treated cotton, are far superior to plastic and worth the extra cost. Canvas covers are waterproof, but the woven fabric allows the passage of water vapor. This "breathing" allows moisture to escape rather than be trapped under the tarp. A good fabric cover is also considerably tougher than a plastic tarp. It can withstand high winds that would tear a plastic tarp to shreds. Canvas lasts long enough under normal use to more than repay its higher initial cost.

The best covers are custom made, usually in a canvas shop, but with a little effort you can make your own. Sunbrella awning fabric is the best cover material, available from Defender Industries in just about every color you can imagine. Sunbrella is expensive at about $13 a yard, but if you're going to put the effort into making a custom cover, use the best materials you can get. Nothing beats this stuff for colorfastness and toughness, and it's light enough (10 ounces) to sew on a home sewing machine.

1. To make a canvas cover, you need the following:
   - A sewing machine capable of stitching through three or four layers of 10-ounce fabric. A zigzag stitch is useful.
   - Plenty of #16 needles for the machine.
   - Seam-basting tape.
   - A small cone of V-69 sailmaker's thread or any stout polyester thread that works in your machine.
   - A sufficient quantity of 46-inch-wide acrylic canvas (Sunbrella or equivalent) fabric. Yards of fabric required = [(length of boat in inches + 54) × (width of boat in inches + 48)] ÷ 1,656. Buy a little extra fabric to cover the possibility that you'll wind up a bit short.
   - A length of ¼-inch braided Dacron line three times the length of your boat.
   - A quantity of ½-inch (inside diameter) brass grommets and an installation tool.
   - One 6-foot piece of ½-inch PVC water pipe for each 2 feet of boat between the transom and dodger.
   - A pair of freshly sharpened shears, a yardstick, and a piece of chalk.

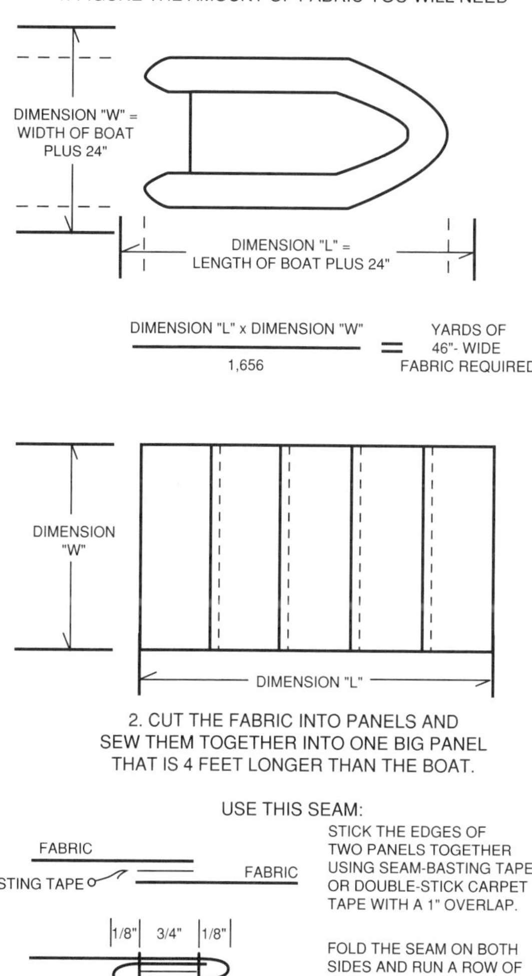

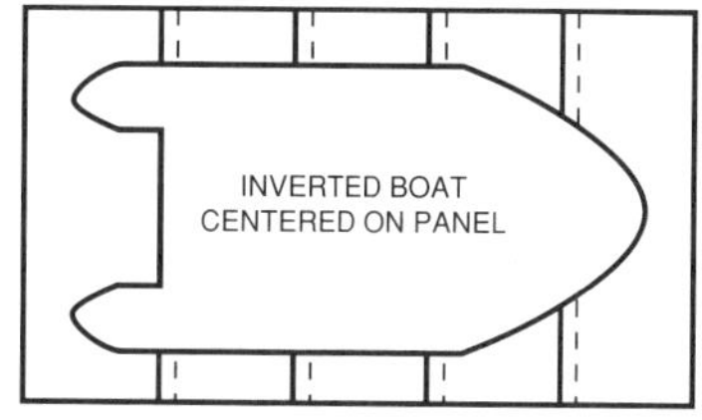

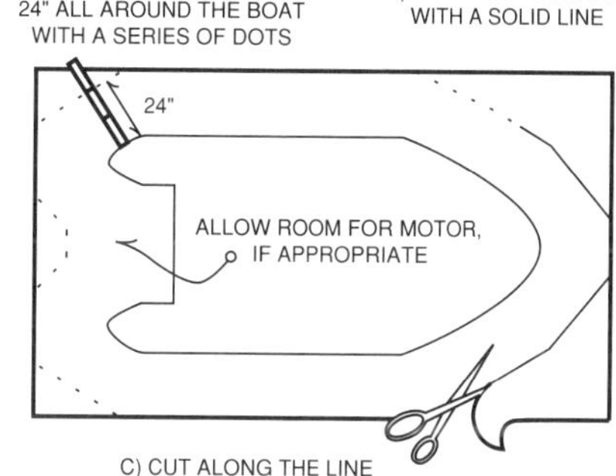

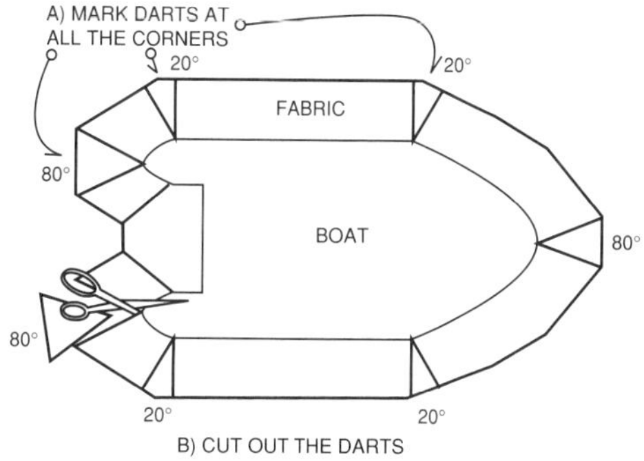

Making a custom boat cover.

2. Cut the canvas into lengths 4 feet longer than your boat is wide. Stitch these pieces together side-to-side, using the seam shown in the illustration, to form a rectangular panel 4 feet longer and wider than your boat.
3. Lay the panel on a large flat surface. A gymnasium floor or a sail loft is ideal, but your driveway, patio, or backyard will work provided you first put down a drop cloth. Invert the inflated boat (without the motor) and center it on the fabric.
4. With the yardstick and the chalk, measure and mark a series of dots 2 feet from the edge of the boat and about 6 or 8 inches apart all around the boat. Connect the dots with a solid line and cut to the line with the shears. You now have a piece of fabric that is 2 feet larger in all dimensions and roughly the same shape as the boat's outline.
5. At all the corners of the boat—the bow, the transom, and the shoulders (where the side tubes transition into the bow tubes)—mark V-shaped darts that have the edge of the boat for their apex and form an angle of about 80 degrees for the stern and bow, and 20 degrees for the shoulders and outboard. For a dinghy, also cut a dart at the center of the transom where the motor is mounted. For a sportboat, make two slash cuts from the corners of the stern indention in the cloth to the stern tubes. Cut out the darts.
6. Remove the boat from the fabric and hem the darts as shown in the illustration. Sew 4-inch square reinforcement patches made from scrap fabric at the apex of the dart on the outside and 3-inch squares on the inside, resulting in three layers of fabric. The pads should be hemmed, which will mean sewing five layers of cloth in their corners and where the hems of the pads cross the hems of the darts. If this is more than your machine can handle, don't try to force it; just stitch these areas by hand.

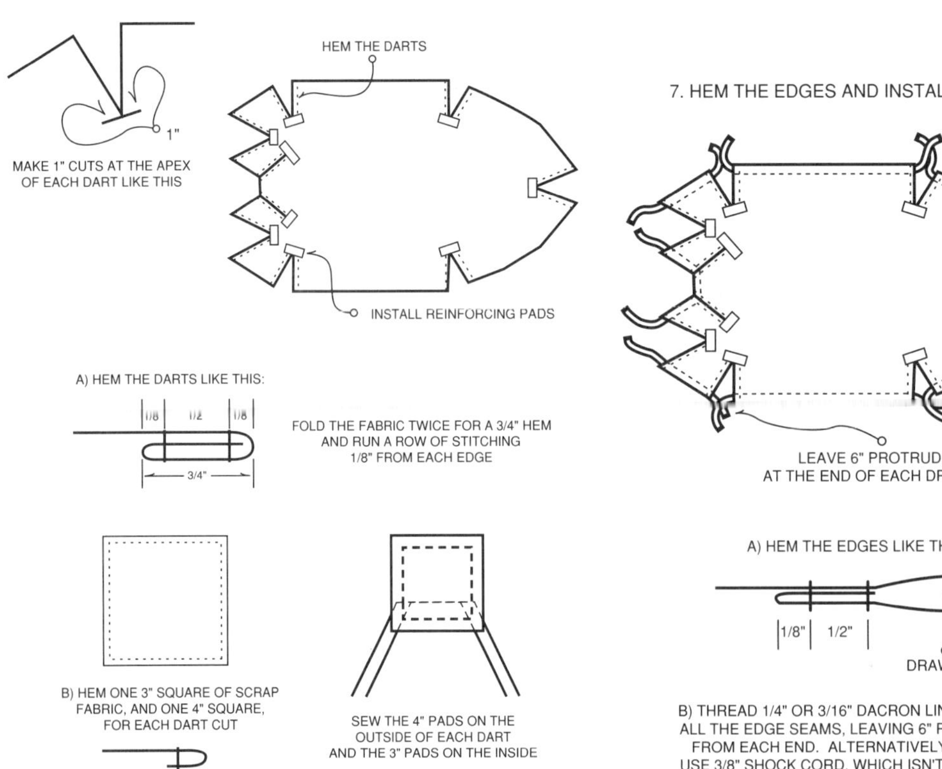

Making a custom boat cover.

7. Sew 1-inch-wide hems (casings) all around the outside edge of the cover, and thread the ¼-inch line through them. Cut the line so that 6 inches protrudes from each end of each hem, and whip the ends so they won't unravel. (Real whippings take about a minute and will last a lot longer than simply burning the line with a match.)
8. Fold the cover lengthwise inside-out to mark the centerline. Mark this centerline with the location of the transom and either the aft edge of the spray dodger or the shoulders. Divide the distance between these two marks into equal sections that are at least 18 inches wide but not wider than 24 inches, and mark them on the centerline.
9. Cut one 3-inch by 8-inch patch from scrap material for each mark and hem the short ends. Place a patch lengthwise across the centerline at each mark and sew the long sides to the inside of the cover. This forms a transverse open-ended pocket for the bows. Space the inside rows of stitching just wide enough for the PVC pipe to slide through with a snug fit. Put a piece of pipe in each pocket.
10. Bend the bows so they are held in position by the sides of the boat, and drape the cover over them. The bows are all too long and need to be cut to fit. Start with the bow farthest aft and cut it so that it holds the cover just clear of the outboard motor in the lifted or towing position. Moving forward, cut each bow 1 or

8. MARK FOR INTERNAL BOWS
INSIDE OF COVER
A) MARK THE CENTERLINE
B) MARK LOCATION OF TRANSOM
C) MARK LOCATION OF SHOULDERS
D) DIVIDE THE DISTANCE BETWEEN (B) AND (C) INTO EQUAL SECTIONS AS CLOSE TO 24" AS YOU CAN

9. INSTALL LOOPS FOR BOWS

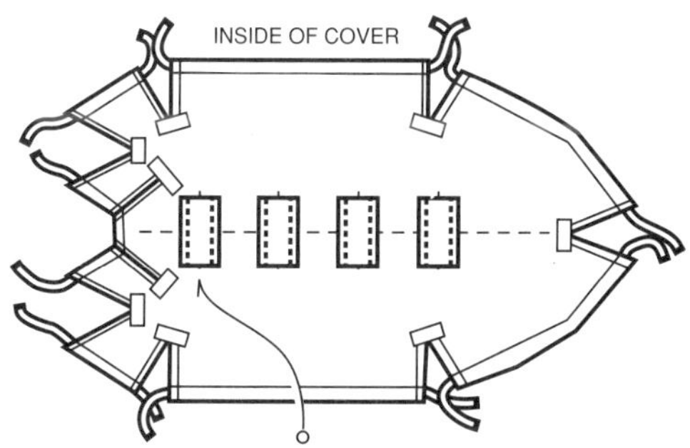

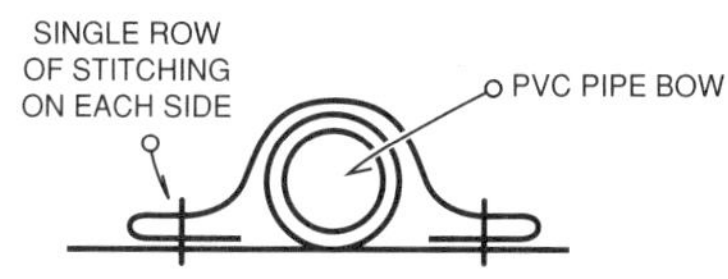

10. CUT AND INSTALL SUPPORT BOWS

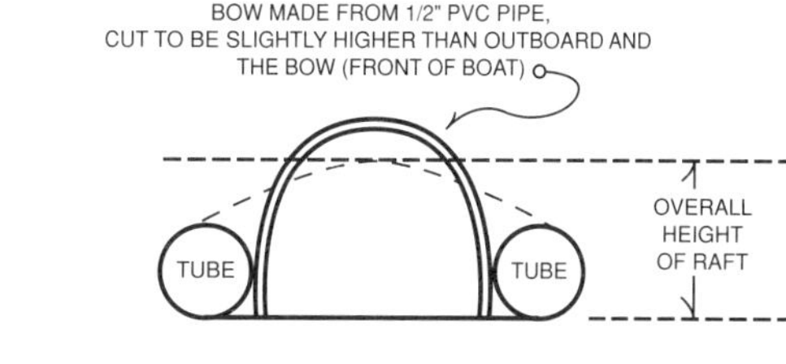

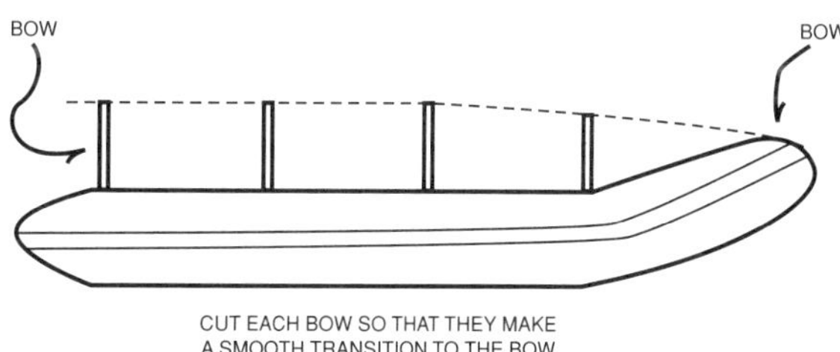

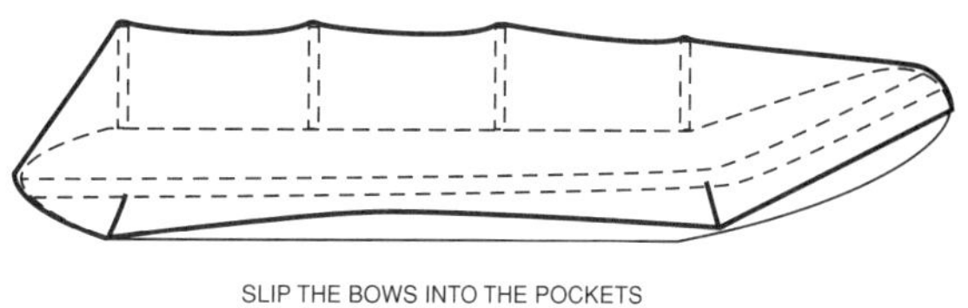

Making a custom boat cover.

2 inches shorter than the one behind it to give the cover a streamlined look. (If you prefer the wagon-train look, or if you plan to carry a lot of stuff in your boat, cut all the battens the same length.) PVC pipe is cheap, so don't worry if you mess up a piece; throw it away and cut another.

11. To install your new cover, place the bows in position, drape the cover evenly over the boat, and draw up and tie together the lines at each dart so the boat looks like it is contained in a giant upside-down coin purse. Work from bow to stern, being careful not to pull the draw lines out of the hems.
12. The cover works just fine as it is, but if you want added security when using it on a trailer, or if you want it to fit a bit more tightly, install grommets in the reinforced squares at the apex of each dart. To the grommets tie lengths of ¼-inch line long enough to secure the cover to the trailer, or make them long enough to pass under the boat and to the grommet on the other side. For the ultimate in security, do it both ways. Tighten these lines with a trucker's hitch.

This cover is designed for use with a boat on a trailer, but you could also put it on a boat in the water if you don't mind the skirt's getting stained. For regular use on a boat in the water, shorten the skirt to halfway down the tubes and install D-rings on the tubes at the darts for attachment.

CHAPTER 8

Inflatable Maintenance

Now that you have finally bought your new (or used) inflatable boat and figured out where and how to store it, let's take a little time to discuss how best to maintain it in mint condition so you aren't faced with making the same purchasing decisions all over again sooner than necessary.

Preventive Maintenance

As tough as they are, inflatable boats are not as rugged or durable as boats built of wood, fiberglass, or aluminum. They require more care and consideration in their use than do conventional boats. And a regular and rigorous schedule of periodic maintenance will help you get the longest possible service life from your boat.

Don't Chafe the Boat

Outside of oxidation and radiation, the biggest killer of inflatable boats is abrasion. Some owners seem to think they can drag an inflatable across rocks and logs with the same impunity as they would a hard boat. Or they don't think twice about leaving their inflatables tied to docks or wharves where wave action rubs the tubes against pilings. I've seen a number of inflatables damaged by the hinge bolts that hold together floating dock sections.

Avoiding abrasion is easier said than done. Common sense suggests keeping your inflatable away from rocky beaches, but that could severely restrict the versatility of your boat—probably one of the big reasons you bought an inflatable in the first place. Instead of avoiding rocky beaches, learn to approach them with care. Try to avoid dragging the boat. Be especially careful around coral and oyster shells.

It's easy enough to pick up a small inflatable and carry it ashore, but large boats present a more difficult problem. Our 12-foot sportboat (with motor and gas) weighs several hundred pounds—too heavy for fewer than four robust adults to lift off the ground, much less carry across a rock-strewn beach. Since half our crew aren't yet adult, and three quarters aren't quite robust (and my robustitude seems to be migrating to my waist as the years progress), we occasionally end up dragging the boat across the rocks, knowing full well we are damaging the bottom fabric. RIBs can handle rocky beaches with the same aplomb as hard boats, but all boats will benefit from minimizing such encounters by using the offshore anchoring system described in Chapter 6.

Lines, ropes, and metal fittings are also a cause of chafe. Slip sections of hose over lines and ropes to protect the fabric where the rope might come in contact with the boat. Use flat nylon webbing instead of rope to tie boats onto trailers. Protect your boat from metal shackles and other hardware with plastic coffee-can lids: cut a slit in the center of the lid the same width as the attachment ring on the dinghy, and slip the lid over the ring before attaching the shackle. The shackle will rub against the plastic lid and not tear up your boat.

Keep It Clean

Cleanliness is next to . . . impossible. Gathering a batch of mussels, for example, without bringing about a ton of mud into your boat is hopeless. Kids playing on a beach can import an amazing quantity of sand into the boat when they climb aboard. With normal use the floor of the boat quickly gets covered with sand and dirt. A significant amount finds its way between the floorboards and the fabric. It sands the finish off the floorboards and eats into the fabric where the side tubes attach to the floor. The resulting small leaks are hard to detect, and their location makes them difficult to repair. In the worst case, the fabric floor must be removed to make the repair—a job for a professional.

The best defense against abrasion damage inside your boat is to stop sand and dirt from getting in there to begin with. Rinse that basket of clams before you load it into the boat. Get the kids to rinse their feet after playing on the beach. Such

measures will help, but they won't keep all the grit out. If you want the longest possible life from your inflatable boat, you will have to give it a periodic and thorough cleaning.

THE WASHDOWN. Every so often, depending on how you use your boat, give it a thorough bath—not just a rinse with the hose but a real washdown. Not just now and then either; the washdown should be a ritual repeated at specific intervals—maybe not as often as going to church but more often than renewing your driver's license.

Spread a plastic tarp on a driveway or a flat area of your lawn to protect the boat and/or the grass. Deflate and disassemble the boat, then reinflate the stripped boat—without the floorboards—with just enough air to keep it in shape.

A shop vacuum is ideal for cleaning inflatables, but a household vacuum cleaner will also do. Thoroughly vacuum the inside of the boat, paying extra attention to the seam between the tubes and the floor fabric. You may find a lot of embedded grit. Don't worry about that now; just get all the loose stuff out. The hardest place to clean is usually the forepeak. With the chambers partially inflated, it is usually possible to compress the bow tubes enough to reach this area, but it is sure to take extra effort.

Pour a few capfuls of strong detergent into a bucket of hot water. Liquid dish soap works fine, as does shampoo (really) or car-wash detergent. Adding a few ounces of ammonia will aid in cutting grease. At least a half dozen soaps intended especially for inflatable boats are on the market, but I suspect they are nothing more than ordinary soap in a special package with a special price. Try one if you like; it can't do any harm.

Scrub the outside of the boat with a medium-to-stiff-bristle scrub brush, then flip the boat over and scrub the inside. Again pay particular attention to hard-to-reach areas where the tubes attach to the floor. This is when you want to concentrate on getting out all embedded grime. Don't try to scrub stains out; learn to love them because they are now part of the boat. When you have thoroughly scrubbed the entire boat, rinse it well with a garden hose and turn it over a few times to let all the pockets of trapped water drain out. Give it a good rubdown with towel or chamois and you're done.

Removing Bottom Growth

If you leave your boat in the water long enough to accumulate growth below the waterline, you'll need to scrub it off, but proceed with caution. Scraping with a metal scraper is out: this will remove the fabric's rubberized coating quicker than it will remove the growth. Sanding is out for the same reason. You can use a plastic scraper if you exercise care.

The safest way to remove marine growth is to kill it by leaving the boat out in the sun for a day or so, then wash the bottom with a strong soap solution and a stiff-bristle scrub brush. Vinegar, ammonia, fabric softener, and bleach are all said to help the process, but there is no substitute for elbow grease. If barnacles have left their little rings on your bottom, don't try to get them off; you will scrub right through the fabric first.

Restorative Agents

Dark-colored boats, particularly red and dark gray, tend to fade with prolonged sun exposure. Interestingly, PVC boats, which are more susceptible than Hypalon boats to UV degradation, are more resistant to fading. This, I am told, is due to the difficulty in coloring Hypalon (black in its raw state) compared with the relative ease in coloring PVC (white in its raw state). Whatever the reason, the dark blue PVC boats from West Marine and the

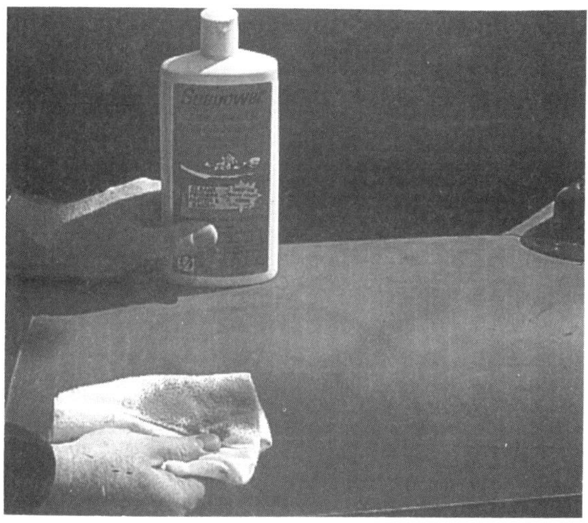

Cleaners/restorers strip away the oxidized top layer of fabric coating.

black ones from Bombard appear to be remarkably colorfast while my red Hypalon Achilles faded to a dull pink after its first season. However, every boat left in the sun too long will eventually have color problems. (Some white boats turn gray, then black.)

You can, if you wish, treat your boat with one of the half dozen or so commercial cleaners/restorers you will find on the shelves of any well-stocked marine store, but there are a few caveats to bear in mind. These cleaners work by stripping away the oxidized top layer of fabric coating, either chemically with solvents or mechanically with fine abrasives. The results can be quite remarkable. However, when these products are potent enough to be effective, they are bound to be harmful to your fabric if used repeatedly. Some contain abrasives that will damage or remove the UV barrier coat from PVC boats.

If you use a cleaner/restorer, be sure it contains no silicones. There is compelling evidence that cleaners or protectants that contain silicones can cause the seams on an inflatable boat to separate. More than one owner has reported that an inflatable simply came apart after he/she "protected" it with Armor All or some other silicone-based treatment. PVC boats are especially at risk, but silicone on any inflatable will make future repairs more difficult because glued patches will not adhere to it. Avoid these problems by reading the label; if the product contains silicones, don't use it on your boat.

I find it best to simply avoid *all* chemical treatments; removing the chalky look does nothing to extend the life of a boat. The best protection against fading is a well-made cover installed on the boat when it isn't in use. If you aren't inclined to use a cover, accept the chalky look as part of the boat—the way you accept verdigris on a bronze statue or patina on antiques.

If you're determined to scrub away that oxidized layer, try Soft Scrub bathroom cleaner. It works just fine on inflatables, but it is strong stuff, so use it sparingly—and only on Hypalon boats. Once you've scrubbed away all that nasty oxidation, you can protect your shiny new finish by spraying it every week or so with 303 Protectant, a nonsilicone UV barrier. But if you want your boat to look like new for a long time, use that cover.

Painting Inflatables

Keep your inflatable outdoors and fail to protect it with a cover, and the finish will eventually deteriorate to where even the strongest cleaner won't help. At that point you might want to consider painting the boat to restore the finish and refresh (or change) the color. A badly faded boat is also likely to leak air right through the fabric, and sometimes this can be stopped or reduced with a few coats of paint. Painting, however, is more repair than maintenance, so we'll save it for the next chapter.

Checking for Leaks

Inflate your clean boat hard. Pour 2 to 3 ounces of liquid dish soap into a cup and add an equal amount of water. Paint the soap solution over all the seams on the boat with a 2-inch throwaway paintbrush. Leaks will be betrayed by a growing column of tiny bubbles. Mark each by circling the bubbles with a red grease pencil. Recruit a helper to hold the boat upright on its side while you can check all the inside seams. Don't forget the inflatable keel if your boat has one. Now paint all the inflation valves. Check these with the caps screwed on tight. It isn't uncommon for the valve diaphragm to leak a little; the cap provides the air-tight fit that prevents the valve from losing air. After valves have been checked, check the outside surfaces of the tubes. Rinse the boat with a hose and you're finished with the first step.

Because the bottoms on most inflatables are not pressurized, finding leaks in the bottom fabric requires a different approach. First leave the boat inflated in a covered, dry location—the garage or the basement—for a few days to make sure it is completely dry. With the boat upside down, coat the bottom with talcum powder. Turn the boat right-side up and support it level and well off the ground. (Sawhorses are ideal for this, but four kitchen chairs will work.) Add about 2 quarts of water to the inside of the boat and have an assistant slosh it around while you watch the underside. Don't slosh too vigorously; you don't want to splash any water out of the boat. Leaks show up as dark wet spots on the light-colored powder. Mark them with your grease pencil. We will fix them in the next chapter.

The Hard Parts

Begin the care of the wooden and metal parts of your boat with a thorough cleaning. Give all the removable parts a good scrubbing with your stiff brush and soap solution. Inspect for scratches and abrasions that violate the surface integrity of the finish. Repair any break in the finish that penetrates to the bare wood or metal before the damage spreads.

Wood Parts

Scrapes and scratches in the surface finish of the wooden parts of your boat admit water into the wood fibers. If they become saturated, the wood can delaminate, warp, or rot. The wooden components on your boat may be finished bright (varnished) or painted with a high-quality two-part polyurethane paint. Maintaining each of these finishes requires a different approach.

VARNISHED SURFACES. Odds are about 10 to 1 that the bright finish on your transom and floorboards is either polyurethane varnish or a commercial polyester finish. These finishes look great when they're new, and they are rugged and durable. But once they begin to deteriorate, they are difficult to repair and keep looking good.

If the finish is polyurethane, you can touch up scratches and scrapes with a small brush and a good marine grade of polyurethane varnish (such as Interlux Clipper). Touch-up repairs won't last forever, but they will protect the wood until the end of the season when you can effect a more permanent repair.

Fortunately not many manufacturers use polyester finishes anymore. If you have an older boat with polyester on the wood, you'll know it as soon as you try to repair it with polyurethane varnish. The finish will become sticky and refuse to dry. If this happens, your best option is to strip all the old finish and start from bare wood.

For wood parts that can't be removed for refinishing, mask all fabric and rubber within a foot of the wood with at least two layers of brown kraft paper—newspaper is too thin. Use #256 Scotch Mark Green masking tape (very good but expensive) or #218 3M Fine Line (cheaper).

Coat the old finish with a high-viscosity paint remover such as Interlux #199. Be careful not to get any remover on the tape, and be absolutely paranoid about getting even a single drop on the fabric. Let the stripper work for about five minutes, then scrape it off with a putty knife or a cabinet scraper. Don't flush it with water as directed in the instructions because you will wash the chemicals onto the fabric. If all the finish doesn't come off on the first try, do it again.

Wipe the stripped wood with clean rags until all the stripper is gone, then wash the wood with denatured alcohol to neutralize any remaining traces. At this point you may want to consider an epoxy/varnish finish, which will outlast straight varnish about five to one. Epoxy application is beyond the scope of this book, but it is covered in vivid prose in *Wooden Boat Renovation* (Jim Trefethen, International Marine, 1993).

Sand the stripped wood with aluminum-oxide paper, starting with 80-grit and finishing with 220-grit. Your transom is probably plywood, so be careful not to sand through the surface plies. Brush on at least six coats of good marine varnish (I like Captain's from Z-Spar), sanding between coats. The more coats, the better; if you want a real show finish, you'll need at least 20.

Another way to treat damaged polyurethane or polyester parts, especially if you aren't sure which you have, is to soak them with boiled linseed oil (available in any paint store). The linseed oil doesn't have any effect on the finish, but it penetrates through the scratch and protects the wood. Refresh the oil every week or so, and the wood parts of your boat will last forever even though they will start to look pretty ragged after a while.

If your varnish deteriorates to the point that the wood is stained and weathered, don't hesitate to paint right over it. There is nothing sacrosanct about varnished woodwork, and often a coat or two of good paint is the best way to make shabby components look new.

If you think all this sounds like too much work, check out the replacement cost for just a set of oars for your boat. The retail price of replacement oars for my Zodiac was $110, and that's for each oar—$220 a set! For that you could buy all the materials to build a good plywood pram, with enough cash left over for a set of new oars.

PAINTED SURFACES. Painted surfaces are easier to maintain than varnished ones. The process is similar—scrub and dry the part, then touch up any scratches—but it is easier to get the repair paint to match the original than it is to get varnish, especially polyurethane, to match. Auto-supply stores sell touch-up paints in just about every color imaginable. You will find it available in both 1-ounce bottles and small spray cans. The paint is usually enamel, which should be compatible with the original paint on your boat. Try it out in an inconspicuous spot first, just to be sure.

To repair a break in a painted surface, take the surface gloss off the repair area with 120-grit aluminum-oxide sandpaper. Cover adjacent areas of fabric with masking tape and newspaper. Spray or brush the paint on according to the instructions on the container. Don't worry if it isn't a perfect match; you can take care of that later when you refinish the wood completely. If you don't want to mess around with touch-up paints and you aren't fussy about having the scratches and scrapes show, the boiled-linseed-oil treatment works just as well on painted surfaces.

Metal Parts

Almost all inflatables larger than a play boat have at least a few parts made from either aluminum, stainless steel, or (shudder) mild steel. My Achilles has all plastic inflation valves, but the oarlocks are stainless steel, and the floorboard rails, floorboards, and oars are anodized aluminum. Outboard brackets on a lot of soft tails are made from mild steel coated in plastic. Some boats have stainless valve parts.

These parts are often neglected because otherwise careful owners assume stainless steel and aluminum won't rust and the plastic coating will protect the mild steel. Nothing could be farther from the truth. All of these materials oxidize readily, and if they come in contact with each other, especially in salt water, they will self-destruct through galvanic corrosion in a remarkably short time. All metal parts need regular inspection and maintenance if you want your boat to last past the warranty period.

STAINLESS STEEL. Stainless steel is the easiest to maintain. Simply keep it clean and give it an occasional shot of WD-40, and it will last forever. Superficial surface blemishes (yes, stainless does stain) can usually be removed and the shine renewed by the vigorous application of a metal polish. My favorite is Noxon, intended for use on stainless-steel cookware and sold in most hardware stores. I'm sure others work equally well. Some boaters report that Penetrol provides a good protective layer on stainless parts.

Once stainless becomes rusted and pitted, more drastic measures are called for. First remove and disassemble the part, then soak it in a weak solution (50-to-1 is usually strong enough) of muriatic acid, sold in hardware stores for masonry cleaning. **Warning!** Muriatic acid is nasty stuff. *Please* observe *all* the precautions listed on the container. The active ingredient is hydrochloric acid, so wear good eye protection and heavy rubber gloves (hydrochloric acid will leave a bright yellow stain on your skin that will defy the strongest soap). The fumes are also toxic, so use acid only in a well-ventilated area.

To use muriatic acid, mix it into a plastic or glass (never metal) container and immerse the parts you want to clean. It will start to boil and bubble like the witches' cauldron in *Macbeth*, but worry not; the toil and trouble are about over. When the commotion in the container stops, remove the parts from the acid. The rust will be gone. Flush the parts with fresh water, then give them a good polishing with Noxon and a squirt of WD-40, and you're ready to reinstall them on your boat.

ALUMINUM. Aluminum can be maintained just like stainless steel except for the muriatic acid treatment—the etching that takes place in oxidized areas goes deeper than necessary in aluminum and can weaken the part. WD-40 does a fine job of removing oxidation. If the damage is deep or extensive, scrub it off with a green Scotch-Brite pad soaked in the stuff. Scratches in anodized aluminum should be sealed a soon as possible with clear lacquer. Clear nail polish works fine.

One problem with several brands of sportboats is the way the plastic end caps on the floorboard side rails are always popping off. Manufacturers glue these caps in place with something that looks like construction adhesive. Whatever it is, it's inadequate for gluing plastic to aluminum. I have found that 3M 5200 polyurethane adhesive does a masterful job of holding together parts made of diverse materials, and now my errant end caps are still in place after several seasons of heavy use.

Many inflatable boats have hollow aluminum parts, notably oars and side rails. These are subject to interior corrosion if water finds its way inside, as it's bound to do sooner or later. In the past there wasn't much you could do, but a relatively recent family of products solves this problem. They are called *corrosion inhibitors,* and the brand I am most familiar with is Boeshield T-9. I buy mine at West Marine, but it is widely available. To protect the inside of hollow-aluminum (or other metal) parts, spray a liberal shot of this stuff into the cavities. That's it.

Unfortunately some parts don't offer ready access to the cavity. In that case, drill a small hole where it won't show or interfere with the operation of the part, and squirt the corrosion inhibitor into the cavity through the hole. Then seal the hole with a pop rivet made of the *same material as the part.* Always use aluminum pop rivets in aluminum parts and stainless pop rivets in stainless parts. If you put an aluminum pop rivet (or other fastener) into a stainless part, the rivet will be destroyed by galvanic corrosion; if you put a stainless pop rivet into an aluminum part, the part will be destroyed for the same reason.

MILD STEEL. The only mild steel parts I regularly encounter are outboard brackets for soft tails. It is beyond my comprehension why manufacturers make these critical parts from a material that is bound to have corrosion problems. I know they do it to save money, but since these brackets are expensive anyway (the bracket for an Avon Redcrest sells at discount for about $115), using stainless steel couldn't possibly add more than 10 percent to the price. Oh well, I guess it was thinking like this that ensured my dismal failure as an entrepreneurial industrialist.

Anyway, if you have one of these brackets, it is imperative that you keep the protective plastic coating intact. If water, particularly salt water, gets between the plastic and the steel, your bracket will evaporate into a pile of rust flakes in a single season.

Two similar products work well for maintaining the coating. One is called *liquid electrical tape* and is available from electrical-supply outlets. It comes in any color you want as long as you want black. The other is called *liquid rubber* and is sold at most hardware outlets as a coating for metal tool handles. I prefer liquid electrical tape because it comes with a handy applicator brush, but the liquid rubber can be applied with an acid brush. To use either, clean the area around the damage with acetone or lacquer thinner, then paint a liberal coat over the damage. Let the first coat dry and apply additional coats until you get the desired thickness—it's as simple as that.

If you notice a bulge in the plastic coating, it is too late for preventive repairs. Water has already gotten under the plastic and caused significant damage to the metal. The bulge is caused by a build-up of rust scale under the plastic, and it will eventually burst the plastic coating. Remedial action is required.

Peel the plastic coating away from the metal enough to expose about an inch of bright steel all around the damaged area. Brush off the loose scale with a wire brush, and clean the rusted area with Ospho (available at hardware stores or industrial cleaning-supply houses). Ospho works much like muriatic acid, but it has a phosphoric acid base (rather than hydrochloric) that reacts with rust to form a black protective coating of iron phosphate on the steel. Brush the Ospho onto the bracket with an acid brush or a small natural-bristle paintbrush. Keep painting it on until the foaming stops. Cover all the exposed steel right up to the plastic. Once the acid stops foaming, let it dry, then flush the entire bracket with fresh water.

When the treated bracket is completely dry, clean the damage area with acetone. Paint multiple coats of liquid rubber over the damage, letting each coat dry (about an hour) before applying the next. Repeat this until the thickness of the rubber is about the same as the thickness of the original material.

This repair keeps moisture away from the corrosion-prone mild steel, but it isn't as rugged as the original plastic and it deteriorates with prolonged ultraviolet exposure. The next step is to wrap the repaired area with plastic tape. Electrician's tape works fine, but your hardware or auto-parts store probably stocks decorative vinyl tape in a wide assortment of colors that will allow your innermost artistic juices to flow forth in a cataract of creative expression to make your restored outboard bracket the snazziest in the fleet.

Bottom Paint

If you must leave your inflatable in the water for more than a few days at a time, the answer to the problem of marine growth is to protect the bottom with antifouling paint. Regular bottom paints don't work well on inflatables because they don't stick well to the fabric and they are too thick to allow the boat to be deflated and stored without cracking the paint. Thinning the paint to the point that it will dry thin and flexible enough to allow the boat to be folded compromises its ability to repel marine growth. Paints that work by leeching the active ingredient (usually cuprous oxide) into the water lose their effectiveness when they dry out. They also rub off onto everything they touch, making handling the boat out of the water messy and unpleasant.

Several bottom-paint systems intended for use on inflatable boats are on the market. I am sure most, if not all, do an acceptable job, but I can vouch only for the one I am the most familiar with. This two-step system requires the application of a primer coat followed by a high-quality cuprous-oxide bottom paint. It is distributed by Inland Marine of Cape Coral, Florida (see Appendix A).

Before the primer (called Hy-Grip) can be applied, the bottom must be clean. Use soap and water to strip marine growth off old boats, then scrub the bottom with solvent—toluene or acetone on Hypalon boats, MEK on PVC boats—until all the oxidized surface material is dissolved. Inland Marine recommends scrubbing until a clean rag soaked in the solvent doesn't show any color when rubbed on the fabric.

New boats have no marine growth on them, of course, but you must remove all surface plasticizers from the bottom fabric. Most can be cleaned with a cloth soaked in the appropriate solvent, but some inflatables use bottom fabrics that telegraph the texture of the base cloth through the coating, making the surface quite rough. Scrub these with a stiff-bristle brush.

If the boat has ever been treated with a restorative agent or any cleaner containing silicone, you *must* remove all traces of these with Interlux #202 solvent wash. Interlux #202 is the only product Inland Marine has found effective for removing silicones. Thorough cleaning is critical. Any trace of plasticizers, oxidized material, or silicones on the surface of the fabric will prevent the primer from sticking, and the system won't work.

Once the bottom is clean, paint the Hy-Grip onto it with a clean brush. The Hy-Grip serves as a bonding agent between the boat and the bottom paint, and it dries so quickly that the bottom paint can be applied almost immediately. Any bottom paint will stick to the Hy-Grip, but the manufacturer recommends and supplies Shipbottom Premium Performance antifouling paint. This is a hard-drying, flexible paint with a very high (62.5 percent) cuprous oxide content. It remains effective from season to season, and the boat can be folded for storage without the paint cracking or flaking or rubbing off.

As with all bottom paints, the paint line on your inflatable should be slightly above the actual waterline of the fully loaded boat. Mask the line with tape to get a workmanlike job. The bottom paint should be good for at least two seasons. The primer should last for the life of the boat unless you abrade the fabric by dragging the boat across the beach or rocks. If you do, touch up the abraded spots (don't forget to clean them) with primer before you apply fresh bottom paint.

Paint the hard bottoms of RIBs the same as any other aluminum or fiberglass boat, but keep in mind that the side and stern tubes of nearly all RIBs are in the water when the boat is at rest. They also need protection. For a first-class job, treat the fiberglass or aluminum bottom with an appropriate primer (your marine paint dealer can help you here) and treat the bottom of the side tubes with Hy-Grip. Paint the entire bottom with Shipbottom.

Registration Numbers and Boat Names

For many years I operated my properly registered inflatable boats with peel-and-stick registration numbers affixed to plastic barge boards laced to the lifelines. One fine summer day I was happily motoring down the Danvers River in eastern Massachusetts when the assistant harbormaster roared up in his Boston Whaler Rampage and proclaimed my registration numbers to be illegal. He further declared that the next time he caught me on his river without numbers properly applied to my boat, he would be forced to exercise his responsibilities as an officer of the law to protect the citizens of Danvers from brigands and outlaws such as me. He didn't elaborate, but because he was aggravated beyond reason by the criminal nature of my numbers, I departed without argument.

Later, still thinking my numbers were perfectly legal, I called both the Coast Guard and the state agency responsible for boat registration. Low and behold the harbormaster was correct. Both agencies require the numbers to be *permanently* affixed to the boat. Lace-on plastic boards just don't make it.

Don't try to use peel-and-stick vinyl numbers; they won't stick to either Hypalon or PVC for more than a half season or so, especially if the boat is rolled or folded. The most permanent way of dealing with names and numbers is with glue-on numbers and letters sold just for inflatables. Your inflatable dealer has them and they are available in most marine-supply stores—white for dark-colored boats and black for light-colored boats. You glue them to the boat just like a repair patch.

Glue-on numbers are a lot of work, however. An easier way of affixing names and numbers is to paint them on using a stencil kit. Some kits come with a primer; others supply a vinyl paint that goes directly onto the boat. The primer kits are probably the more permanent, but the sides of most boats aren't subject to the same degree of torture as the bottom. You'll have to decide if the extra durability is worth the extra work.

This chapter may seem to some readers, especially those indolent mendicants used to letting their small boats take care of themselves, as nitpicking and compulsive. But when you consider the price of inflatable boats in light of their abbreviated life spans when not treated and maintained properly, and when you consider that a properly maintained boat will last at least twice as long as one that isn't properly maintained, it's easy to see that time spent in taking proper care of your inflated investment is like putting money in the bank.

Chapter 9

Repairs You Can Do Yourself

No matter how careful you are with your inflatable boat, there will likely come a time when it sustains damage severe enough to require repair. This can range from minor to catastrophic, from a pinched inflation tube when you're inflating the boat to a boat washed ashore and torn apart by the surf and rocks when it breaks loose from its tether. Even without an "event," leaks caused by wicking or minor abrasions grow worse as the boat ages. Every degree of damage is handled differently, so we will consider them separately, starting with the easiest to repair.

Minor Damage

You can often repair minor damage on the spot using the emergency repair kit that comes with most boats. Small leaks may be caused by punctures, pinched fabric, and abrasions that occur or are discovered as the boat is being launched or is in use. You will likely make the repair on a beach or launch ramp, or somewhere else where conditions are less than ideal.

Most instruction manuals say emergency repairs made with the repair kit are temporary and should be replaced with a proper patch as soon as it is convenient to do so. My old Zodiac had a number of "temporary" repairs that lasted longer than five years and were still holding when the boat self-destructed. As a rule of thumb, if a patch is holding air and its edges aren't starting to curl, I don't mess with it regardless of how it was applied. Like the man said, "if it ain't broke, don't fix it."

The Emergency Repair Kit

I have only been caught once without an emergency repair kit. Since that incident (which I will relate shortly), I never go anywhere in an inflatable boat without one. I have since encountered many situations that called for the kit, but I've never again been stranded.

When you buy your inflatable you should become familiar with the repair kit that comes with it. They differ little from boat to boat. A typical kit will contain the following:

- An assortment of round patches ranging in size from about 1 inch to about 4 inches in the appropriate material and color for your boat.
- A tube of one-part contact cement appropriate for the type of material used in your boat.
- A coarse stone or waterproof sandpaper for abrading the fabric around the repair.
- A set of instructions for effecting repairs of different types.

The basic kit is adequate for one or two small repairs but would be insufficient for more serious damage. Augment the kit by adding the following:

- Extra patches and a 3- × 6-inch piece of repair fabric. If your boat has more than one color and you're fussy about its appearance, you'll need patches for both colors.
- A stout sewing needle. A #15 sailmaker's needle is ideal but any robust needle will do.
- Five or six yards of stout three- or five-ply polyester thread.
- At least one extra tube of glue. Several small tubes are better than one large tube.
- One or two single-edge razor blades.
- Several acid brushes.
- A permanent felt-tipped marking pen (such as a Sharpie).
- A spare valve diaphragm (if appropriate).

Emergency repair kit.

- Spares of any other small odd parts for your boat or outboard that might break or get lost and ruin a trip.

Needless to say, this kit should go with the boat at all times if you want to avoid being stuck.

A Typical Small Repair

My fishing buddy Steve and I were drifting with the current on the Connecticut River several miles downstream from Wilder Dam on a terrific New England summer day. We were using the oars to stay about 20 yards from the Vermont shore and casting plugs into the weed beds along the bank for big walleye. Thinking I had a strike, I snapped the fishing rod back to set the hook. What I had snagged was not a trophy walleye but a log floating just below the surface. When I jerked the rod, the lure pulled free and shot like a bullet out of the water and into the side of the boat. Two of the treble hooks buried themselves deep into the fabric right at the waterline. The hiss of air and the sound of bubbles left no doubt that we would be glad we had remembered to bring along our trusty repair kit.

The leak wasn't severe enough to cause immediate problems. Steve was quick to point out that leaving the lure embedded would minimize the damage since the barbs of the hooks were bound to enlarge the holes were we to remove them. Thus we continued fishing with bubbles blowing, air hissing, and lure dangling, one of us stomping on the foot pump a few times every 10 or 15 minutes to replace the lost air. But we still had a long run upstream to get back to our car. A soft boat will float along with the current just fine, but it won't motor worth a damn, so there was no question that the leak would have to be fixed before the end of the day. Trying to operate a boat with a soft tube at planing speeds can be dangerous. The soft side creates excess drag and makes the boat difficult to control.

We drifted along and soon came upon a small sand beach where a tributary drained into the main river. Since it was lunch time and the fish weren't cooperating anyway, we decided to land, stretch our legs, eat our lunch, and fix the leak. First we emptied all the gear from the boat and removed the outboard. Then we carried the boat up on the beach and positioned it for maximum exposure to the drying sun. After lunch we spent a pleasant half hour futilely casting our entire assortment of plugs and lures from the beach, letting the bottom of the boat dry completely. By then the leaking tube had practically deflated, so it was an easy matter to complete the deflation.

The two holes were about an inch apart. We selected a single patch from the repair kit that was 3 inches in diameter—large enough to cover both punctures and allow at least an inch of overlap. The punctures were within an inch and a half of one of the main tube seams. Because an overlapping patch is difficult to seal, we decided to butt the patch to the seam. On a handy fallen tree trunk, we trimmed about a half inch of the patch (using the razor blade from the kit) to give it a straight edge where it would meet the seam (see illustration, page 91).

Next we spread the tube over the log and roughened the area around the holes with the abrasive stone from the kit. We did the same to the contact surface of the patch, paying particular attention to the edges, where the bond is most critical. We positioned the dry patch over the punctures and drew its outline on the boat with the felt-tipped pen.

When we punched a knife blade through the seal on the top of the little tube of glue in the kit, we found the glue had dried in the tube and was useless. This is not at all unusual, but this time the gremlins that delight in this particular mischief were disappointed because we had thought to bring several tubes. The second one was fine.

We coated the outlined area and about a quarter inch beyond, then we coated the patch. After about 15 minutes, when the first coat was dry to the touch, we gave both surfaces a second coat. When that coat would no longer stick to a finger, we pressed the patch into position. With the boat draped over the log so that the patch rested on the top, we used the handle of a sheathed hunting knife as a roller to apply as much pressure as we could directly to the patch.

The boat could have been inflated immediately, but we decided to do a bit more fruitless casting to give it extra time to cure. More than two years later our "temporary" patch is still holding. If you're up by Wilder Dam and you see a guy in a red Achilles and a funny-looking hat flailing away in an energetic but futile attack on the walleye population, stop by and I'll show it to you.

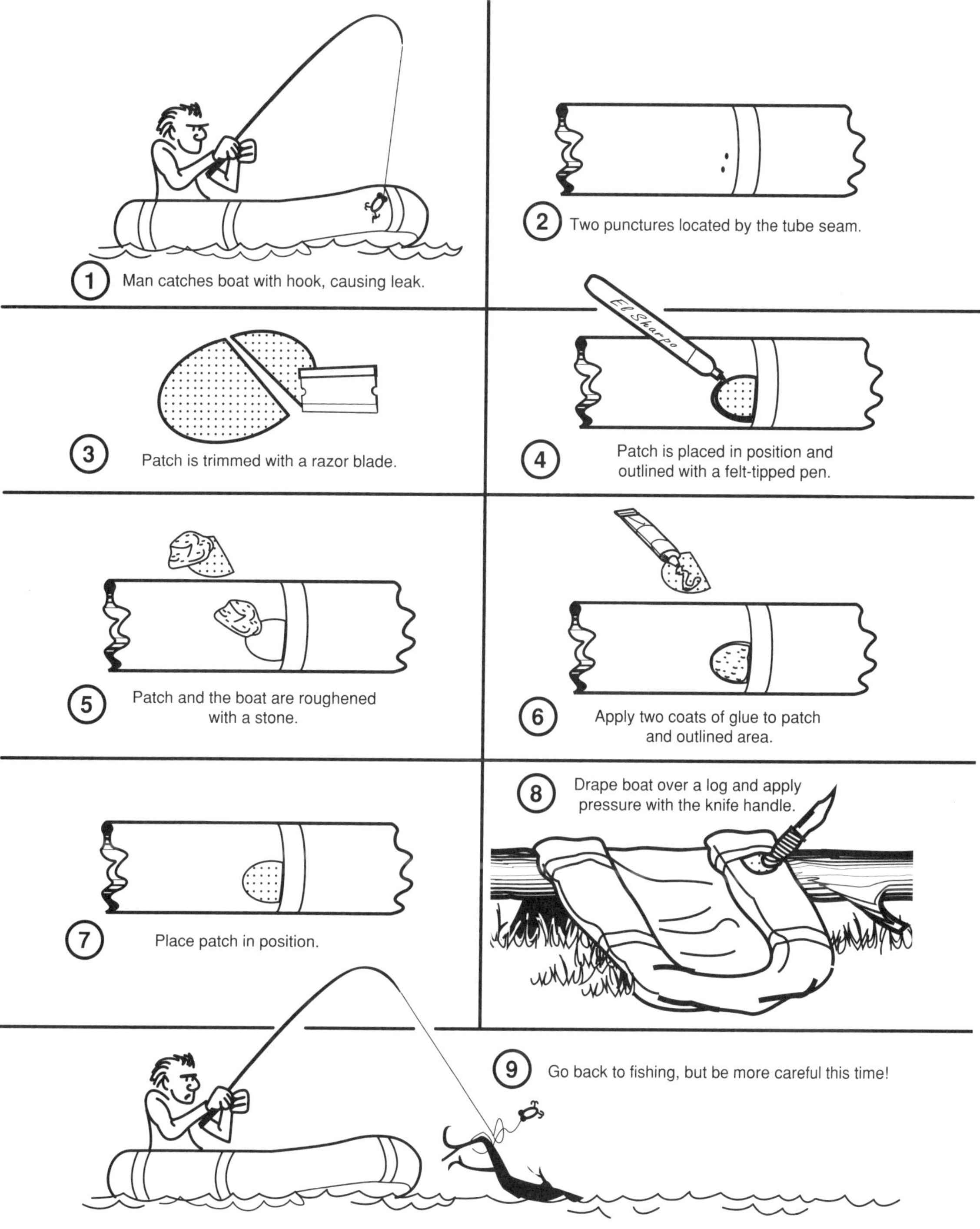

Fixing a minor leak.

Leaking Seams

A leaking seam can be anything from a minor annoyance to a major catastrophe, depending on the degree of damage causing the leak and on the willingness of the manufacturer to make good on the warranty. Almost all leaking seams are caused by problems in manufacture rather than any use or misuse by the owner. Overuse of cleaning solutions and solvents or the application of silicone protectants are about the only things an owner can do to destroy the seams in a boat. In general, repairing opened seams is a job for a professional inflatable repair shop regardless of whether it is covered by warranty.

Wicking and Leaking Fabric

Frequently, seam leaks are not caused by glue or weld failure but by wicking—the tendency of air to escape from the inflation chambers by following the threads in the cloth. Wicking occurs more frequently in more expensive boats because their heavier fabrics don't become completely impregnated with the Hypalon, neoprene, or PVC. While wicking might be merely a nuisance in a new boat, it can worsen over time until it becomes severe enough to require repair.

If a boat has been subjected to abrasion over a large area, air can effectively wick out where the exterior coating has been scraped away. Even without significant abrasion, very old boats sometimes start to leak air right through the fabric. The procedure for repairing all of these conditions is exactly the same: you can paint the outside, you can seal the inside, or you can do both.

INFLATABLE PAINTS. Wicking and fabric leaks may be undetectable with a soap-bubble solution, but your boat will be limp and saggy by the end of the day and will require frequent pumping to keep it hard. By the time your boat gets to this condition, it is probably also faded and dull and can't be revived no matter how hard you scrub. A couple of coats of paint could solve both problems.

Before you start, make sure all visible leaks are well patched. The US Army tested the paint we will discuss below and found it effective in stopping leaks caused by pinholes as large as .045 inch. That's pretty impressive, but bullet holes and bayonet slashes still needed to be patched.

Several brands of paint just for inflatable boats are available, and several boat manufacturers sell paints under their company names. Some of these paints are appropriate for only one type of fabric (Hypalon or PVC) while others work on both. One of the best treatments for shabby Hypalon boats is a coat or two of liquid Hypalon, sold in black and gray by International Watercraft. The paint I am most familiar with is made by Inland Marine, so that's the one I'm going to detail; if you select a different product, the application will be similar.

Inland Inflatable Boat Paint comes in standard inflatable colors (white, gray, red, blue, and black) plus a few that aren't standard (orange and yellow), and they will be happy to mix just about any color you like. They custom mix camouflage paint for the US Army and a few dedicated duck hunters. The Inland paint is a vinyl, water-based formula that works on both Hypalon and PVC, and it sticks to vinyl, neoprene, and even wood. In fact, it has nonskid qualities that make it an excellent paint for wooden floorboards.

You apply inflatable-boat paint directly to the boat—without a primer. First disassemble, clean, and dry the boat (as detailed in Chapter 8), and support it on sawhorses in a dry area protected from direct sunlight. If you have a PVC boat, wash the entire boat with MEK until it loses its luster and has a dull, flat surface. Wash a Hypalon boat thoroughly with acetone. Using good masking tape, tape off all areas you don't want to paint. I like #218 Fine Line tape by 3M. Good tape costs about $5 a roll. The stuff you buy in the hardware store for 99 cents is worthless and will ruin your paint job.

Pour about half a pint of paint into a 1-quart paper bucket. Thin it with a few ounces of water and mix it thoroughly. With a good-quality 4-inch china-bristle paintbrush, apply the first coat. Start at the top and work toward the bottom. Brush the paint well to get a thin application. Don't worry about what it looks like at this point. Take special care at the junction of the floor and the inflation tubes, and any other areas where there is an overlap of fabric. You may have to hold the floor fabric away from the tubes with toothpicks or Popsicle sticks. When you have a uniform coat on the entire boat (or at least the part you want to paint), check for drips and runs, then let the first coat dry for a few hours.

Apply the second coat full strength. Lay it on as thick as you can (without letting it run) until you have a uniform coat free of drips and sags. You don't need to worry about brush marks: vinyl paint has good self-leveling qualities, and it will dry to a smooth surface in about four hours.

If you're painting your boat the same color it was originally, or if you're painting a dark color over a light color, two coats should give you adequate coverage. If you're changing colors, especially if you're trying to cover a dark color with a lighter color, you'll need three or even four coats. Additional coats are applied just like the second coat, but they may take a little longer to dry. Let the paint cure for at least a day before you launch.

Inland's paint costs about $35 a quart, which is enough for two coats on a 10-foot boat, provided you thin the first coat properly. It is tough stuff, but sooner or later any paint will wear through where the boat rubs against docks or is dragged across the beach. Keep leftover paint for touch-ups.

INFLATABLE SEALANT. When it is impossible or impractical to stop multiple small leaks by patching on the outside, you need to patch from the inside. Internal sealant kits designed specifically for this purpose are available from Boat/U.S., West Marine, and just about every other full-line marine outlet.

Always repair leaks with external patches if you can, even if it means making a lot of small patches. Use a sealant kit only when patching is not an option—to repair serious wicking, widespread abrasion, or excessive wear at the floor-to-tube juncture, for example.

To use internal sealant, remove the floorboards, clean the boat, and check it for leaks with a soap solution. Mark their locations with a grease pencil. Drain all residual water from the tubes and inflate the boat to its operating pressure. Make sure you know which inflation chamber is leaking and which valve gives access to it. This is usually fairly obvious, but it can be more confusing on a large inflatable. If your boat has a cross-connect feature allowing the entire boat to be inflated from a single valve, make sure the cross-connect valve is closed. Inflate just the chamber that is leaking if it makes the job easier.

Install the injection nozzle on the sealant container and insert it through the valve as far as it will go. Squirt about an ounce of sealant into the tube; it is thin and works best in small quantities. Immediately remove the nozzle and reinflate the boat to operating pressure, turning the boat at the same time to orient the leaks you marked with a grease pencil at the lowest point in the chamber. Gravity will carry the sealant to the leak. Work fast. As soon as sealant starts bubbling through the leak, release the pressure in the chamber, leaving just enough air to keep the tube barely inflated.

Wipe off any sealant that seeps out through the leak. Both water- and acrylic-based sealants clean up easily (with water or alcohol, respectively) before they dry, but they set quickly. Once set, they are very difficult to remove.

Give the sealant that has seeped into the leak a minimum of three hours to cure, then inflate the boat hard and check the repaired area with soapy water. If it is still leaking, repeat the entire process. Major seam leaks may require as many as three or four applications of sealant. Don't try to rush the process by squirting a larger quantity into the tube; all you'll do is make a mess and waste material. If you have more than one area or seam that needs treatment, completely seal one before you move on to the next.

Whatever you do, don't try to substitute tubeless-tire sealant (sold in auto-supply stores). This black goo may work on tires, but it is designed to remain semiliquid. When your boat is deflated with this stuff in the tubes, the sides of the tubes will stick together, making a mess of mind-boggling magnitude.

Catastrophic Damage

Catastrophic damage renders a boat unusable until repaired and is extensive enough to be beyond the capabilities of the emergency repair kit. This might include a tear or cut large enough to cause the complete and immediate collapse of a major inflation tube, a major tear in the bottom fabric, the separation of the transom from the side tubes, or extensive abrasion resulting in multiple small leaks. All too often catastrophic damage is terminal. A boat washed onto sharp rocks can sustain damage that is impossible to repair. I've seen cases of vandalism where the tubes were slashed to such an extent that the boat couldn't be saved.

Less severe forms of catastrophic damage don't result in the destruction of the boat but do require the services of a professional inflatable-boat repair shop. A transom that has come loose from the side tubes is one example of a repair that shouldn't be attempted by an owner. Seams that come unglued are another. Many times damage of this nature is covered by a warranty that would be voided by amateur attempts at repairs, so it's a good idea to check with the dealer before attempting to fix any major damage yourself, particularly if it isn't the result of abuse or unusual circumstance. Most name-brand inflatables carry 5- to 10-year warranties on seams and fabric, which the manufacturer may honor even if you bought your boat used. Almost all have authorized repair facilities scattered around the country. Your dealer can advise you where you can send your boat for major repair, overhaul, or warranty service.

But let's take for our example a major repair that definitely isn't covered by warranty. My fishing buddy Steve and I were camped for a few days on the eastern bank of the Magalloway River in northern New Hampshire. Steve was using a large, sharp hunting knife to eviscerate the day's catch of brookies and rainbows when the blade slipped and eviscerated the starboard tube of my Avon instead. In a fraction of a second my previously seaworthy soft tail was rendered useless with a 6-inch gash in the tube.

The Avon was our only means of transportation to the opposite bank where our car was parked. The alternative was a 10-mile hike through cedar swamps and pine ridges that would have defied Tarzan. Swimming was not an option, as anyone familiar with the icy water that flows in the Magalloway knows. We were in dire straits. This is the one (and last) time I was without a repair kit, but I doubt that a basic kit would have helped much anyway. We were faced with making the repairs with materials at hand—and a resourceful attitude.

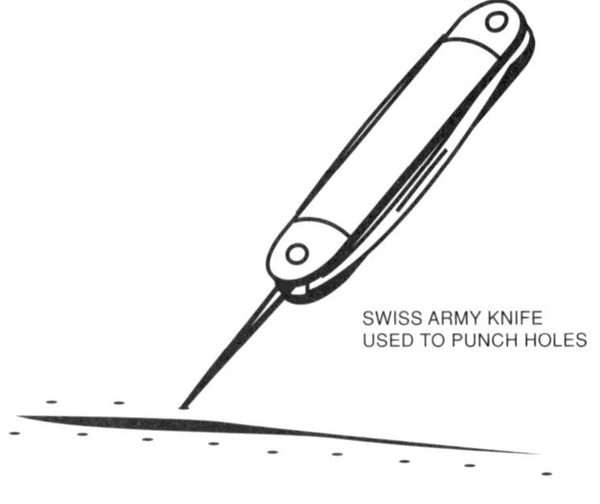

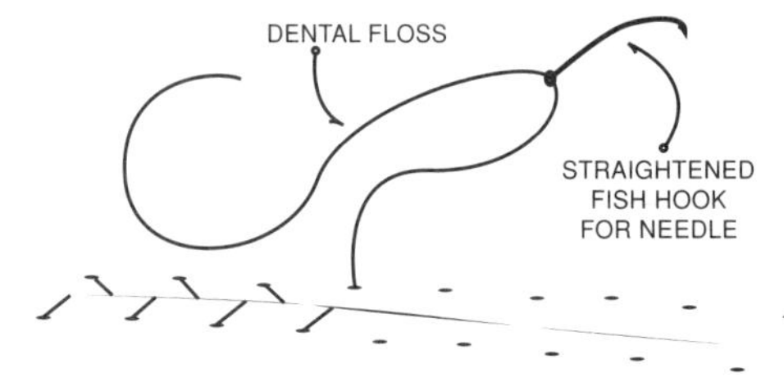

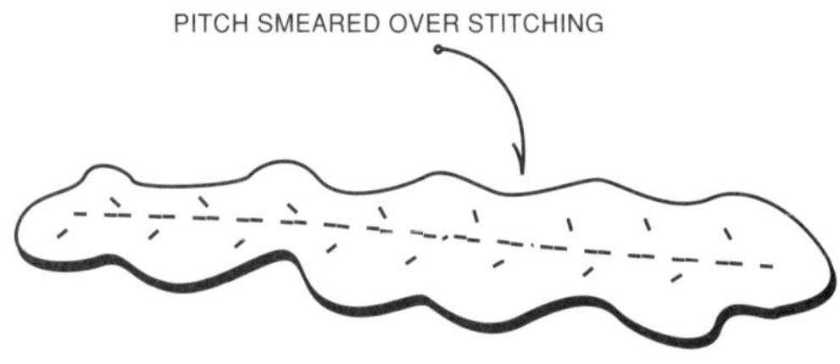

Repairing a gash without patch material.

Major Emergency Repairs

We inserted a short piece of split pine kindling, flat side up, into the slash. With the wood serving as a backboard, we used the awl on a Swiss Army knife to punch a series of holes about a half inch apart and about a half inch back from the cut along both edges. We removed the piece of pine.

With the gash prepared for stitching, we began to search for a suitable thread. Steve suggested we dispatch a moose and use its sinews, the way the original inhabitants of this wilderness had stitched together their birch-bark canoes. I was about to suggest, since he had caused the damage, that his sinews were much closer to hand and would work just as well, but then I remembered the dental floss in my toilet kit (or I could've used some light fishing line). Straightening out the largest fish hook we had to fashion a crude but workable needle, we used the dental floss and a baseball stitch to close the gaping hole.

Finally, we smeared the stitches with a liberal coating of spruce gum, available in that part of the world from the trunk of any large spruce tree. The spruce gum dried hard by the next day. Our repair bore an uncanny resemblance to a Frankensteinian

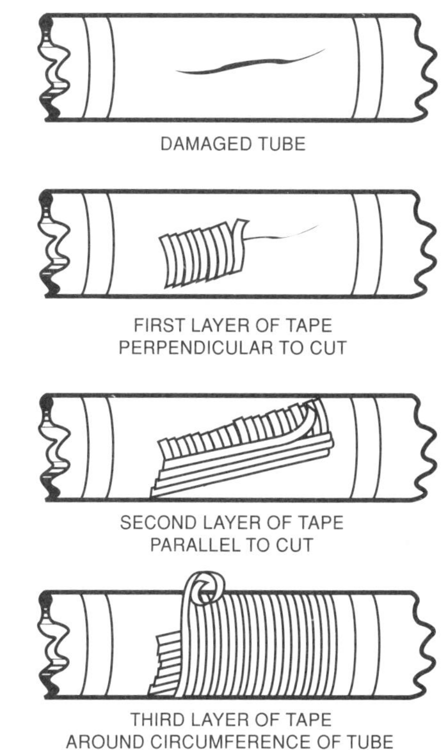

Repairing a leak with duct tape.

neck joint, but the boat worked—not as good as new, but good enough to get us back across the river. We didn't dare inflate the boat to its normal pressure for fear of tearing out the stitching.

The spruce gum, it turns out, was superfluous. The stitching by itself would have held air in the tube long enough for us to cross the stream, but dental floss alone lacks the appropriate woodsy touch for a story like this. Still, using floss to effect the repair was easier, far less dramatic, and complied more closely with extant wildlife laws than trying to fell a moose with a fly rod.

Duct-Tape Repairs

Duct tape provides another way of making emergency repairs on catastrophic damage. The trick is to use lots of tape. Deflate the damaged inflation chamber (this is probably already done or you wouldn't need the repair) and thoroughly dry the boat. Lay on 8-inch strips perpendicular to the rip or cut, overlapping the strips by half their width. Cover the entire area plus several inches past each end. Cover these with a second layer of tape laid perpendicular to the first, also overlapping each strip by about half. Inflate the boat just hard enough to hold its shape, then apply a third layer of tape *perpendicular to the tube,* with each strip going as far around the circumference of the tube as it will reach. This layer reinforces the tube so that it doesn't expand and tear the first two.

You now have three layers of tape (six counting the overlap): the first is perpendicular to the damage, the second is perpendicular to the first, and the third is perpendicular to the tube. A friend repaired a large slash in the bow of his Avon this way, and the repair held for several months—long enough for him to finish out the season. He made more enduring repairs in the winter at his leisure.

Permanent Repairs

When I got home after our adventuresome trip on the Magalloway, I had a bit of a mess on my hands. The spruce gum had softened in the heat of the car trunk and spread everywhere. And of course, the dental floss stitching needed to be replaced with something more appropriate.

After I cleaned the pitch from the fabric with turpentine and lots of clean rags, I removed the floss. I roughened the fabric with my abrasive stone—easier to do now than after the stitching. With a proper needle and a much finer stitch, I neatly restitched the entire slash with doubled polyester sailmaker's thread (any strong polyester thread will work). I used a baseball stitch again, but this time the stitches were about ¼ inch

Inflatable Desperation

The missionary who took our Zodiac when it fell apart in Florida (Chapter 4) was faced with the Herculean task of patching all those deteriorated seams. All the inflation tubes were intact, but practically everything that was glued to the tubes, including the oarlocks, side handles, bow dodger, and transom, had fallen off. I want to share with you his unique repair technique without necessarily recommending it.

He first disassembled all the loose seams and cleaned them of all traces of the old glue with a strong solvent. Then he stuck the whole thing back together with 3M 5200, an industrial-grade polyurethane adhesive sealant available in most chandleries. He also put a coat of 5200 on all the tube seams to stop wicking, and he let the repairs cure for several days in the sun. When the boat was launched, the lines of white squeeze-out at all the seams gave the boat the striped appearance of a badly assembled zebra, but the last time we saw our old Zodiac, the missionary, his wife, two other adults, two kids, and a dog were happily paddling off into a spectacular Florida Keys sunset.

Since then I've seen this same technique used to inject a season or two of vitality into several other boats that were otherwise beyond repair. As I said, I'm not recommending this course, but if you find yourself with an inflatable basket case that you're thinking of taking to the landfill, a $10 tube of 5200 might just buy you another season or so of inflatable fun.

apart—about what you see on a regulation baseball.

With the slash properly stitched, I was almost ready to put a patch over the entire area. The patches in a repair kit may not be big enough to cover a large rip or cut. Larger pieces of patching material that match in type, weight, and color the material in your boat should be available from your distributor, or you can get them from International Watercraft (see Appendix A). Major repairs need at least two layers of material to be permanent.

Professional repair shops forgo the stitching and start major repairs with a patch inside the tube. This undoubtedly works well, and the extra strength of a patch on the inside of the tube where it is held against the damaged area by air pressure is a definite advantage. Unfortunately, cleaning and abrading the inside of the tube is beyond the capabilities of my stubby fingers, and getting the glue and patch to cooperate without making a horrendous mess is, for me, nearly impossible. If your fingers are more adept, you may want to try this method.

Inflatable Glues

Not all glues work on all boats, so glue selection is important. The best course is to follow the suggestions of the boat's manufacturer. In the absence of that, you will need to determine the best glue on your own. Glues for inflatable repair can generally be categorized as single-part and two-part glues.

ONE-PART GLUES. Single-part glues are not as strong as two-part glues, but they have a few advantages that should be considered. They are much less expensive, they are easier to use, they have a longer shelf life, and they are strong enough to last several seasons or longer. One of the largest inflatable repair facilities in New England uses one-part glues for all patching jobs short of a major rebuild. They use the same glue on Hypalon and PVC, and they guarantee the repair for the life of the boat. The manager claims he has never had a customer complain that a patch didn't hold. This bears out my experience with one-part glues. I have festooned numerous boats with numerous patches using several kinds of one-part glue. The few failures were directly attributable to improper application of the glue; the rest of the patches have lasted for years and years.

One-part glues are generically known as *contact adhesives*. They are similar to the rubber cement you might use to paste clippings into a scrap book, but much stronger. The tube in your emergency repair kit contains a one-part glue. Numerous brands are available, and I've had good luck with several, including Dura-Bond, Elmer's, and Barge Cement. Most marine stores, catalogs, and good hardware stores carry one of these products.

TWO-PART GLUES. Two-part glues are also contact adhesives, but while one-part glues cure by the evaporation of a solvent, two-part glues cure by a catalytic process. As their name implies, they come in a kit containing the glue and a catalytic agent.

Mixing two-part adhesive.

Two-part glues are a lot more expensive than one-part glues, they are more difficult to use, and the catalytic agent is highly volatile, meaning they have a very short shelf life. Once the bottle of activator is opened, you must use the glue within a few days or throw it out. Two-part glues are stronger and tougher than the one-part variety, however, and if you're faced with a major repair, they can be worth the extra work and expense.

It is imperative that you select a glue appropriate for the fabric in your boat and that you follow the manufacturer's instructions closely. The following general procedures apply to most two-part glues.

Bostik, a brand that has given me good results, is typical of two-part glues. It comes in a 2-ounce can with a tiny bottle of activator and retails for about $17 at discount houses. Because of the short shelf life, don't buy any more glue than you need for your immediate repair.

Mix the glue in proportion to the amounts supplied in the kit. In other words, if you need half the glue in the can, you add half the activator to it. It is difficult to judge the correct relative amounts of the two parts when mixing very small quantities. The manufacturer of Bostik recommends that you not mix less than half the kit at any one time, but that's a lot of glue. With a judicious eyeball and a steady hand, you can mix as little as a quarter of the kit with consistent success.

Pour all the glue into a graduated plastic beaker. Note the total, then pour ¾ of the glue back into its can, leaving ¼ in the beaker. The quantity of activator is too small to be measured in the same way as the glue, but it comes in a handy glass bottle in the Bostik kit and others. (Glue brands with the activator in a tube are more difficult to mix in fractional quantities.) Scrape away part of the label to expose the glass, then holding the bottle to light, divide the contents into equal halves with a small pencil mark on the remaining label. Divide the halves into halves again to give equal quarters. Pour the activator into the glue in the beaker a few drops at a time until you have poured exactly ¼ from the bottle. Cap the remaining activator tightly; it evaporates quickly if it has any access to air. Stir the two parts together thoroughly and the glue is ready for use. The mixed glue will last about four hours before it becomes useless, so there is no need to hurry your repair.

Applying the Glue

Trim the first patch to size with a pair of heavy-duty shears so that it overlaps the area to be repaired, including the stitching, by at least 2 inches on all sides. Position the patch and outline it on the boat fabric. Clean the fabric inside the outline with acetone or lacquer thinner if the boat is Hypalon and with MEK if it's PVC. Roughen both the fabric and the bottom surface of the patch with 80-grit (medium) sandpaper or an abrasive stone. (If this is a stitched repair, you should have abraded the repair area before sewing it.) Pay particular attention to the edges of the patch where a good bond is of utmost importance. Clean up the roughened dinghy and patch with your solvent; they are clean when nothing discolors your solvent-dampened cloth. Let the areas dry thoroughly before applying the glue.

The best tool for applying the glue (one-part or two-part) is an acid brush, available at your hardware store for less than a quarter. Prepare your glue and brush a uniform layer onto the repair area and the patch. Be especially careful on PVC boats to keep the glue within the outline of the patch; you can clean excess glue off Hypalon boats later but not off PVC boats. Let the coated surfaces sit for about 10 to 30 minutes, then brush a second coat of glue over the first. When the second coat is tack free—usually after about five minutes—you are ready to apply the patch.

Position it over the repair with *extreme* care. Once the surfaces touch, the bond will be

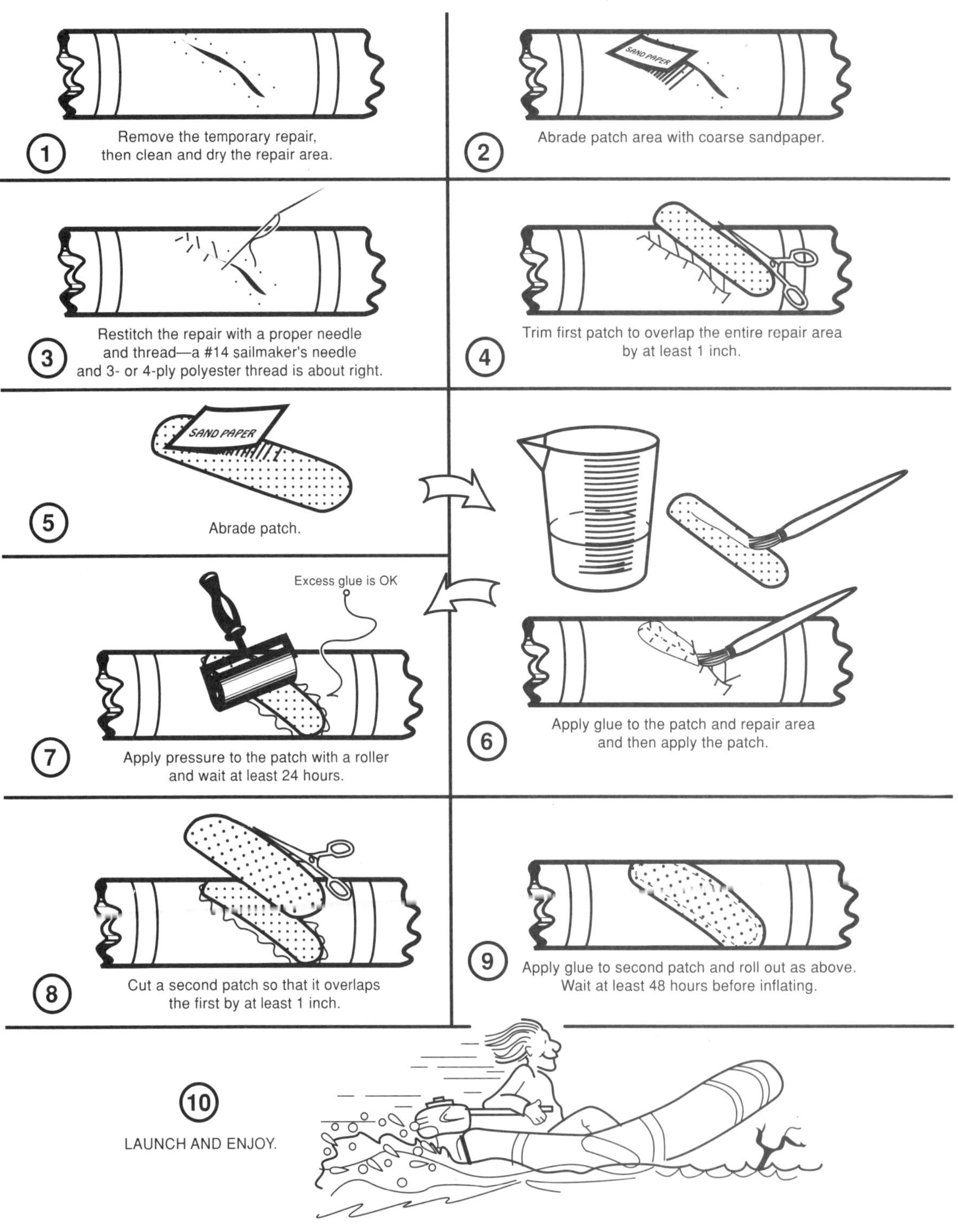

Permanent repairs.

instantaneous, and any attempt to reposition the patch will tear the glue from either the boat or the patch, necessitating doing the entire job over.

When the patch is in position, apply as much pressure as you can with a roller. The best is a "J" roller, used primarily for the installation of plastic laminate (Formica). For small repairs you can use a wallpaper seam roller. On larger repairs, I have been known in a pinch to surreptitiously borrow Susan's rolling pin from the kitchen.

Let this first patch set for at least 24 hours (some glues require about a week to cure completely), then cut a second patch that overlaps the first by 2 inches—an inch if you're using two-part glue. Apply this second patch over the first in exactly the same way you applied the first patch over the stitching.

Clean excess glue off Hypalon boats with acetone, lacquer thinner, or toluene. Do this after the glue sets but is still slightly soft—generally about two hours after the patch is applied. Just *dampen* your rag with the solvent; if you let it run into the seams or under the new patch, you'll cause worse damage than you started with.

Don't try to clean the excess glue off PVC boats with solvent; any solvent strong enough to dissolve the glue will also dissolve the boat. If you're a neat freak, just be careful to keep the glue within the outline.

Let the boat sit again for at least 48 hours (a week is better), then inflate it hard and check it for leaks. No leaks? Great! Now launch and enjoy your good-as-new boat, and don't worry if the new patch doesn't exactly match the old material. Inflatable boats wear their patches like veterans wear their medals—with pride and dignity. A lot of conspicuous patches, like a lot of medals, will set you apart as one who has been there and doesn't have to talk about it to anyone.

Repairs to Ancillary Equipment

It is one thing to be equipped to patch a hole in your trusty inflatable, but what do you do if you break your only paddle while shooting Class III rapids? Or what do you do when your motor quits? Or your boat deflates and your pump is broken, what then? Well, keep reading.

Outboard Motors

No, we're not going to talk about how to repair outboard motors. (That sound you hear is my editor's sigh of relief.) We don't have the space, nor do I have the expertise to do the subject justice. Besides, there are already plenty of books on outboard repair (try *Keep Your Outboard Motor Running*, International Marine, 1992). My contribution to this subject is only to help you prepare for an unexpected engine failure.

If your inflatable is fitted with an outboard motor, it is probably more a necessity than an option. You may take your inflatable far back into wilderness or far out to sea and depend *entirely* on the outboard to get you back safely. And while modern outboards are incredibly reliable, taking this reliability for granted can be dangerous. I've taken my inflatable boats into places where it would have been nearly impossible to row or paddle them out, and I've had engines quit on me in the worst of circumstances. When your outboard quits, there is always a moment of shocked disbelief, a lot like finding a picture of Granny in the monthly *Playchick* centerfold. The trick is to be prepared for the failure no matter how unlikely. With a little pluck and a lot of luck, I've always gotten back.

The very first thing you should do when you buy a new outboard is to buy the shop manual that goes with it. Then *read* it. With this manual in hand, remove the motor cover and review the carburetor, the fuel system, the ignition system, and the throttle linkage. You don't have to become an engine mechanic, but you should become familiar enough with how these critical systems work to be able to recognize when they aren't working properly. Remove and replace the prop so you'll know how. Locate the cooling-water outlet so you can check for proper operation of the water pump each time the engine is started. Also find the water intake so you can clear it if it becomes clogged.

You will need a few tools aboard—the tool kit that came with your motor is inadequate. Buy a *good* spark-plug wrench of the correct size (get a spare set of spark plugs while you're at it). Also buy a 6-inch adjustable wrench, a pair of Vise-Grip pliers, a small pair of needlenose pliers with wire cutters, and a pair of screwdrivers (slotted and Phillips). From your outboard dealer buy two or three spare fuel filters, a carburetor repair kit, shear pins (if appropriate), a spare water-pump impeller, and any other small parts easily broken or lost that your dealer recommends. Put tools and spare parts together in a small plastic fishing-tackle box. Add a spool of fine stainless safety wire, a role of electricians tape, and a tube of five-minute epoxy to the box, and you're ready to fix about 90 percent of the things that kill outboards.

If you venture into areas where losing your outboard could prove catastrophic, make sure you also take your emergency grab bag (Chapter 3) and a handheld radio. These won't help your outboard repair a bit, but they may make life easier when Old Betsy gives up the ghost. The radio will be invaluable if you find yourself adrift in the middle of a shipping lane just as a fog bank rolls in. When that exact thing happened to your intrepid (and often fog-bound) author right in the entrance to Portland Harbor in Maine, the ability to call the Coast Guard on VHF radio was literally a lifesaver.

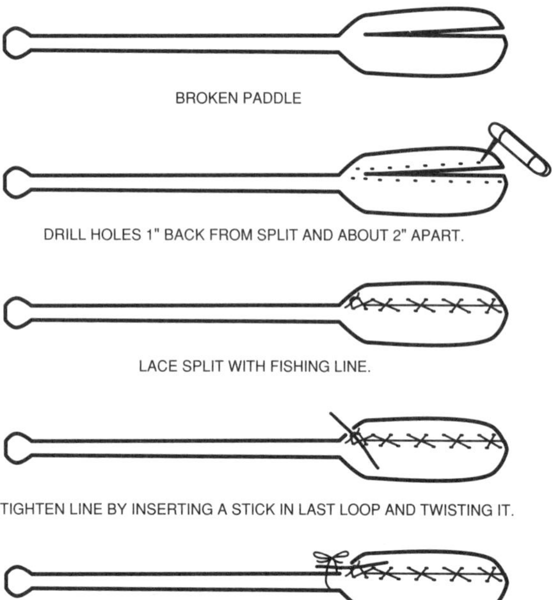

Repairing a split blade.

Oars and Paddles

A broken or lost oar or paddle can be as serious as a dead outboard. The ability to repair a paddle or fashion a new one quickly and efficiently is a valuable skill.

REPAIRS In my experience the most common oar or paddle failure is a split in the blade. The split first appears at the tip where the wood is thinnest, but it quickly extends up into the handle or off to one side, often causing a section of the blade to fall off. Repair splits as soon as they appear because once they start, they migrate quickly and render the paddle or oar useless.

You can temporarily repair a split blade by simply wrapping it tightly with duct tape (or even electrician's tape), but lacing the blade through drilled holes on either side of the split will give a more durable repair. With the awl on a Swiss Army knife (if you have one), or with any sharp piece of metal, drill a series of holes about an inch back from the split (on both sides) and about 2 inches apart. It's a lot easier than you might think because the wood is thin and often a fairly soft variety. In a pinch you could burn the holes with a piece of stiff wire heated red-hot on a campfire, but I've never found this necessary.

Use any cord or string that's handy. If what you have isn't strong enough, double it and double it again until it is. Six or eight strands of 5-pound-test fishing line twisted together will make a cord strong enough for your repair. If you have any glue, use it in the split regardless of the type. Epoxy works best, but the contact cement in your emergency repair kit will help strengthen the repair, even if it won't last very long.

The trick behind an effective repair is to get the lacing absolutely tight. This requires a small Spanish windlass. Pull the cord as tight as possible and secure it with a square knot, then slip a short stick through the lacing at the handle end and twist it to draw the lacing tighter. Secure the stick with another piece of line and you're ready to paddle off.

AN EMERGENCY OAR OR PADDLE. Fortunately well-made paddles and oars seldom break, but they are sometimes lost when a boat swamps (inflatables don't often capsize, even in the rapids). The technique of making an oar or paddle from scratch was taught to me by an old-time fishing guide in Maine. It's not hard to do, and so far in my short but exciting life I've had to use the skill twice, so it will be space well used to pass it on to you.

I was taking a break from fly-fishing for salmon on the eastern terminus of Grand Lake

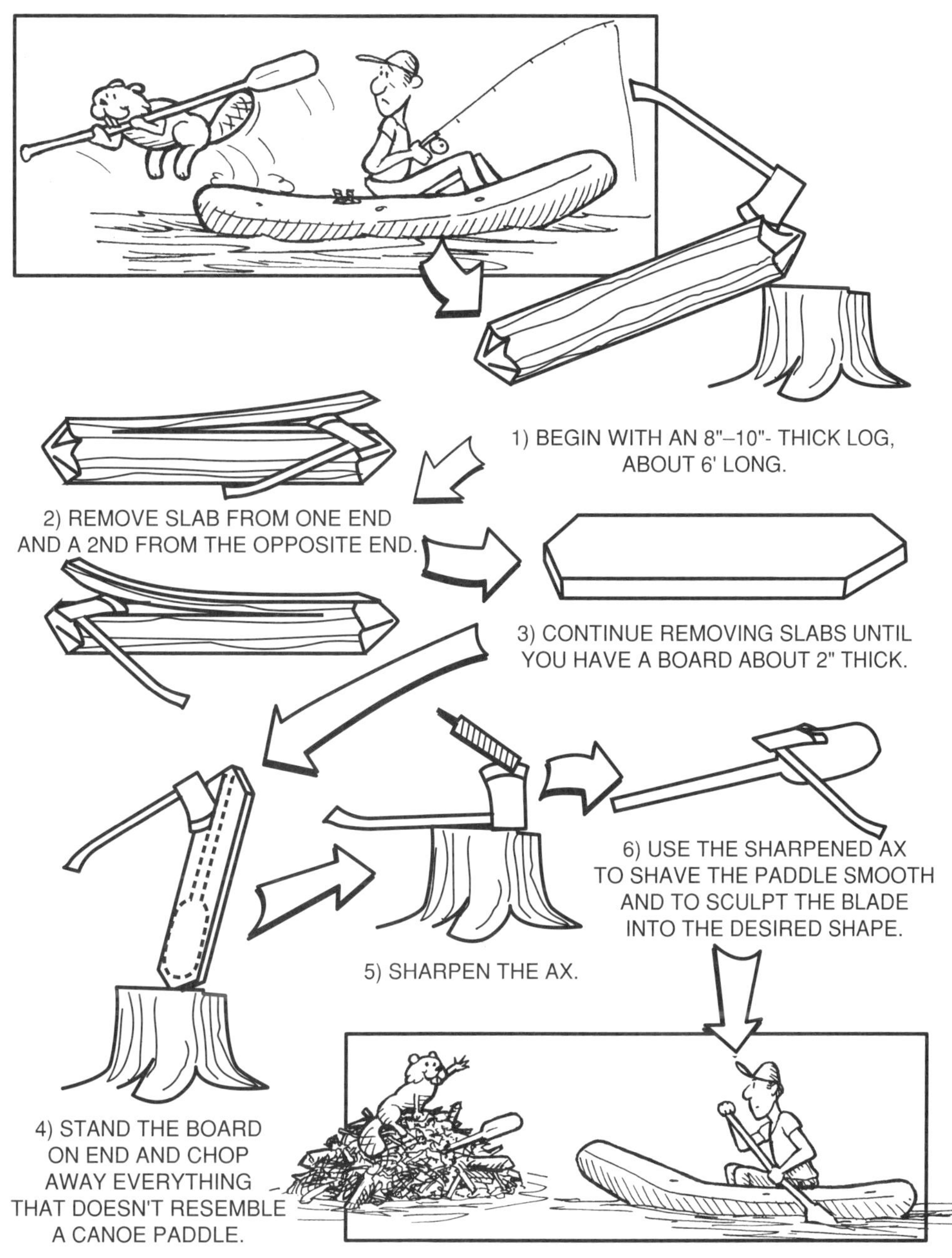

Making an emergency paddle.

Stream—not far from where it empties into East Grand Lake—when a local guide showed up towing a huge canoe known as a Grand Lakes Guide Boat. I helped him get the boat off the trailer and the outboard mounted and was rewarded with an incomparable Down East scowl; he had somehow forgotten his paddle and was loath to go fishing without one. More annoyed than upset, he produced a small ax and a pair of heavy leather gloves from a box in his pickup and disappeared into the brush. When the sounds of energetic chopping stopped, the guide emerged carrying the trunk of a small spruce tree about 10 inches in diameter and about 6 feet long.

Propping the log against an old stump, he swung the ax in a wide arc over his head, driving the blade deep into one end of the log about 2 inches from the center and causing the wood to split. Pulling on the split piece while chopping lightly into the split with the ax, he quickly removed a large slab from one side of the log. The slab was tapered and didn't run the full length of the log, stopping about a foot from the opposite end. He flipped the log over and repeated the exercise on the other end. Then he did it again on the other side. After about 10 minutes and about a dozen peeled slabs, he had reduced the log to a rough but reasonably flat plank.

Holding the ax near the head, he used it like a hatchet to chop away at the sides with short deliberate strokes until he had fashioned the board into the shape of a rough paddle. This crude paddle would have been adequate in an emergency just as it was, but my laconic friend wasn't quite finished. He fetched a large file from the box and sharpened the ax to a razor's edge. Holding the paddle in place on the stump with his knee, he grasped the head of the ax with both hands and guided the edge with his thumbs to shave long, even curls of sweet-smelling spruce from the paddle's blade and handle until they were smooth and flawless. He finished off the edges with his pocket knife and carefully whittled the knob end to fit his hand. Sighting along the blade, he gave a grunt of satisfaction, hopped into his guide boat, and with a little wave and a wink that says thanks in Maine, he was off across the lake.

Thirty five years later I watched another woodsman, a Quiché Indian, perform this same ritual on the banks of a river in Central America. His boat was a dugout canoe, and he used a machete instead of an ax, but the grunt of satisfaction was exactly the same.

There is one last thing to remember before you try to make your own paddle or oar from standing timber. Trees aren't as plentiful as they used to be, and on most public (and private) woodlands, strict laws prohibit chopping them down. So forbear, and except in the case of dire emergency, make sure you know who owns the tree you are about to destroy and that you have his/her permission before you start swinging away with your ax.

Air Pumps

Air pumps catch hell. They usually end up rattling around on the floorboards by the fuel tank where they are kicked, stomped, and left roasting in the noontime sun. The varnish disappears, cracks appear in the fabric bellows, the hose gets kinked, and sooner or later the tip breaks off. The amazing thing is that the pump still pumps, even if it does take twice as many stomps, but eventually it will stop working and you'll have to patch the thing up. (Note: Those with the foresight to keep their pumps in some sort of protective bag can skip this section because the pump will likely outlast the boat; the other 99½ percent of us can read on.)

Most pump repairs are common sense. Use electrician's tape to repair breaks or leaks in the hose and to reattach a broken-off tip. Temporarily repair leaking air valves by smearing them with grease or Vaseline. Sometimes spare diaphragms for the valves on the boat will also fit the valves on the pump; it's worth checking.

Patch tears in the bellows with the contact adhesive and any thin plasticized material. In a pinch, a piece of shirttail is better than nothing. Don't use the boat's patch material because it will be too stiff. Bellows repairs are always temporary, and the leaking bellows should be replaced as soon as possible. Remove the old bellows by prying out the staples or nails and use it as a pattern to make a new one from any appropriate material. Reattach the bellows with *copper* upholstery tacks—available in most hardware stores.

I once replaced the bellows on my Zodiac's pump with material from the back of an old yellow slicker I scrounged from a dumpster in the Camden Harbor, Maine, parking lot. As I was removing the slicker from the dumpster, I overheard two lobstermen talking about Walter Cronkite, whose boat had sailed away from the dock not 10 minutes before my arrival.

"Well then, it must'a been him who put this here slicker in the dumpster," I said to the older and therefore wiser of the two.

He looked at the slicker, then at me. "Aaayup," he said. And so far no one has been able to dispute my claim to have spent years pumping up my boat with Walter Cronkite's slicker.

APPENDIX A

Sources of Supply

Many of the products mentioned in this book are available at your local marine store or from the popular mail-order catalogs. The following companies carry inflatable boat supplies that may be difficult to obtain elsewhere.

Inland Marine USA, Inc.
1017-C S.E. 12th Avenue
Cape Coral, FL 33990
(813) 458-0302

International Watercraft, Inc.
2389 S.E. Dixie Highway
Stuart, FL 34996
(407) 283-0933 or (800) 780-7238

APPENDIX B

Inflatable Boat Companies

The following is a list of recreational inflatable boat manufacturers and distributors. This industry is a dynamic one, and companies change alliances, names, addresses, and product lines frequently. Although the author and editors have tried to make this list as accurate as possible at the time of publication, some companies have undoubtedly been omitted and changes will occur. Inflatable boat producers and distributors are urged to send International Marine information to be included in future editions of this book.

AB Inflatables of North America, Inc.
(Artigiana Battelli)
5593 N.W. 72nd Ave.
Miami, FL 33166
(305) 887-9899 or (800) 229-2446

Achilles Inflatable Craft
P.O. Box 517
355 Murray Hill Pkwy.
East Rutherford, NJ 07073
(201) 438-6400

Achilles Inflatable Craft
1407 80th St., S.W.
Everett, WA 98203
(206) 353-7000

Action Marine Distributors, Inc. (Caribe, Zeppelin)
57A Lafayette Ave.
Suffern NY 10901
(914) 368-3798

Airconcept Pneumatics
1485 E. Joliet-Curie
Boucherville, Quebec
J4B 7L9 Canada
(514) 449-2498

AIRE
P.O. Box 3412
Boise, ID 83703
(208) 344-7506

Alliance R.I.B., Inc.
6323 Bay Club Dr. #4
Fort Lauderdale, FL 33308
(954) 772-7330

Apex Inflatables
919-A Bay Ridge Rd.
Annapolis, MD 21403
(410) 267-0850 or (800) 422-5977

Avon Marine East
4740 126th Ave. North
Clearwater, FL 34622
(813) 571-3616

Avon Marine, Inc.
1851 McGaw Ave.
Irvine, CA 92714
(714) 250-0880 or (800) 854-7595

B&A Distributing Co. (Riken Kayak)
201 S.E. Oak St.
Portland, OR 97214
(503) 230-0482

Bear (see *Defender Industries, Inc.*)

Boat/U.S. (Seaworthy)
880 S. Pickett St.
Alexandria, VA 22304
(703) 823-9550 or (800) 937-BOAT (-2628)

Bombard
P.O. Box 400
Stevensville, MD 21666
(410) 643-4141

California Inflatables Co., Inc. (Storm)
2608 Temple Heights Dr.
Oceanside, CA 92056
(619) 724-8300

Caribe Inflatables USA
14372 S.W. 139 Court
Unit 7
Miami, FL 33186
(305) 253-4822

Crewsaver Life Rafts (see *SMR Technologies*)

Custom Inflatables
P.O. Box 80
Albright, WV 26519
(304) 329-2359

Defender Industries, Inc. (Dynous and Bear)
255 Main St.
P.O. Box 820
New Rochelle, NY 10801-0820
(914) 632-3001 or (800) 628-8225

Dunlop-Beaufort Canada
12351 Bridgeport Rd.
Richmond, B.C.
V6V 1J4 Canada
(604) 278-3221

Dynous (see *Defender Industries, Inc.*)

Eastern Aero Marine (Topaz and Triumph life rafts)
3850 N.W. 25th St.
Miami, FL 33142
(305) 871-4050 or (800) 843-7238

Givens Ocean Survival Systems Co., Inc. (life rafts)
35 Lagoon Rd.
Portsmouth, RI 02871
(401) 683-7400

HBI Hard Bottom Inflatables
P.O. Box 256
Sherborn, MA 01770
(508) 653-3366

Hyside Whitewater Inflatables
12100 Sierra Way
Kernville, CA 93238
(619) 376-3723 or (800) 868-5987

Jack's Plastic Welding, Inc. (Pack Cat)
115 S. Main St.
Aztec, NM 87410
(505) 334-8748 or (800) 742-1904

Metzeler (now distributed by *Sevylor* under the trade name Jumbo; see *Sevylor*)

Nautica International, Inc.
6135 N.W. 167th St.
Suite E-17
Miami, FL 33015
(305) 556-5554

Northwest River Supplies
2009 S. Main St.
Moscow, ID 83843
(208) 882-2383 or (800) 635-5202

Novurania of America
4775 N.W. 132 St.
Miami, FL 33054
(305) 685-2464

OMC
200 Seahorse Dr.
Waukegan, IL 60085
(708) 689-7645 or (800) 888-4662

Pack Cat (see *Jack's Plastic Welding, Inc.*)

Plastimo/Elliot (life rafts; see *SMR Technologies, Inc.*)

Quicksilver Inflatables (a division of *Mercury Marine*)
P.O. Box 1939
W6250 W. Pioneer Rd.
Fond du Lac, WI 54936-1939
(414) 929-5204 or (414) 929-5000

Revere Survival Products (life rafts)
3 Fairfield Crescent
West Caldwell, NJ 07006
(201) 575-8811

Riken Kayak (see *B&A Distributing Co.*)

Sea Eagle
200 Wilson St.
Port Jefferson, NY 11776
(516) 473-7308 or (800) 852-0925

Sea Star Yachting Products (Tinker)
1120-C Ballena Blvd.
Alameda, CA 94501
(510) 814-0471

Seaworthy (see *Boat/U.S.*)

Sevylor USA, Inc.
6651 E. 26th St.
Los Angeles, CA 90040
(213) 727-6013 or (800) 821-4645

Simpson Lawrence U.S.A. (M.L. Lifeguard life rafts)
6208 28th St. E.
Bradenton, FL 34203-4123
(813) 753-7533 or (800) 946-3527 (WIN-DLAS)

SMR Technologies, Inc. (Crewsaver, Plastimo, and Elliott life rafts)
P.O. Box 326
1420 Wolf Creek Trail
Sharon Center, OH 44274-0326
(216) 239-1000 or (800) 858-RAFT (-7238)

Soar Inflatables
3152 Cherokee St.
St. Louis, MO 63118
(800) 280-SOAR (-7627)

Storm (see *California Inflatables Co., Inc.*)

Switlik Parachute Co. (life rafts)
1325 E. State St.
Trenton, NJ 08609
(609) 587-3300

Tinker (see *Yachting Services* and *Sea Star Yachting Products*)

Viking Life-Saving Equipment (life rafts)
1625 N. Miami Ave.
Miami, FL 33136
(305) 374-5115

Vista Recreation
P.O. Box 147
Almond, NC 28702
(704) 488-8594

Water Wolf, Inc.
P.O. Box 169
Telluride, CO 81435
(800) H2O-WOLF (426-9653)

West Marine
500 Westridge Dr.
Watsonville, CA 95076
(800) 538-0775

Yachting Services (Tinker)
P.O. Box 1045
Pointe Claire, Quebec
H9S 4H9 Canada
(514) 697-6952 or (800) 618-6748

ZED (now the Serie Z; see *Zodiac*)

Zeppelin Technologies, Inc.
411 St.-Valier
Granby, Quebec
J2G 7Y2 Canada
(514) 375-0508

Zodiac of North America, Inc.
P.O. Box 400
Stevensville, MD 21666
(410) 643-4141

Index